ENCOUNTERING PALESTINE

Cultural Geographies
+ Rewriting the Earth

Series Editors
Paul Kingsbury, Simon Fraser University
Arun Saldanha, University of Minnesota

ENCOUNTERING PALESTINE

Un/making Spaces of
Colonial Violence

Edited by Mark Griffiths and Mikko Joronen

University of Nebraska Press | Lincoln

"Elegy for Return" was originally published
in Zena Agha, *Objects from April and May*
(Hajar Press, 2022) and is reproduced here
by kind permission of Hajar Press.

The University of Nebraska Press is part of a land-
grant institution with campuses and programs
on the past, present, and future homelands of
the Pawnee, Ponca, Otoe-Missouria, Omaha,
Dakota, Lakota, Kaw, Cheyenne, and Arapaho
Peoples, as well as those of the relocated Ho-
Chunk, Sac and Fox, and Iowa Peoples.

♾

Library of Congress Cataloging-in-Publication Data
Names: Griffiths, Mark (Research fellow),
editor. | Joronen, Mikko, editor.
Title: Encountering Palestine: un/making
spaces of colonial violence / edited by
Mark Griffiths and Mikko Joronen.
Description: Lincoln: University of
Nebraska Press, [2023] | Series: Cultural
geographies + rewriting the earth | Includes
bibliographical references and index.
Identifiers: LCCN 2023004041
ISBN 9781496232588 (hardback)
ISBN 9781496237491 (paperback)
ISBN 9781496238023 (epub)
ISBN 9781496238030 (pdf)
Subjects: LCSH: Settler colonialism—Palestine. |
Arab-Israeli conflict—1993—Social aspects. |
Palestinian Arabs—Social conditions—21st
century. | Violence—Palestine. | Palestine—Social
conditions. | BISAC: SOCIAL SCIENCE / Jewish
Studies | SOCIAL SCIENCE / Human Geography
Classification: LCC HN660.A8 E56 2023 |
DDC 303.6095694—dc23/eng/20230712
LC record available at
https://lccn.loc.gov/2023004041

Designed and set in Minion Pro by L. Welch.

Contents

Illustrations

Acknowledgments

Like most books, *Encountering Palestine* has been a long time in the making. From our initial idea to this final version, we have been supported by a great many people. For their encouragement and enthusiasm, we would like to thank the editors of the Cultural Geographies + Rewriting the Earth series, Arun Saldanha and Paul Kingsbury, as well as the patient—and always kind!—guidance provided by the editor in chief at the University of Nebraska Press, Bridget Barry. Our thanks also go to a band of colleagues and friends who have read and commented on the manuscript in various iterations, especially Derek Ruez, who gave valuable feedback on the introduction. We would like to further thank those authors whose work is collected here for their willingness to stick to the book project, especially during the first years of the pandemic that hit when the writing of the chapters had only just begun. Each of you has offered critical work and shown an openness to respond to both our and external reviews. To those reviewers (we count four total), we are indebted for the ways that you pushed us to think further about different themes and to improve the coherence of the text as a whole. On behalf of the authors, we are also grateful for the willingness of people in Palestine to share their experiences and allow them to be documented in texts such as this one.

MARK AND MIKKO

ENCOUNTERING PALESTINE

Introduction

Encountering Palestine, Un/doing Power

Mark Griffiths and Mikko Joronen

The question of Palestine is an inherently geographical one. It is not only a question of land and people—or of the walls and segregations, checkpoints and (im)mobilities, borders and (b)orderings, territorializations, compartments, and strangulations—but also of places and spaces of everyday living that are profoundly marked by colonial violence. On the one hand, Israel's practices of governing, segregating, and subjugating, though founded in longer genealogies of colonial power, survive on innovative and sometimes experimental modes of control that touch all aspects of Palestinian political and cultural life. On the other, this is never a determining relationship; it is not that Israel's techniques of control *control* Palestinian life but that they present a claim to be *made, encountered,* and *undone.* Colonial encounter in this sense is *mutually constituted,* a meeting point that is never fixed and always generative of new and unstable power relations with claims on lands, dwellings, infrastructure, and belonging. Colonial spaces are thus not so much *made* (i.e., a completed state) as *in the making,* a crucial distinction that denotes a certain unfinished-ness and opens us to the processes of *unmaking* space. With close attention to these spatial dynamics of power, the chapters collected in *Encountering Palestine: Un/making Spaces of Colonial Violence* elaborate various themes and intellectual registers—from apartheid to gender, vulnerability to war, queer theory to cultural expectations, vortical maneuvers to failing apparatuses of power—to present original critiques of contemporary colonialism in Palestine. As such, they compose a work of critical geography that addresses the question of Palestine as one of un/making colonial spaces at multiple sites of encounter.

At base, *encounter* is conceived here as that point where political violence meets the culture of living, where Israel's colonial project manifests in and targets everyday lives of Palestinians. Politics and culture thus coalesce, each an expression of the other, and neither is satisfactorily comprehensible without a focus on both. Edward Said (1993, 7), of course, articulated this so clearly, emphasizing particularly the *spatial* entanglements of politics and culture: "Just as none of us is outside or beyond geography, none of us is completely free from the struggle over geography. That struggle is complex and interesting because it is not only about soldiers and cannons but also about ideas, about forms, about images and imaginings." Said's (1978) earlier classic is lucid testimony to this: *Orientalism* offers a view of a political production of imaginative geographies, ones that are all too familiar within historical and contemporary framings of Palestinians as, for instance, terroristic, violent martyrs; ruthless suicide bombers; uneducated barbarians; and so forth (see also Massad 2006; Puar 2007). While the rich tradition of postcolonial thought reveals the inextricability of culture from geographies of power (and politics from cultural geographies), the frameworks and analyses elaborated in *Encountering Palestine* are less aligned with the production of "images and imaginations." Instead, they are angled toward more embodied or entangled *geographies* of power. This is of course not to deflect from important critiques of racist colonial representations and their tangible and destructive consequences but rather to shift emphasis to those *geographies of encounter* through which everyday cultural forms of living in Palestine are denigrated, persist, and, at times, transcend mechanisms of political oppression. From the production of political images *of* Palestine, we thus move to the politics of (cultural) life *in* Palestine—or, in more specific terms, to the forms of life that are not only productive of but also irreducible to various entanglements with power: its apparatuses, forms, techniques, and imaginaries (see Agamben 2013; Anderson 2020; Joronen 2017).

As the authors included here cumulatively make clear, domains of life—family, art, civil society, care, reproduction, hopes, expectations, and so on—exist in particular tension with colonial politics such that the two become not merely collapsible but also aligned in irreducible yet affirmative geographical reciprocity. Just as there is cultural work that sustains occupation so, too, is there a proliferation of forms of life that does precisely the opposite. In a context of settler colonialism, arguably *the* dominant critical framework in research on Palestine over the last two decades, this relationship has been overshadowed in works keenly focused on various eliminatory capacities of power. Much of this has leaned on the work of Patrick Wolfe (2006, 388) and the often-quoted base observation that "settler colonisers come to stay: invasion is a structure not an event." It is difficult to overstate the influence of this idea on academic work on Palestine/Israel, even if it is not without pointed critique (e.g., Barakat 2018; Englert 2020) and even though settler colonial studies, by now an established subdiscipline, too often overlook antecedents written by Palestinians (e.g., Abu-Lughod 1971; Sayegh 2012; see also Joronen in chapter 10 of this volume). For readers perhaps new to the specific regional focus here, settler colonialism may provide an open way into the text, not only as a methodological approach in dialogue with diverse contexts (e.g., the United States, Australia, Canada, Northern Europe) but also as a readily communicable political critique that has also transcended academia into spaces of public discourse and activism. The contributions here are very much concerned with the politics of settler colonialism—and so we hope with a wider appeal—without confining analysis to the (albeit valuable) tools of settler colonial studies. If we can distill a conceptualization that runs through this book, it might read as follows: settler colonialism *forms through* the colonial encounter, one that is not oriented so unidirectionally toward elimination or replacement, and has many steps along that way—if, indeed, that is the way at all. We aim for readings that see settler colonialism less as a success story and more as a complex set of claims incapable of irreducibly returning everyday life to its (often) structured machinations of power.

It is this possibility, firmly grounded on the irreducibility of life, that we intend to keep—or prize—open. The reason for this is quite simple: such an approach learns from an emerging body of works (Abu Hatoum 2021;

Griffiths 2022; Hammami 2019; Joronen and Griffiths 2019) that begins from the endurance of indigenous voices, agency, and forms of living by looking at how they work against or beyond various methods of elimination, subjugation, exploitation, and dispossession. This move attends to debates on de/colonization that, importantly, bring a past "decoloniality" of the indigenous/colonized culture alongside a forward-looking emphasis on the potentials of decolonized subjectivities (see, e.g., Appadurai 2021; Mbembe 2021). In both temporal movements, indigenous cultures—as forms of life, as ways of knowing and being, as a collection of modes of subjectification—are not (yet *or ever*) wholly subsumed by the claims of those who arrive with designs on control, land, and resources. And yet (we cannot emphasize this point enough), to recognize an irreducibility of life to power is neither to understate colonial violence nor to romanticize nativism as a form of life "free" of power relations. As Lana Tatour (2019) has argued, it is precisely the existence of settler colonialism—essentially focused on the land and the occupation of territories already inhabited by (racialized) others—that brings forth the "native" as a political category, thus further underlining the need to understand culture as a deeply political and *politicizing* category (for a similar argument, see Coulthard 2014; Chandler and Pugh 2022). While there is an irreducibility of life, and its forms, to colonial politics, we must also face a complex politics of culture while training our critical faculties on encounters between the cultural and the political in Palestine.

In a context defined by more than a hundred years of colonialism, seventy years of military occupation, and continuous cycles of explosive and quotidian violence—all centered on the geographical questions of land claims and the right to dwell—it is understandably hard to avoid conceptualizations that render, often a priori, all aspects of living as permeated by the machinations of power. Certainly, this tendency reveals as much about academic work and intellectual conceptualization as it does about the situation itself. But it is also the case that deep colonial legacies lend some comprehensibility—as well as visibility—to the ways in which colonialism inheres in various, often indirect, normalized, and mundane modes of military, legal, administrative, economic, and non-state violence (see Azoulay and Ophir 2009; Berda 2017; Khalidi 2020). Consequences of this can be seen in every moment of living in Palestine, often through multilayered and complex (spatial) arrangements through which various vulnerabilities, structural injustices, and forms of violence are engendered, maintained, and embodied. First, such a ubiquity of violence requires a certain methodological sensitivity: by taking the ways in which Palestinians encounter overlapping modes of colonial violence as a shared starting point, we begin to see more clearly the unspectacular and slow modes of colonial violence that constantly and incrementally harm or impede mundane forms of living (see Griffiths et al. 2022; Hammami 2019; Harker 2020; Joronen 2021; Peteet 2017).

At a base level, a focus on encounter thus offers a way to recognize various overlapping forms of colonial vulnerabilities as they operate through less spectacular forms of everyday life, or the culture of living. Moreover, when the very existence of a culture, and the forms of life it contains, is under a constant threat of being denied, hampered, displaced, incapacitated, assimilated, or even wiped out entirely, a mere steadfastness of holding on to existing forms of living, often by simply continuing to reside within the spaces of colonial violence, can metamorphose culture into a form—or a weapon—of popular resisting. As is documented by many (e.g., Leshem 2015; Meari 2014; Ryan 2015), Palestinian steadfastness (*sumud*) in remaining on native lands and in native homes, despite significant threats to living, has become a crucial cultural component of political resistance against decades of colonial subjugations. The politicization of the everyday realm of living thus might operate through acts of less visible domination, including self-regulating governmentalization, but it cannot prevent forms of life from becoming something the oppressed can embody, mobilize, and cling to so as to refuse or render inoperative its maneuvers. In the middle of various forms of domination, we can hence catch glimpses of a realm of living that contains an aspect, or a residue, that may engender spaces that, while connected to violent realities, always reside partly beyond them—as *inexhaustible* to their violent organizations of space. Indeed, the chapters collected here are precisely testament to this inexhaustibility of life to violence and domination, one that we hope to do justice to in these opening words.

A key aspect that thus runs through *Encountering Palestine* is a call to examine this inexhaustibility and irreducibility—or, more properly, the *ungovernability*—of Palestinian life (Joronen and Griffiths 2022). This does not refer to a simple juxtaposition of cultural histories against the legacies of political violence—the native against the settler, or heroic counter to a regime of control—but to a discussion of power and the ungovernability of life in those spaces where they meet and co-constitute. In this encounter, various (re)configurations of power and culture are set in motion, as each author shows in detail: from swift movements and mirroring tactics to queering and creative openings, from intimate biopolitics to failures and incapacities. This multiplicity to spaces of encounter, one that is foregrounded throughout, leads us to critical thresholds that run analogously to that between politics and culture: governing and ungovernability, violence and life, colonization and decolonization. At these encounters we can more clearly see the *complexity* of colonial violence while also maintaining a certain *ethical sensibility* toward the lives, voices, and experiences of those who must dwell within the destructive ramifications of power and who are, most notably, directed to the sites of emergence that not only reform, reclaim, and renew but also *undo* geographies of power. *Encountering Palestine* is not merely about the making of colonial space but also, and crucially, about an *ethical sensibility toward the complexity of its unmaking.*

Here, we arrive at the second key aspect addressed in this book—an approach to the question of power as a process of *un/making*. To some extent, this point follows the former—from the ungovernability and inexhaustibility of life (and forms of life) to power—as encounters with power always reveal something of the making of violent forms and techniques of governing: their incompleteness, fragility, and open-endedness. To be sure, this does not entail excluding important elaborations focused more explicitly on techniques of power or their genealogical formations over decades of colonizing presences in Palestine. As several chapters that follow also underline, colonial formations and techniques go hand in hand with the evolution of modernity and capitalism in as much as they contain modes of violence and power—from biopolitics to thanato-politics—that are well addressed in existing work in geography and beyond (see Englert 2020; Ghanim 2008; Gregory 2004; Griffiths and Repo 2018; Joronen 2016; Medien 2019; Saldanha 2020; Shalhoub-Kevorkian 2016). What is offered here is an elaboration of such forms from a particular perspective, where they are seen explicitly through their sites of formation—through the makings that are always unfinished, paradoxical, interrupted, incapable, on the move, and, importantly, unmade. While this obviously highlights the problems related to armchair geographies and (geo)political remote sensing that reduce Palestine to buzzwords that, often in the name of theoretical coherence, can appear plausible (only) from afar, above all it helps to underline the *nonstrategic* as a key aspect for thinking at the threshold between making and unmaking of various modalities of power. Regardless of whether these formations in un/making contain more widely known modes of power (e.g., biopolitics, neoliberalism) or yet-to-be-named ones, what we want to emphasize here is less their use as analytical frameworks and more their presence as interpretive reservoirs for analyses that start, not from the strategic success stories or the coherencies of power, governing, or domination but from the messy sites of encountering and un/doing power. At such sites, the structures of power break down into the *claims* of power—that is, into claims upon life and in which encountering is never reducible to a form, a tactic, or a domination that these claims contain (see Joronen and Rose 2020; Rose 2007). What emerges are detailed accounts of encounter that recognize colonial forms as primarily a *response* to the problem of governing life; thus, as a response, colonial power remains always—whether greatly or marginally—secondary to life's multiplicity, ungovernability, and irreducibility.

The focus on encounter—the irreducibilities that it underlines, the processes of unmaking that it contains—serves to guard against becoming enchanted by the claims colonial apparatuses make upon its efficacy. Encounters, we hold, open a view of various forms of (colonial) power, not simply in their process of making but also through the lives of those who must dwell in its violent spatialities. This is as much about underlining the complexity of power and colonial violence as it is about an ethical sensibility toward life that is always inexhaustible in its movements. Encounter, in other words, brings us to those *sites* where power becomes not only exercised, claimed, complex, and made but also escaped, canceled, mitigated, refused, and unmade. It is to this threshold of un/making that we orient this book.

Making Space for Encounter

It is not via an overly complex justification that we arrive at the theme of encounter, especially given that this is a context where colonizer and colonized lives—culture and power, indigeneity and politics—are so intimately entwined. To be sure, it is not only in Palestine that colonizers have arrived and, in addition to ruling and exploiting, made sovereign claims on lands already inhabited by others. As an invigorating body of research has (re) emphasized in recent years, wider struggles against settler colonialism—for instance, those of First Nations in Canada (Coulthard 2014), Aboriginal peoples in Australia (Howlett and Lawrence 2019; Povinelli 2016), and Native Americans in the United States (Byrd 2011; Simpson 2014; Van Sant, Milligan, and Mollett 2021)—and other forms of colonial relations (Davies and Isakjee 2019; Naylor et al. 2018; Radcliffe 2017; Sundberg 2014) are very much ongoing and politically pointed in even the most quotidian sites of encounter. Yet, a definite degree of antagonism, experimentation, and proliferation in making the colonial frontier marks the *intensity* of Israel's colonial project in Palestine, where the pervasive creep of colonial expansion and the vastly different topologies it en/forces consist in such starkly contested geographical terms. The extremist settlers who occupy Palestinian homes in Hebron, the settlement extensions that threaten Bedouin homes in the South Hebron Hills, the strangulation of Palestinian villages amid vast settlement blocks—each of these and innumerable other sites are products and productive of encounters between colonial bodies and logics that alternatively simmer and erupt as various forms of spatial and embodied violence. It is only here, conversely, that encounter is so strictly

GRIFFITHS AND JORONEN

delimited; for instance, walls and roads segregate (and make) neighbors and enemies, creating parallel topologies that maintain a simultaneous separation and proximity. It is only here that such a vociferous animosity toward the colonized foments normalized moves from both right and left of the political spectrum, from scarcely believable calls for "settler rights" or against "miscegenation" to more liberal sensibilities to "save" Palestinian queer and women victims of primitive patriarchy. It is only here that these become more than questions of representation and pass into embodied or entangled forms of encounter that are continually in formation both in the name of settler incapacity and the irreducibility of colonized forms of life.

Our turn to encounter, then, emerges from a context where difference and definition form through a particular presence of the Other—the settler and the native, colonizing aims and decolonizing ruptures, captures and escapes—with demarcations that can only be understood as *irreducibly co-constitutive*. And nothing is stable or decided in advance; the "contact zone" of colonial encounter is a space where "cultures meet, clash, and grapple with each other," as Mary Louise Pratt (1991, 33) famously wrote. Further, in that most violent grapple, we are forced to reckon with Gloria Anzaldúa's (1987, 25) evocative figure of an "open wound" that bleeds "and before [a] scab forms it haemorrhages again, the lifeblood of two worlds merging to form a third country." These now-canonical characterizations serve as notable antecedents in an intellectual project of realizing something of the full critical concept of encounter.

For contemporary geographers in particular, encounter has shifted from a normative (and, it must be said, somewhat naive) assumption that it precedes a greater "tolerance of difference" toward a more dynamic opening of a "distinctive event of relations . . . within the remit of difference, rupture and surprise" (Wilson 2017, 452; see also Cockayne, Ruez, and Secor 2020; Ruez 2016). *Rupture* and *surprise* are key correctives; they indicate nothing is given and that while encounters are prefaced by preexisting power relations, they are also productive of *different* ones—ones that might be formed through or simply *happen* unpredictably in the encounter. Indeed, encounters are not only about reciprocal makings, where two poles—

colonized and colonizers, structures and agencies—make and unmake one another. Encounters also expose the strategic to the unpredictable, claims to ruptures, machinations to surprise. As Françoise Dastur (2000, 183) writes, it is precisely the nature of the event to force out not only difference but also the possibility of what to some extent seems at first *impossible*; by "coming to us without coming from us," events lay before us something unexpected that nevertheless does happen, thus making the "impossible possible." These unexpected ruptures and surprises come not only from the reciprocity of power relations but, importantly, to *interrupt* them. Here, the *irreducibility* in the phrase "irreducibly co-constitutive" speaks most clearly: while ruptures and surprises constantly remake and undo power relations, they also make visible the irreducibility of the encounter to the strategic and, effectively, to the relational itself (see Harrison 2007). Encounters, in other words, are never simply about recognizing the constitutive role of relational other(s)—the settler and *its* native, the native and *its* settler. Encounter is also about the facticity of the situation happening and forcing itself to become encountered and thought. Encounter, in this regard, is never reducible to relations or produced through "representations"; it is rather a call for participation, to think and act in its sites and spaces.

Encounter thus lends itself to thinking around power and life, and their forms, cultures, and politics in Palestine. First, it encourages an approach to questions of power that is not tied to preset "structures" (such as *the* settler colonial structure of elimination) or to assumptions of always-capable agencies that heroically make and counter. Encounter directs us toward the spaces of *un/making*: to structures in their incomplete processes of emergence (e.g., Stoler 2016), to agencies whose possibilities are disclosed (and foreclosed) in the process of contact (e.g., Athanasiou 2016; Griffiths 2017; Hammami 2019; Simandan 2019), and to ruptures that emerge in and from those same comings together (e.g., Pyyry and Aiava 2020; Wilson 2017). Seen through encounter, agencies are, almost without exception, less capable than they claim; structures, less complete than their articulations suggest; and strategic forms, rationalizations, and preconfigured techniques, more reassuring than what their blueprints indicate. Second, the notion of encounter sharpens a focus on precisely what emerges as part of these spaces of making. This not only signposts the incompleteness and (im)potentiality to all processes of making but also underlines the constant *undoing* of power in those relations in which it becomes actualized. Again, undoing should not be understood as a mere *capacity* to (un)do but also through that stubborn aspect of life that remains always ungovernable—the surprises and unexpected events that, to reuse Dastur's (2000) neat formulation, "come to us without coming from us." Third, as the reference to events and surprise also underlines, encounters contain aspects that are not simply returnable to the relational constitutions of power and life, settlers and natives, politics and culture but that come to these relations as givens. These surprises—which are never reducible to the strategic—prompt or even force responses (see Joronen and Häkli 2017). Events in this regard are a call for encounter, and thus for a response and (re)action, or even escape. But such an irreducibility to the strategic and its dialectical reciprocities contains more than just a call: it might point toward what happens to us and forces us to respond, yet it also guides toward the *irreducibility* of life (and the forms it takes) to various techniques of governing and control. The machinations and maneuvers of power can never wholly capture, in other words, the *ungovernability* of life: its events, its surprises, its irreducibilities.

On these three fronts—the relational constitution, the processes of (un)making, the irreducibility of life to governing—we can open up encounter as a versatile and elastic concept. Indeed, with these qualities we are not aiming to enclose possible frames that limit the vocabularies through which encounters should and could be approached. By doing so, we wish instead to open the notion of encounter to various uses. Whether angled toward the relational, processual (un/making), or ungovernable—or to some combination of them—each chapter of this book offers its own conceptual and thematic dealings with encounter.

In the opening chapter, Kathryn Medien's contribution locates the site of encounter in the (bio)politicization of the body. In particular, she documents and critiques an Israeli civil society organization, Yad L'Achim, that intervenes in mixed Palestinian-Israeli relationships by "rescuing" Jewish

Israeli women whom it sees as "preyed upon" by Palestinian men. Medien makes the careful and substantiated argument that such practices—carried out by a readily mobilized cohort of Israeli volunteers—reveal a biopolitical dynamic where mixed Palestinian-Israeli relationships exceed the heteronormativity and biologized categories at the center of the idea of the state. This critical intervention broadens the account of colonialism in Palestine to Israeli civil society organizations and shows how bodies themselves are sites of encounters within the broader logics of settler colonial (bio)power. Sophie Richter-Devroe follows this in chapter 2 with a focus on state capitalist expropriation of the commons and an account of Bedouin women's struggles with space, ownership, and forms of living in the Naqab region. In particular, Richter-Devroe attends to the logic of the "witch hunt" in settler capitalist (re)organizing of communal lands, labor relations, and reproductive capacities of female bodies, showing also the ways Bedouin women undo various aims to dispossess and eliminate them from the commons and indigenous forms of living. Tales of modernization and development are held to the light here and, as is so often the case, exposed for their intimacy with colonialism and the ways that narratives of progress preface the dispossession of native lands. Richter-Devroe articulates social, cultural, and political spaces that not only encounter but also counter and remain beyond the biopolitical and modernizing logics of Israeli settler capitalism.

In the third chapter, Wassim Ghantous moves the focus to settler-state assemblages in rural areas of the West Bank. Through an elaboration of the Deleuzian notion of the "War Machine," or that which names the assemblage of state and non-state actors (settler organizations and hybrid security bodies), Ghantous shows how violence issues from spatial-affective relations where a constant threat—or "imminent (in)security"—makes every village, every home, every structure, and every Palestinian body a site of an always-possible eruption of spectacular violence. The figuring of Palestinians as imminent security threats, Ghantous argues, allows the assemblages of the Israeli War Machine to target Palestinian bodies and spaces with a "speedy, unpredictable, and geographically unbounded" mode of "vortical violence." It is via the notion of encounter that the account is further enriched: Palestinians caught within this "vortical violence" are never entirely subsumed as they find new—complementing but not wholly derivative—modes of machinic and rhizomatic sumud in their steadfast protection of their homes and livelihoods. In chapter 4, Mark Griffiths remains with the sphere of (settler) civil society to track the operations of Regavim—an Israeli "settler human rights NGO" (nongovernmental organization)—in the southern West Bank, where it collects data to petition Israeli courts for demolition orders on Palestinian structures. Its growth and successes have made Regavim a primary node of Palestinians' encounter with colonialism, where the state is alternatively a facilitator of and a check on Regavim's particularly extremist approach to eliminating native structures and presences on the land. Regavim's capacities to carry out its work rest on a prominent donor-targeted marketing campaign that, Griffiths suggests, can be understood productively as a mediated "hyperreality" in which the proliferation of images effaces "other realities." Crucially, he further documents, targeted Palestinian communities are active in the (re) making of these power dynamics by adapting Regavim's tactics for their own ends in the practices of grassroots advocacy and publicity that show, with no glorification or romanticization, a mode of anticolonial resistance that is as dynamic as it is subtle.

Rhys Machold contributes chapter 5 and turns to Israel's image as a tech-savvy "start-up nation" and to the specific case of its Iron Dome missile interception system. By looking at various encounters with critical views that question the system's capacities and its "success stories," Machold demonstrates how "staying with the trouble"—the failures and shortcomings of Iron Dome—can reveal the ways in which certain ideas of Israel's progressiveness, superiority, and modernity are formed, assumed, and diffused. In particular, Machold argues that by following the failures of Iron Dome, it becomes possible to challenge not only the representations of Israel as an effective and innovative start-up nation but also the key presumptions related to settler colonial forms of power in Palestine/Israel (and beyond). Moving toward more coded forms of violent space making,

Haim Yacobi and Moriel Ram's chapter 6 elaborates the scalar politics of neo-apartheid in contemporary Jerusalem. A focus on the scale of the city, they show, forces us to look at the broader regime of separation as a messy politics, where state mechanisms of segregation, coded forms of discrimination, violent dispossession, and neoliberal restructuring intersect and become encountered as lived reality. Jerusalem thus offers a scalar view on how apartheid as a political project is dependent on other forces and rationalities that shape settler colonial spaces and structures of control in Palestine/Israel. Here, ways of dispossessing Palestinians are shown to contain encounters that also engender odd anomalies, perhaps most clearly present in the figure of Palestinians living in settlements normalized as part of the urban milieu of Jerusalem, that further highlight the importance of examining forms of domination in relation to their scalar specificities.

In the seventh chapter, Tiina Järvi examines the lived realities of encounter in Palestinian refugee camps in the West Bank and in Lebanon. By paying close attention to Palestinian family life, Järvi takes us to the at once mundane yet profound decisions made by Palestinian refugee families in their efforts to safeguard the—or a—future. With a particular focus on the tension between cultural expectations and anticipations of what is possible in the context of lacking opportunities, she demonstrates the ways that encounter can be temporal, where colonial and cultural impositions coalesce and demand anticipatory response. In chapter 8, Arun Saldanha moves to more surrealist visions of Palestinian future/s in an examination of expressions of decolonization and state power in Elia Suleiman's 2002 film *Divine Intervention*. Saldanha shows how Suleiman's surrealist cinema creates a poetic space for encounters that, by blurring the boundaries between reality and imagination, "probes into the occupation's more ridiculous dimensions." Through ironic twists, humorous scenes, and ambivalent images, Saldanha shows how Suleiman's often bizarre cinema offers an alternative view of a Palestinian future, one that ridicules the absurdities of state power while pointing toward less militant and anti-nationalist forms of decolonization.

In the book's penultimate chapter, Walaa Alqaisiya writes evocatively and politically on "queering esthesis," a form of native cultural resistance to the violence of the colonial sensual regime, or "pinkwashing." Alqaisiya exposes the logics of power that underpin that regime in the example of Israel's victory at the 2018 Eurovision Song Contest before discussing the ways that different Palestinian artists queer the settler colonial configuration of sex and sense. The artists' works are as creative as they are political: the medium of film exposes the collusion between sexual modernity and the negation of violence, reworked folk songs map native return, and dance reinscribes native queerness into the colonized landscape. Each of these examples, Alqaisiya shows, not only (further) highlights the conceit to Israel's (self-)image as a sexually liberated (and thus modern) sanctuary but also challenges the amnesia of settler colonialism by remaking the space in the image of the native. In the final chapter, Mikko Joronen problematizes the commonplace framing of Palestinian spaces through narrow readings of settler colonialism, questioning specifically the abilities afforded to notions of colonial power. By moving the focus from power's capacities to its woundedness, Joronen suggests a reading where power does not emerge as a particular type or a preset form but through its own incapacity to maintain what it claims for itself. And yet, Joronen further argues, power is not only inherently vulnerable and fragile, a wounded power, but also epiphenomenal to the original receptivity and exposure of life. This reveals a double movement between a wounded life and epiphenomenal power that is always seeking another form, technique, or maneuver in the face of its own impotence. Through examples drawn from fieldwork in the West Bank communities, Joronen demonstrates how this woundedness (of and to power) offers an original scene of encounter for research on the colonization of (everyday) spaces in Palestine.

Encountering Palestine is brought to an eloquent close with Zena Agha's "Elegy for Return," a four-part poem animated by the photography of Dorothy Allen-Pickard. The words are mournful and powerful. We leave them to speak with their full force.

Encounters take place, it seems, not simply between the colonizers and the colonized but also on various fronts: in bodies, cinema, and simulacra;

through failures, vulnerable exposures, and vortical and rhizomatic move-ments; in relation to future, artistic queering, and urban spaces; between the state, settlers, and existing forms of living. By drawing critical attention to these fronts of encounter, the contributors grasp through various com-binations of themes, trends, and intellectual registers—be they old, new, or both—spaces that are emerging and failing, capable and incapable, in the *making* and *unmaking*. In this focus on un/making, we—the editors and the authors—wish to amplify the voices of the colonized, the oppressed, and the subaltern as they encounter forms of violence. Still, we also aim a little further: to move the focus to sites where these voices remain multiple, formative, and inexhaustible, often emerging in a fashion that is chaotic but nevertheless posed in some relation to, or at least in the shadows of, various claims of oppressive political violence. Indeed, whether claimed or ignored, maintained or refused, forced or decolonized, enclosed or unfolded, these spaces are caught up in what has already called forth an encounter, a site of encounter. It is to this geography of power, the sites of unmaking, that the following encounters will lead us.

References

Abu Hatoum, Nayrouz. 2021. "Decolonising [in the] Future: Scenes of Palestinian Tem-porality." *Geografiska Annaler: Series B, Human Geography* 103 (4): 397–412.

Abu-Lughod, Ibrahim. 1971. *The Transformation of Palestine: Essays on the Origin and Development of the Arab-Israeli Conflict*. Evanston IL: Northwestern University Press.

Agamben, Giorgio. 2013. *The Highest Poverty: Monastic Rules and Form-of-Life*. Stanford: Stanford University Press.

Anderson, Ben. 2020. "Cultural Geography III: The Concept of 'Culture.'" *Progress in Human Geography* 44 (3): 608–17.

Anzaldúa, Gloria. 1987. *Borderlands: La Frontera*. San Francisco: Aunt Lute Books.

Appadurai, Arjun. 2021. "The Future of Postcolonial Thought." *The Nation*, March 6, 2021.

Athanasiou, Athena. 2016. "Nonsovereign Agonism (or, Beyond Affirmation versus Vul-nerability)." In *Vulnerability in Resistance*, edited by Judith Butler, Zeynep Gambetti, and Leticia Sabsay, 256–77. Durham NC: Duke University Press.

Azoulay, Ariella, and Adi Ophir. 2009. "The Order of Violence." In *The Power of Inclusive Exclusion*, edited by Adi Ophir, Michal Givoni, and Sari Hanafi, 99–140. New York: Zone Books.

Barakat, Rana. 2018. "Writing/Righting Palestine Studies: Settler Colonialism, Indigenous Sovereignty and Resisting the Ghost(s) of History." *Settler Colonial Studies* 8 (3): 349–63.

Berda, Yael. 2017. *Living Emergency: Israel's Permit Regime in the Occupied West Bank.* Palo Alto CA: Stanford University Press.

Byrd, Jodi. 2011. *The Transit of Empire: Indigenous Critiques of Colonialism.* Minneapolis: University of Minnesota Press.

Chandler, David, and Jonathan Pugh. 2022. "Interstitial and Abyssal Geographies." *Political Geography* 98.

Cockayne, Daniel G., Derek Ruez, and Anna J. Secor. 2020. "Thinking Space Differently: Deleuze's Möbius Topology for a Theorisation of the Encounter." *Transactions of the Institute of British Geographers* 45 (1): 194–207.

Coulthard, Glen Sean. 2014. *Red Skin, White Masks: Rejecting the Colonial Politics of Recognition.* Minneapolis: University of Minnesota Press.

Dastur, Françoise. 2000. "Phenomenology of the Event: Waiting and Surprise." *Hypatia* 16 (4): 178–89.

Davies, Thomas, and Arshad Isakjee. 2018. "Ruin of Empire: Refugees, Race and the Postcolonial Geographies of European Migrant Camps." *Geoforum* 102 (June): 214–17.

Englert, Sai. 2020. "Settlers, Workers, and the Logic of Accumulation by Dispossession." *Antipode* 52 (6): 1647–66.

Ghanim, Honaida. 2008. "Thanatopolitics: The Case of the Colonial Occupation in Palestine." In *Thinking Palestine*, edited by Ronit Lentin, 65–81. New York: Zed Books.

Gregory, Derek. 2004. *The Colonial Present: Afghanistan. Palestine. Iraq.* Oxford: Wiley-Blackwell.

Griffiths, Mark. 2017. "Hope in Hebron: The Political Affects of Activism in a Strangled City." *Antipode* 49 (3): 617–35.

———. 2022. "Thanato-Geographies of Palestine and the Possibility of Politics." *Environment and Planning C: Politics and Space* 40 (8). https://doi.org/10.1177/23996544221099461.

Griffiths, Mark, and Jemima Repo. 2018. "Biopolitics and Checkpoint 300 in Occupied Palestine: Bodies, Affect, Discipline." *Political Geography* 65:17–25.

Griffiths, Mark, Yael Berda, Mikko Joronen, and Lara Kilani. 2022. "Israel's International Mobilities Regime: Visa Restrictions for Educators and Medics in Palestine." *Territory, Politics, Governance.* https://doi.org/10.1080/21622671.2022.2095008.

Hammami, Rema. 2019. "Destabilizing Mastery and the Machine: Palestinian Agency and Gendered Embodiment at Israeli Military Checkpoints." *Current Anthropology* 60 (19): s87–s97.

Harker, Christopher. 2020. *Spacing Debt: Obligations, Violence, and Endurance in Ramallah, Palestine.* Durham NC: Duke University Press.

Harrison, Paul. 2007. "How Shall I Say It . . . ? Relating the Nonrelational." *Environment and Planning A* 39 (3): 590–608.

Howlett, Catherine, and Rebecca Lawrence. 2019. "Accumulating Minerals and Dispossessing Indigenous Australians: Native Title Recognition as Settler-Colonialism." *Antipode* 51 (3): 818–37.

Joronen, Mikko. 2016. "Death Comes Knocking on the Roof: Thanatopolitics of Ethical Killing during Operation Protective Edge in Gaza." *Antipode* 48 (2): 336–54.

———. 2017. "'Refusing to Be a Victim, Refusing to Be an Enemy': Form-of-Life as Resistance in the Palestinian Struggle against Settler Colonialism." *Political Geography* 56:91–100.

———. 2021. "Unspectacular Spaces of Slow Wounding in Palestine." *Transactions of the Institute of British Geographers* 46 (4): 995–1007.

Joronen, Mikko, and Jouni Häkli. 2017. "Politicizing Ontology." *Progress in Human Geography* 41 (5): 561–79.

Joronen, Mikko, and Mark Griffiths. 2019. "The Affective Politics of Precarity: Home Demolitions in the Occupied West Bank." *Environment and Planning D: Society and Space* 37 (3): 561–76.

———. 2022. "Ungovernability and Ungovernable Life in Palestine." *Political Geography* 98:1–10.

Joronen, Mikko, and Mitch Rose. 2020. "Vulnerability and Its Politics: Precarity and the Woundedness of Power." *Progress in Human Geography* 45 (6): 1402–18.

Khalidi, Rashid. 2020. *The Hundred Years' War on Palestine: A History of Settler Colonialism and Resistance, 1917–2017*. New York: Metropolitan Books.

Leshem, Noam. 2015. "'Over Our Dead Bodies': Placing Necropolitical Activism." *Political Geography* 45:34–44.

Massad, Joseph. 2006. *The Persistence of the Palestinian Question: Essays on Zionism and the Palestinians*. London: Routledge.

Mbembe, Achille. 2021. *Out of the Dark Night: Essays on Decolonization*. New York: Duke University Press.

Meari, Lena. 2014. "Sumud: A Palestinian Philosophy of Confrontation in Colonial Prisons." *South Atlantic Quarterly* 113 (3): 547–78.

Medien, Kathryn. 2019. "Palestine in Deleuze." *Theory, Culture & Society* 36 (5): 49–70.

Naylor, Lindsay, Michelle Daigle, Sofia Zaragocin, Margaret Marietta Ramírez, and Mary Gilmartin. 2018. "Interventions: Bringing the Decolonial to Political Geography." *Political Geography* 66:199–209.

Peteet, Julie. 2017. *Space and Mobility in Palestine*. Bloomington: Indiana University Press.

Povinelli, Elizabeth A. 2016. *Geontologies: A Requiem to Late Liberalism*. Durham NC: Duke University Press.

Pratt, Mary Louise. 1991. *Imperial Eyes: Travel Writing and Transculturation*. London: Routledge.

Puar, Jasbir. 2007. *Terrorist Assemblages*. Durham NC: Duke University Press.

Pyyry, Noora, and Raine Aiava. 2020. "Enchantment as Fundamental Encounter: Wonder and the Radical Reordering of Subject/World." *Cultural Geographies* 27 (4): 581–95.

Radcliffe, Sarah. 2017. "Decolonising Geographical Knowledges." *Transactions of the Institute of British Geographers* 42 (3): 329–33.

Rose, Mitch. 2007. "The Problem of Power and the Politics of Landscape: Stopping the Greater Cairo Ring Road." *Transactions of the Institute of British Geographers* 32 (4): 460–76.

Ruez, Derek. 2016. "'I Never Felt Targeted as an Asian . . . until I Went to a Gay Pub': Sexual Racism and the Aesthetic Geographies of the Bad Encounter." *Environment and Planning A: Economy and Space* 49 (4): 893–910.

Ryan, Caitlin. 2015. "Everyday Resilience as Resistance: Palestinian Women Practicing Sumud." *International Political Sociology* 9 (4): 299–315.

Said, Edward. 1978. *Orientalism*. London: Penguin.

———. 1993. *Culture & Imperialism*. London: Chatto & Windus.

Saldanha, Arun. 2020. "A Date with Destiny: Racial Capitalism and the Beginnings of the Anthropocene." *Environment and Planning D: Society and Space* 38 (1): 12–34.

Sayegh, Fayez A. 2012. "Zionist Colonialism in Palestine (1965)." *Settler Colonial Studies* 2 (1): 206–25.

Shalhoub-Kevorkian, Nadera. 2016. "The Biopolitics of Israeli Settler Colonialism: Palestinian Bedouin Children Theorise the Present." *Journal of Holy Land and Palestine Studies* 15 (1): 7–29.

Simandan, Dragos. 2019. "Revisiting Positionality and the Thesis of Situated Knowledge." *Dialogues in Human Geography* 9 (2):129–49.

Simpson, Audra. 2014. *Mohawk Interruptus: Political Life across the Borders of Settler States*. Durham NC: Duke University Press.

Stoler, Ann Laura. 2016. *Duress: Imperial Durabilities in Our Times*. Durham NC: Duke University Press.

Sundberg, Juanita. 2014. "Decolonizing Posthumanist Geographies." *Cultural Geographies* 21 (1): 33–47.

Tatour, Lana. 2019. "The Culturalisation of Indigeneity: The Palestinian-Bedouin of the Naqab and Indigenous Rights." *International Journal of Human Rights* 23 (10): 1569–93.

Van Sant, Levi, Richard Milligan, and Sharlene Mollett. 2021. "Political Ecologies of Race: Settler Colonialism and Environmental Racism in the United States and Canada." *Antipode* 53 (3): 629–42.

Wilson, Helen F. 2017. "On Geography and Encounter: Bodies, Borders, and Difference." *Progress in Human Geography* 41 (4): 451–71.

Wolfe, Patrick. 2006. "Settler Colonialism and the Elimination of the Native." *Journal of Genocide Research* 8 (4): 387–409.

1   An Intimate Occupation

Governing Love in Occupied Palestine

Kathryn Medien

In November 2018 the Israeli orthodox organization Yad L'Achim posted an
article titled "Youth Cruelly Cut Off from His Mother and Raised in Arab
Village, Reunited with His People." The article tells the story of Binyamin
(formally named Kamal), aged nineteen, who "was born in a hostile Arab
village in the north of Israel to a Jewish mother and an Arab father" (2018).
Binyamin had been raised by his Palestinian father following his parents'
divorce but had later ended up estranged from all family. After being "put
in touch with Yad L'Achim by a Jew who heard his story and understood
that his true desire was to return to the Jewish people" (Yad L'Achim 2018),
the organization arranged for Binyamin to take lessons in Hebrew and
Judaism and provided him with access to necessities such as food and
clothes. Detailing Binyamin's *hatafas dam* bris ceremony, whereby he formally converted to Judaism and received his new name, the article ends
by stating that such "success stories only motivate us to continue and treat
thousands of others with similar stories who are crying out for help. We
won't rest or be quiet until we bring them back home" (Yad L'Achim 2018).

"Back home," for Yad L'Achim, refers to the Jewish faith and the state of
Israel, understood as the exclusive homeland of the Jewish people. Formed
in 1950 and working under the motto "We don't give up on even a single
Jew!" Yad L'Achim runs a range of services: "rescue missions" of Jewish
women in relationships with Palestinian men, a hotline to report mixed
Palestinian-Israeli relationships, social reintegration programs for the "sur-
vivors" and children of mixed relationships, belated circumcision and bar

mitzvah ceremonies for children raised in non-Jewish households, and campaigns against Christian missionaries working in Israel. In so doing, the organization reports that the "phenomenon [of mixed relationships] is growing, and hundreds of cases a year are reported to Yad L'Achim" (Yad L'Achim n.d.c). Organized and carried out by Yad L'Achim and its self-described activists, its activities take place within a broader context where intimate relations between Palestinians and Israelis are deemed taboo and are understood as a threat to the Israeli state and its colonial project (Hakak 2016; Ihmoud 2018). Other organizations that similarly partake in anti-miscegenation activism to intervene in mixed Palestinian-Israeli intimate relationships include Lehava, Lev L'Achim, and Derekh Hayim, while in some Israeli cities Jewish citizens have formed vigilante patrols to break up mixed relationships (see Lee 2013; Freedman 2009). In this chapter, I examine the reports and articles concerning "rescue missions" carried out by Yad L'Achim, exploring how these activities support the settler colonial project of the Israeli state by serving Zionism's biopolitical and geopolitical demographic drive to keep separate Palestinians and Israelis, and to prevent population mixing, while also seeking to decrease the overall Palestinian population (Shalhoub-Kevorkian 2015b; Shragai 2010; Yiftachel 1999). At the same time, in analyzing these so-called rescue missions that stage the body as a site of encounter, I ask how such Israeli citizen-led infrastructures of surveillance and control can help us better understand the quotidian ways in which bodies are spatially disciplined within regimes of occupation and how central to such infrastructures is the regulation of family life, intimacy, and reproduction.

In Israel's mode of colonial occupation, "the 'need' for a Jewish majority" (Yuval-Davis 1989) has resulted in the proliferation of an intricate system of colonial rule that privileges "the lives of Zionist settlers at the expense of the Palestinians and their homes and livelihoods" (Griffiths and Repo 2018, 18), producing a territory that is "fragmented, shattered by colonisation and closure" (Tawil-Souri 2012, 155). In spatial terms, Eyal Weizman's (2007, 6) analysis of the post-1967 occupation of the West Bank, East Jerusalem, and the Gaza Strip demonstrates how the state of Israel has sought to impose and maintain a porous, flexible system of micro-borders aimed at colonizing and controlling Palestine and the Palestinian people, and at producing what he names as an "elastic geography" of occupation. Scholars studying this elastic geography of occupation have importantly elaborated on the various Israeli state tactics and strategies of governance and control that are brought to bear upon Palestinians and their land. In the most recent phase of occupation after the Oslo Accords (1993)—a set of agreements that were purported to serve as a "peace treaty"—Helga Tawil-Souri (2012, 155) has noted that "Israel's unique colonial project is focused on incorporating as much (Palestinian) territory but with as few Palestinians as possible." To realize this, Neve Gordon (2008) has argued, the Israeli state has increasingly focused on attempts to "separate" the Palestinian and Israeli populations. This intricate micromanagement of Palestinian populations, which are both separated from Israelis and from one another, is facilitated via a range of technologies and infrastructures, such as checkpoints, roadblocks, radars, X-ray machines, security walls, remote-controlled bulldozers used for house demolitions, drones, identity cards, work permits, and the creation of closed military zones, administrative divisions, and seam zones, among other land categorizations. At the same time, as Tawil-Souri (2012, 164) further argues, this infrastructure of occupation often leaves the Jewish-Israeli population unaffected: "Jewish-Israeli mobility is largely un-bounded either in Israeli or Palestinian spaces, whereas Palestinians are often forbidden from moving within their own spaces, let alone in/out of Israel."

Social scientists examining these infrastructures of colonial occupation have drawn attention to how such technologies survey, monitor, and manage the Palestinian population and territory, "penetrating the most seemingly imitate spaces of everyday life" (Ritchie 2015, 623). Here, scholars have drawn on and developed Michel Foucault's analytic of biopower to examine how a productive politics of life, death, and debilitation shape Palestinian subjectification, movement, and daily life through the creation and perpetuation of heteronormative gendered hierarchies and divisions of labor and reproduction (Abu Awwad 2016; Boano and Martén 2013; Griffiths and

Repo 2018; Hamayel, Hammoudeh, and Welchman 2017; Parsons and Salter 2008; Puar 2017; Pugliese 2020). Taking Checkpoint 300 as their site of analysis, Mark Griffiths and Jemima Repo (2018, 19) argue that checkpoints function as a productive biopolitical site, producing "a heteronormative sexual division of labour that is conducive to Israeli state biopolitics." In her analysis of the Israeli state control over Palestine agriculture, Nida Abu Awwad (2016, 557) argues that land confiscations and restrictions produce a productive "colonialist exploitative gender ideology" whereby the Israeli authorities issue "permits only for women . . . they exploit the common notion that women are weak and unable to take on all these tasks, and assume that if women cannot complete the work, Palestinian agricultural fields behind the separation wall will be destroyed." In common across this scholarship is an attempt to examine what operates against and in excess of technologies and mechanisms of separation and how Palestinians "actively and relentlessly 'work'" through such technologies to keep "surviving in the present" (Hammami 2015, 14–15).

This chapter builds on this literature both by examining a site of spatial and bodily encounter that is deemed in excess of infrastructures of separation and by exploring how the non-state regulation and control of mixed Palestinian-Israeli relationships form part of the broader intimate infrastructure of colonial occupation in Palestine/Israel. While much scholarly attention has been given to Israeli state attempts to regulate the intimate everyday lives of Palestinians, less scholarly attention has been directed at moments of intimate encounter *between* Palestinians and Israelis, and how non-state organizations form part of the colonial security infrastructure. As a non-state organization that operates to intervene in and govern relationships between Palestinian men and Jewish Israeli women, Yad L'Achim organizes incursions into Palestinian villages and towns to "take back" Jewish women and their children who are understood as part of the state of Israel's body politic. While these incursions differ from the Israeli military–led invasions involving drones, tanks, bulldozers, and armed forces, they nonetheless work in the service of state biopolitics by governing relationships that pose a threat to the contours of Israel's colonial state–building project. Importantly, in analyzing the regulation and governance of mixed Palestinian-Israeli relationships, I do not suggest that such relationships function as sites of liberation, resistance, or freedom from occupation. Indeed, in settler societies, racial mixing, or "miscegenation" as it is often termed, has been differently instrumentalized and governed to keep populations separate and biologically "pure" via a tactic of indigenous "absorption" (Ellinghaus 2006, 2009; Wolfe 2001) and as a technology through which to declare a "post-racial" society (Mahtani 2014; Nyong'o 2009). Rather, I take these relationships, and the strict regulation of them, as sites through which we can deepen our understanding of gender, sexuality, and reproduction in the context of Israel's occupation of Palestine and specifically elaborate how the activities of Yad L'Achim operate as a form of intimate regulation—that is, an encounter structured by colonial violence—that supports the broader project of settler colonial occupation.

The rest of this chapter forms three sections. In the following section, I outline the theoretical framework for the chapter with a specific focus on how, in the context of Israel's occupation of Palestine, biopower operates through intimate, reproductive politics. In so doing, I situate Yad L'Achim's anti-miscegenation activism within a longer history of reproductive and intimate control. The second section examines reports and articles produced by Yad L'Achim, specifically focusing on how relationships between Palestinian men and Israeli women are framed as an extension of "Palestinian warfare," a scheme that justifies and ushers in citizen-led incursions and population-wide surveillance. The third section considers the politics of rehabilitation, a process that takes place after "successful" rescue missions. I argue that rehabilitation functions as a patriarchal disciplinary site of power that (re)produces the state of Israel through the biologized, yet shifting, category of Jewishness. I close by considering the contributions of this chapter to the broader study of intimacy and colonial occupation.

Sexuality and Reproduction in Occupied Palestine

Alongside and entwined within the militarized technologies of surveillance and control outlined above, as feminist scholars of biopower and settler colonialism have long argued, the regulation and management of the family, reproduction, and intimacy provide key vectors through which colonial control is exercised over both settler and indigenous populations. In her seminal work on Foucault's mapping of biopower, Ann Laura Stoler (1995) suggests that any account of biopower that doesn't take seriously the ways in which discourses of racial survival and sexual regulation in Europe were influenced by the figuring of colonized subjects as posing a sexual and racial threat misses a large part of the history and emergence of biopower. In examining the colonial society of the Dutch East Indies, Stoler (1995, 35) argues that it was "imperial-wide discourses that linked children's health programs to racial survival, tied increasing campaigns for domestic hygiene to colonial expansion, made childrearing an imperial and class duty, and cast white women as the bearers of a more racist imperial order and the custodians of their desire-driven immoral men." By linking imperial expansion to gender and the rise of sexual technologies of biopower, Stoler demonstrates how the political economy of population that Foucault identified was tied to and influenced by sexual practices in the colonies and by associated fears of the demise of the white race. Complementing Stoler's analysis and responding to recent scholarship that has focused heavily on the biopolitics of race, Repo (2016, 112) has further argued that the "exclusive focus on race elides the sexual politics that transforms bodies into productive and reproductive machines through processes of regulation, discipline and subjectification." Building on Foucault's (2003, 255) assertion that sexual biopolitics operates through a racist logic, "separating out groups that exist within a population" in the service of the "cleanliness of the social body" (Foucault [1978] 1998, 54), this scholarship helps us understand how birth rates, reproduction, the family, and other intimate political technologies and institutions become central to the racializing colonial disciplining and regulating of populations. Indeed, for Foucault (2003, 82), it was through ideas of race becoming entangled with sexuality and state sovereignty that "the appearance of what might be called State racism, of a biological and centralized racism," was able to emerge. Thus, rather than managing sexuality—"the birth rate, the mortality rate, longevity, and so on" (Foucault 2003, 243)—to promote the vitality of all, state racism fractured and differentiated the social body by determining which lives should be promoted, regulated, and maximized, or secured for reproduction. Or, as Repo (2013) has put it, "Race is not just a new means of carrying out the death function of sovereign power, but it is a central part of determining whose lives to defend, preserve and regulate." My focus on this intimate sexual politics of occupation, and how the regulatory management of intimate Israeli and Palestinian population mixing, is tied to the broader apparatus of Israeli colonial occupation. I thus concentrate on how bodies are ordered, sorted, produced as governable, and targeted for intervention through a racializing sexual and reproductive politics.

The intimate regulatory surveillance of intimacy and reproduction that Repo identifies is a salient and long-standing feature of Israeli settler colonialism and occupation, and the production and governance of Palestinian and Israeli subjectivities, as well as other groups who live under Israeli rule. Scholars analyzing early Zionist ideology and settlement in Palestine have examined how sexuality and reproduction were key to both the "reinvention" or "regeneration" of Jewish settlers and to the cultivation of Palestinian land, a process that also laid the foundations for the politics of population separation outlined above. In seeking to naturalize Jewish identity in the land of Palestine by drawing out and making concrete the historical links between the Jewish people and their exile from Palestine, early Zionism figured settlement in Palestine as a "return" to a previous state of affairs (Abu El-Haj 2012; Bhandar 2018). Surveying the role that gender and sexuality played in these Zionist narratives of nationalist regeneration, Raz Yosef (2004, 18–19) has argued that early Zionist advocates longed "for a new kind of strong, healthy, proud, and heterosexual Jewish masculinity that would contradict the image of the diaspora Jew as weak, queer, and 'feminine.'" It was this reinvented subject who would create and build the settler state of Israel or, as Brenda Bhandar (2018, 118)argues, it is "through the mixing of his sweat with the soil of Palestine that the exiled Jew would redeem himself, re-forming his attachment to the land of Zion, while at the same time creating a viable and sustainable Jewish economy in Palestine." Through undertaking this nationalist project, Edward Said (1979, 82) has argued that Zionism drew on the logics of European colonialism and the "racial concepts of European culture" and, in so doing, drew "a sharp line between Jew and non-Jew . . . [a category] to which the Arab never belonged" (107).

Building on the project of Jewish regeneration, in the years following the formal establishment of the state of Israel, reproductive health and fertility held immense importance to the state. It is widely accepted that through its wide-ranging investment in Jewish Israeli reproductive capacities, the state of Israel is a world leader in pronatalist policy, which is commonly attributed to a range of factors, including the biblical commandment "be fruitful and multiply," the Holocaust, and what is termed the Palestinian "demographic threat" (Birenbaum-Carmeli 2004; Sperling 2010). These pronatalist policies, often targeting the bodies of Jewish settler women, have been present since the founding of the state in 1948. For example, in 1949, Israel's first prime minister, David Ben-Gurion, announced the award of a symbolic monetary prize for "heroine mothers" who delivered a tenth child (Birenbaum-Carmeli 2004). This policy was subsequently supplemented with a range of other initiatives, including the 1962 setting up of the Natality Committee and the 1968 establishment of the Demographic Centre, which aimed to "carry out reproductive policy intended to create a favourable climate, such that natality will be encouraged and stimulated; an increase in natality in Israel being crucial for the future of the whole Jewish people" (Birenbaum-Carmeli 2004, 902). And today Israeli state pronatalism takes the form of expansive assisted reproductive technology (ART) provision (Nahman 2013), including for posthumous reproduction (Landau 2004), and access to certain ARTs and adoption for lesbian, gay, bisexual, transgender, and queer (LGBTQ) populations. While these policies are often situated within broader Israeli state discourses of sexual and gendered liberalism and rights, they also take place within a context where Palestinian reproduction is strictly regulated. As a result, Puar (2017, 113) has argued that the "excelling of ART in Israel has a biopolitics of population racism intrinsic to its logic," while Sigrid Vertommen (2016, 208) importantly asserts that "Israel's (in)famously pronatalist assisted reproductive policies have been co-produced within a Zionist demographic logic of elimination which aims to create and consolidate a 'Jewish majority in a Jewish state' by containing Palestinian fertility."

Through the literature discussed thus far, we can begin to see how foundational to the Israeli state-building project was the production of Palestinians as antithetical to Israeli modernity and how the biopolitical regulation and proliferation of Jewish Israeli reproduction and fertility take place against the restrictive and invasive regulation of all aspects of Palestinian life. It also allows us to understand how sexuality and gender came to be embedded within the machinery of Israel's occupation and how all bodies in Palestine/Israel are biopolitically governed and ordered toward different but entwined demographic ends. For my analysis of the "rescue missions" carried out by Yad L'Achim, we can understand mixed Palestinian-Israeli intimate relations as sites in which Israel's seemingly pronatalist stance toward Jewish Israeli reproduction and the figuring of Palestinian reproduction as a "demographic threat" meet. A meeting, or encounter, that takes place despite the Israeli state's efforts to separate these populations threatens the biologizing racial logics of the setter colonial state. Indeed, as Sarah Ihmoud (2018, 99) has argued, "The anti-miscegenation movement's focus on the protection of Jewish women and their bodies, and attempts to exercise control over their sexual choices . . . stems from the Zionist construction of women as reproducers of the Jewish nation, and a discourse framing Palestinians as a demographic threat to the security of the nation."

Understanding the historic and present centrality of demographic and reproductive politics to the Israeli settler state provides a vital backdrop within which to situate present anti-miscegenation activism and helps us better understand the certain organizations' investment in intervening in such relationships. Indeed, if the presence and proliferation of mixed Palestinian-Israeli intimate relationships, almost exclusively reported as relations between Palestinian men and Israeli women, threaten the maintenance of Israeli colonialism and the notion of a racially pure Jewish state, then this presents a concern for all those invested in the Israeli state project. Invoking the sanctity and purity of the Jewish woman's body, which plays a central role in the reproduction of the nation, the activities of Yad L'Achim point to a further site where intimacy, family life, and reproduction become a biopolitical target within Israel's occupation of Palestine.

Sexual Warfare

People must understand that Jewish-Arab marriages are part of the larger Israeli-Arab conflict. These girls are in distress, they are wandering the streets and the Arabs take advantage of them. They see it as their goal to marry them and ensure that their children aren't raised as Jews. This is their revenge against the Jewish people. They feel that if they can't defeat us in war, they can wipe us out this way. We must fight this threat as well; it's a matter of national security.

—YAD L'ACHIM n.d.b

Taken from an account of a rescue mission undertaken by Yad L'Achim titled "Non-Conventional Warfare," the quote above offers an insight into how the organization understands the intimate relationships between Palestinian men and Jewish Israeli women. Situating mixed Palestinian-Israeli relationships as part of the broader "conflict" and hailing them as a matter of national security, Yad L'Achim firmly places mixed heterosexual intimate relationships as an act of warfare Palestinian men carry out on the bodies of Israeli women. Posing a threat to the contours of the state of Israel as the exclusive homeland of global Jewry and to the sanctity of the national female body, intimate Palestinian-Israeli relations sit outside national understandings of the family, love, and intimacy. Indeed, despite being heterosexual, such relationships exceed the sexual normativity of that state. Not only are such relationships themselves understood as acts of Palestinian warfare, but they are also articulated as posing a threat to the state's expansive security infrastructure. In September 2014 Yad L'Achim (2014b) reported on the case of an Israeli woman who had been sentenced

An Intimate Occupation

to a year in prison after using her "position as an inspector at a security checkpoint to allow her Arab husband to slip into Israel illegally." Claiming there have been a number of such cases, Yad L'Achim (2014b) states "that the problem of assimilation and intermarriage has a security as well as spiritual component. As such, it represents an existential threat of the highest order." Thus, for Yad L'Achim, rather than miscegenation being understood as a mechanism through which Palestinian populations can be absorbed in the service of a politics of elimination (Wolfe 2001, 2006), mixed Palestinian-Israeli relationships offer us an insight into a different strategy of settler colonial governance and control. Indeed, while the organization does not tolerate the mixed unions, it welcomes both Jewish women and the children born from mixed Palestinian-Israeli relationships "back" into the Israeli state and subjects them to discourses and programs of rehabilitation. This practice, I would suggest, attempts both to maintain the politics of separation and to incorporate both Jewish women and the children born from mixed relationships into the Israeli state. This incorporation, I argue, hinges on understandings of Jewish-ness as formed through what Foucault ([1978] 1998, 149) terms a "thematics of blood," which allows those newly incorporated subjects to "become Israeli" and thereby able to "participate in the process of accumulation by dispossession" (Englert 2020, 1660).

In publishing and narrating mixed relationships within a frame of sexual warfare, Yad L'Achim's reports of rescue missions almost always emphasize patriarchal control and domestic and sexual violence on the part of the Palestinian partner that they attribute to Arab and Muslim culture. For example, in a report detailing the "rescue" of an Israeli-born Jewish woman from the Palestinian village of Umm el-Fahm, Yad L'Achim (n.d.a) noted that after marrying a Palestinian man, the woman "was expected to be completely subservient to her husband, in keeping with Islamic practice." However, following her rescue, "she entered the rescue car and we sped out of town. We took her to an apartment in a secret location that was equipped with food and clothing for the mother and child, as well as warm, supportive social workers" (Yad L'Achim n.d.a). Drawing on the much broader discursive production of Palestinian men as sexually violent, irrational, and intolerant vis-à-vis the purported framings of Israel as a liberal, democratic, and civilized state (Ihmoud 2018; Puar 2017; Shalhoub-Kevorkian 2015a), Yad L'Achim sharply distinguishes between the kinds of modern love, care, and family life found in the state of Israel and that found in Palestine.

Through this figuring of mixed Palestinian-Israeli relationships as a national "existential threat" and its claims that the physical and spiritual safety of Jewish Israeli women is at risk, Yad L'Achim is able to invade Palestinian villages, towns, and cities, "taking back" children and women deemed part of Israel's body politic. While scholarship examining Israeli incursions into Palestinian land often focuses on bureaucratic and militarized technologies of occupation, the incursions carried about by volunteer Yad L'Achim activists represent another axis of Israel's "demographic war" (Faitelson 2009) against Palestinians. Delimiting the ability of Palestinians to create and live out family life, such incursions also point to the precarious nature of being at home in Palestine (Griffiths and Joronen 2019). The articles of rescue missions examined for this chapter contain numerous detailed accounts of such incursions, which were often carried out in coordination with the Israeli military. In July 2012 Yad L'Achim reported the rescue of Dina—an Israeli Jewish woman who grew up in Lod, a city close to Tel Aviv—and her children. Dina married a Palestinian man and had been living with her husband and children in the West Bank city of Tulkarm. As the report (Yad L'Achim 2012) explains:

> Three weeks ago, in a stunning development, Dina contacted a relative in Israel. It was the first sign of life from her in 25 years. The relative called Yad L'Achim's hotline and provided operators with Dina's phone number and whatever information she had gleaned from her conversation with her.
>
> Yad L'Achim wasted no time in setting up a team to plan her rescue. The sense of urgency, and emotion, was particularly strong in light of this poor woman's name: Dina bat Leah, whose biblical namesake had been held captive by Arabs in Shechem (Nablus), and who was ultimately rescued by her two brothers Shimon and Levi. . . .

Yad L'Achim completed its rescue plan for Dina and her two young children, an eight-year-old son and a 10-year-old daughter. Her older children would have to remain behind, for now. Contact was made with a senior official in the office of the IDF's [Israel Defense Forces'] Coordinator of Government Activities in Yehudah and Shomron, who agreed to issue Dina and her children a special visa to enter Israel. Soldiers at the border crossing were given instructions to open the gates to the rescue car. . . .

When the call came from the soldiers at the border crossing—"We see her with the children!"—a weight was lifted from the shoulders of those manning the command room at Yad L'Achim.

After the car crossed into Israel and came to a stop, Dina emerged with her children. She burst into tears at the realization that her nightmare of 25 years was finally over. She and her children were home and could begin the journey back to their people.

They were welcomed at the checkpoint by social workers from Yad L'Achim, headed by S, who was Dina's liaison in the weeks prior to the rescue. The two maintained ties under the nose of the hostile Arab husband.

Dina related that during their drive in the rescue car, when she revealed to her children that they were on a one-way trip to Israel, the children, who had themselves suffered from their father's abuse, shouted in excitement: "Promise us that we won't ever go back there!"

At the checkpoint, while they sipped from glasses of cold water and calmed down from their stress of recent weeks, Dina removed her jalabiya and scarf and asked a Yad L'Achim staffer to "thrown it in the garbage."

In that moment, she shed her Arab dress and took on the appearance of a Jewish woman taking her first steps back to her people and birthplace. There wasn't a dry eye at the checkpoint; even hardened soldiers cried unashamedly.

Dina's story is one of many told by Yad L'Achim. From the account of her rescue, it is clear that such interventions into mixed Palestinian-Israeli relationships function as part of the broader security apparatus that maintains the occupation of Palestine, and they point to wider structures and dimensions of citizen-led surveillance and militarism. Central to the justification of such rescues is the active construction of Palestinian patriarchy as temporally distinct from Israeli modernity. Providing a structural basis for the necessity of rescue, Palestinian family life and culture, and Palestinian men in particular, are painted as violent and irrational against the safety of the Israeli state. This structural framing takes on wider significance when considering the state of Israel's broader biopolitics of sexuality and intimacy. In response to the plethora of scholarship that has arisen around Israeli pinkwashing—the practice whereby the occupation of Palestine is obscured by promoting Israel in a frame of sexual modernity with exemplary LGBTQ rights while targeting Palestine as a site of violent homophobic repression (see, e.g., Maikey 2017)—Puar (2017, 124–25) maintains that a singular focus on the politics of pinkwashing can

> actually work as a foil to the pronatalist, eugenically orientated practises of sexual reproduction—both homo and hetero—mapping certain ableist prototypes of homosexuality as a form on capacity that can potentiate, on the side of life. . . . Given these interconnected and multiple rubrics, enacted in the name of sex, sexual freedom, and stellar technological achievement (as with ART), any anti-pinkwashing stance that does not address the biopolitics of reproduction and regeneration may come dangerously close to reiterating the ableism not only of the Israeli state but also of (secular) queerness itself. Whereas the effeminate Jew was antithetical to the project of Zionism, and homosexuality was considered an Orientalist (and therefore, Arab) vice, the rehabilitation project of the Israeli state now embraces the potential for the new muscular Judaism to be the muscular homosexual Jew. The rehabilitation of the effeminate sickly Jew of the diaspora realizes its apex in the child-rearing gay Israeli man.

Arguing that the proliferation of identity-based sexual freedoms in the Israeli state masks the strict biopolitical regulation of heterosexual intimacy and reproduction, Puar ties the proliferation of Jewish reproductive capacity to the older project of Jewish regeneration. Here, the project of regeneration remaps itself, encompassing new biopolitical coordinates of sexual and gendered life (e.g., "the child-rearing gay Israeli man") that can be put to use in the service of Israeli demography and the occupation of Palestine. In the case of Yad L'Achim's rescue missions, the Orientalist constructions of Palestinian patriarchy not only justify the need and urgency of rescue but also concomitantly creates a distance between the modern, caring Jewish family and the violent Palestinian family, with the latter placed outside the confines of Israeli family life. In the next section, following the rescue of Jewish women who had formed intimate relationships and forged lives with Palestinian men, new biopolitical coordinates of regeneration and rehabilitation are produced to integrate the women and children into the Israeli state.

Rehabilitation

> Despite the difficulties and dangers, the rescue is the easy
> part. Then comes the rehabilitation.
> —YAD L'ACHIM, n.d.a

In this final section, I examine how discourses of the rehabilitation and reintegration of Israeli women and their children following their rescue produce a new biopolitical coordinate of Jewish regeneration that serves the interests of Israeli demography. I argue that the practice of rehabilitation—an attempt to "fix" and reintegrate Jewish women who have gone astray—functions as a disciplinary site of power through which the state of Israel is (re)produced through the biologized and racialized, yet shifting, category of "Jewishness."

Following rescue missions, Yad L'Achim uses many rehabilitation techniques, including Hebrew lessons, religious education and ceremonies, safe houses, the provision of food coupons and other welfare services, and psychological treatment and social workers. Central to this rehabilitation is the pathological production of the Jewish woman—although such women have often converted to Islam and spent years living and raising their children as Muslim—as naive, vulnerable victims of deceitful intimate Palestinian warfare. In his analysis of transcripts from Israeli parliamentary committee meetings in which mixed relationships were discussed, Yohai Hakak (2016,

986) argued that "depicting 'other men' as dangerous, deceitful and violent, and Jewish women as weak victims unable to protect themselves provides justification for intervention and helps maintain the separation between communities." Indeed, in the story of Dina told in the previous section, Yad L'Achim (2012) emphasizes that after a difficult childhood, "severe emotional distress led her to sever ties with her family and, at the age of 20, to make a hasty decision that condemned her to a life of severe abuse and unbearable suffering." The rescue missions thus depend on this construction of female vulnerability and victimhood—such relationships would not be formed if the woman was in the "right" frame of mind—and of the Palestinian man as deceitful, opportunistic, and barbaric, materialized through the continual emphasis on domestic and sexual violence. This double production of female victimhood and male aggression subjectifies both the Israeli-born women and Palestinian men by perpetuating the logics of pinkwashing that not only situate Palestinian sexuality as perverse but also mask the patriarchal workings of Jewish Israeli society and the regulatory reproductive control exercised over Jewish women's bodies. Notably, within these discourses, Palestinian women and the myriad ways they are affected by the intimate machinery of occupation are absent.

Casting Palestinian and Israeli society as materially distinct, rescue and rehabilitation create a break, or caesura, within an undesirable social order that is antithetical to the biopolitical logics and aims of colonial occupation. Operating at the level of the body through what Foucault ([1978] 1998, 139) names as a set of "regulatory controls" that seeks to survey and manage sexuality and reproduction through a biopolitics of a racialized population, rehabilitation also draws on older Zionist logics that sought to "fix" or civilize Jewish populations. Exploring the links between medicalization, nation-building, and race, Meira Weiss (2001, 98) traced the migration of Yemeni Jews to Israel in the late 1940s and 1950s, arguing that "the attitude of the new Zionist state toward the Yemenite immigrants was very similar to that of the colonial missionaries and medical troops that had set out to 'civilize' the 'primitives.'" Held in transit camps upon their arrival in Israel, North African and Middle Eastern Jewish immigrants were subjected to an array of immunizations and fitness examinations developed though "a complex system of welfare workers, nurses, and doctors . . . striving not only to heal immigrants, but also to educate them in a host of areas, from infant care to matters of personal hygiene" (Davidovitch and Shvarts 2004, 153). And while these public hygiene programs notably took their inspiration from European and North American racial science and social eugenics (see Davidovitch et al. 2005), they "also arose—at least in part—from the Zionist establishment's conception of creating a 'new man'" (Davidovitch and Shvarts 2004, 15). While the subjects and context of Yad L'Achim's rehabilitation programs are different from the racialized Jewish populations kept in transit camps, such programs nonetheless draw on this older Zionist strategy and logic holding that Jewish people and their bodies, or people with Jewish parentage, can be fashioned anew.

At the same time, rescue and rehabilitation point to Foucault's ([1978] 1998, 149) notion of a "thematics of blood" to Israeli conceptualizations of race and religion, and the attendant logics of rehabilitation. Arguing that modernity required a shift from a thematic of bloodlines to one of sexuality, Foucault suggests that a facet of modern biopolitical racism manifested in their overlap—that is, the space in which a concern for the purity of bloodlines was replaced or complemented by a desire to manage the biological processes of sexual reproduction. In the context of Yad L'Achim's activities, we see a thematics of blood emerge through the rehabilitation of children born in Palestine to Palestinian fathers and Israeli-born mothers. In June 2016 Yad L'Achim reported on the rescue of "A," a then thirty-six-year-old woman who had spent eighteen years living with her Palestinian husband and their six children. Following the "rescue," the woman and her children were placed "in a secure hideaway, where they began a period of rehabilitation under the guidance of a Yad L'Achim social worker." The report details:

> The children, who didn't know a word of Hebrew, began to blend in carefully and gradually, in their Jewish schools, with the help of mentors sponsored by Yad L'Achim.

A. recently underwent a "return to Judaism" procedure and wanted to mark her escape from the Arab village with a symbolic visit to the Western Wall together with her children. . . . "We were very moved to hear A.'s request to visit the Western Wall together with her children, who had been educated in Islam," said an official at Yad L'Achim. "We have been in close contact with the family throughout their rehabilitation and it never ceases to amaze us how the Jewish feeling burns so strong, even after 20 years in an Arab village, cut off from her people." (Yad L'Achim 2016)

The term "rehabilitation" implies a "process of returning to a healthy or good way of life" (*Cambridge Dictionary*). Thus, the contours of rehabilitation not only reinscribe the notion that life in Palestine is violent and uncivil but also imply that the children here are returning to their natural and healthy state. Through a disavowal of their Muslim upbringing and Palestinian parentage, and hinged on the notion that such qualities can be rehabilitated and reoriented toward Judaism, the process of rehabilitation points to the elasticity of racialized biology and its refashioning in the service of Israeli demography and colonial occupation. Indeed, through the incorporation of these rescued subjects, the Israeli state is able to gain more settler-citizens, who in turn may be put to future use "in the processes of accumulation by dispossession through the occupation of lands, the elimination or exploitation of indigenous peoples, and the extraction of expropriated resources" (Englert 2020, 1658).

In May 2014 Yad L'Achim reported helping a woman who had grown up "thinking she was a Muslim and condemned to life imprisonment in a violent marriage" to become Jewish once again (Yad L'Achim 2014a). Reportedly for this Palestinian woman, who had grown up without knowing her mother was Jewish, "hearing that her mother was Jewish didn't mean anything to her since according to Islam the child's religion goes after the father" (Yad L'Achim 2014a). But a rescue mission was nonetheless carried out, with Yad L'Achim transferring her to a safe house inside Israel's 1948 boundaries, "where she drew closer to Judaism with the assistance of a Yad L'Achim mentor" (Yad L'Achim 2014a). Yad L'Achim's activities, framed around its motto "We don't give up on even a single Jew," thus reinstate not only the centrality of Jewishness to the state of Israel but also the biological inscription of Jewishness as an innate ethno-religious category that triumphs despite one's upbringing and paternal relations. In this inscription, the complex process of rehabilitation receives its "justification from the mythical concern with protecting the purity of the blood and ensuring the triumph of the race" (Foucault [1978] 1998, 149).

Conclusion

In this chapter, I have argued that the rescue missions and rehabilitation programs carried out by Yad L'Achim seek to intervene in and regulate Palestinian and Israeli mixed relationships in ways that are tied to the broader demographic objectives of Israel's colonial occupation. While much existing literature has developed and enhanced our understanding of the intricate state security apparatus that regulates Palestinians' lives under occupation, this chapter has drawn attention to how non-state organizations similarly engage in militarized practices that seek to regulate and order Palestinian and Israeli life. This focus, I have suggested, may enrich our understanding of how Israeli citizens form part of the infrastructure of occupation and are called upon to survey and intervene in the lives of those who fail to conform to nationalist ideas of sexual normativity, which are structured around Jewishness and against Palestine and Palestinians. At the same time, I have suggested that the activities and stated aims of Yad L'Achim may point to a different set of settler colonial logics than that encapsulated by the "logic of elimination" (Wolfe 2001), a logic that is commonly theorized as central within the academic field of settler colonial studies. Indeed, by attempting to maintain a politics of Palestinian and Israeli separation while also seeking to incorporate both Jewish women who married Palestinians and the children born from these mixed relationships back into the Israeli state, the activities of Yad L'Achim violently attempt to produce new or rescued settler-citizens. In this sense, to understand the activities of Yad L'Achim as an *encounter with colonial violence* extends beyond the violent encounter of rescue and points to the broader encounter with settler dispossession that their activities are both grounded in and perpetuate.

Drawing on feminist analyses of biopower and literature examining reproduction in Israel, I have suggested that the activities of Yad L'Achim are embedded in older and broader logics of rehabilitation and reproduction. Putting these broader discourses to use in new, productive ways, the rescue and rehabilitation of Israeli-born women who form intimate relations with Palestinian men operate as political technologies that regulate both Israeli and Palestinian populations across all territories under Israeli control. Drawing on Puar's (2017) scholarship, which calls on us to broaden our sexual analytics beyond pinkwashing, I have underscored how the regulation of mixed heterosexual intimacy and reproduction is ordered and surveyed in ways that seek to maintain and perpetuate the Israeli settler state project. Here, Puar (2017, 119) argues that "in this oscillation between disciplinary societies and control societies, sexuality is not only contained within bodies but also dispersed across spaces." The case of Yad L'Achim's rescue missions allows for an elaboration of this point. Indeed, rather than directly targeting bodies through sexual identity per se, the infrastructure of rescue and rehabilitation targets and orders bodies through a racialized colonial biopolitics. Such a politics, I have suggested, draws on the patriarchal logics that hold Jewish women as sacred to the Israeli nation and harnesses the logics of Foucault's "thematics of blood" to secure the reproduction of Jewish subjects within an exclusively Jewish state and against the existence and reproduction of Palestinian life. Responding to relationships that are posited as an extension of Palestinian "warfare," rescue missions operate as an additional site through which Palestinian family life is subjectified and regulated, and points to the uneven and fiercely ordered dispersal of intimacy, family life, and reproduction across the racialized geographies of occupation.

As I noted in the introduction, it is important to caution against understanding mixed Palestinian-Israeli relationships as an act of resistance or as inherently working against colonial occupation; however, we also must reckon with the threat that such intimate relations are understood to pose to the contours of the Israeli state. In rupturing or causing a break in the separation of bodies that maintains the occupation and by operating as a site where various overlapping, yet oppositional, demographic projects meet, mixed Palestinian-Israeli relationships present the occasion to deepen our understanding of how bodies themselves are sites of encounters within the broader infrastructure of settler colonial occupation. Indeed, throughout this chapter, we can see how gendered and racialized bodies are sites that carry and embody demographic concerns, ideas of threat and warfare, and, for the Israeli state and Zionist project, the settler promise of "return" and "rehabilitation." But for Palestinians, the encounter is one of violence and dispossession, where the possible threat of family separation haunts life under occupation.

References

Abu Awwad, Nida. 2016. "Gender and Settler Colonialism in Palestinian Agriculture: Structural Transformations." *Arab Studies Quarterly* 38 (3): 540–61.

Abu El-Haj, Nadia. 2012. *The Genealogical Science: The Search for Jewish Origins and the Politics of Epistemology*. Chicago: University of Chicago Press.

Alatout, Samer. 2009. "Walls as Technologies of Government: The Double Construction of Geographies of Peace and Conflict in Israeli Politics, 2002–Present." *Annals of the Association of American Geographers* 99 (5): 956–68.

Bhandar, Brenda. 2018. *Colonial Lives of Property: Law, Land, and Racial Regimes of Ownership*. Durham NC: Duke University Press.

Birenbaum-Carmeli, Daphna. 2004. "'Cheaper than a Newcomer': On the Social Production of IVF Policy in Israel." *Sociology of Health & Illness* 26 (7): 897–924.

Boano, Camillo, and Ricardo Martén. 2013. "Agamben's Urbanism of Exception: Jerusalem's Border Mechanics and Biopolitical Strongholds." *Cities* 34:6–17.

Davidovich, Nadav, and Shifra Shvarts. 2004. "Health and Hegemony: Preventive Medicine, Immigrants and the Israeli Melting Pot." *Israel Studies* 9 (2): 150–79.

Davidovitch, Nadav, Shifra Shvarts, Rhona Seidelman, and Avishay Goldberg. 2005. "Medical Selection and the Debate over Mass Immigration in the New State of Israel (1948–1951)." *Canadian Bulletin of Medical History* 22 (1): 5–34.

Ellinghaus, Katherine. 2006. *Taking Assimilation to Heart: Marriages of White Women and Indigenous Men in the United States and Australia, 1887–1937*. Lincoln: University of Nebraska Press.

———. 2009. "Biological Absorption and Genocide: A Comparison of Indigenous Assimilation Policies in the United States and Australia." *Genocide Studies and Prevention* 4 (1): 59–79.

Englert, Sai. 2020. "Settlers, Workers, and the Logic of Accumulation by Dispossession." *Antipode* 52 (6): 1647–66.

Faitelson, Yakov. 2009. "The Politics of Palestinian Demography." *Middle East Quarterly* (Spring): 51–59.

Foucault, Michel. (1978) 1998. *The History of Sexuality*. Vol. 1, *The Will to Knowledge*. London: Penguin.

——. 2003. *Society Must Be Defended: Lectures at the Collège de France, 1975–1976*. New York: Picador.

Freedman, Seth. 2009. "Israel's Vile Anti-Miscegenation Squads." *The Guardian*, September 29. https://www.theguardian.com/commentisfree/2009/sep/29/israel-jewish -arab-couples.

Gordon, Neve. 2008. *Israel's Occupation*. Oakland: University of California Press.

Griffiths, Mark, and Jemima Repo. 2018. "Biopolitics and Checkpoint 300 in Occupied Palestine: Bodies, Affect, Discipline." *Political Geography* 65:17–25.

Griffiths, Mark, and Mikko Joronen. 2019. "Marriage under Occupation: Israel's Spousal Visa Restrictions in the West Bank." *Gender, Place & Culture* 26 (2): 153–72.

Hakak, Yohai. 2016. "'Undesirable Relationships' between Jewish Women and Arab Men: Representation and Discourse in Contemporary Israel." *Ethnic and Racial Studies* 39 (6): 976–93.

Hamayel, Layaly, Doaa Hammoudeh, and Lynn Welchman. 2017. "Reproductive Health and Rights in East Jerusalem: The Effects of Militarisation and Biopolitics on the Experiences of Pregnancy and Birth of Palestinians Living in the Kufr 'Aqab Neighbourhood." *Reproductive Health Matters* 25:87–95.

Hammami, Rema. 2015. "On (Not) Suffering at the Checkpoint: Palestinian Narrative Strategies of Surviving Israel's Carceral Geography." *Borderlands* 14 (1): 1–17.

Ihmoud, Sarah. 2018. "Policing the Intimate: Israel's Anti-Miscegenation Movement." *Jerusalem Quarterly* 75:91–103.

Landau, Ruth. 2004. "Posthumous Sperm Retrieval for the Purpose of Later Insemination or IVF in Israel: An Ethical and Psychosocial Critique." *Human Reproduction* 19 (9): 1952–56.

Lee, Vered. 2013. "Love in the Time of Racism: The New, Dangerous Low in the Campaign to Stop Interracial Relationships." *Haaretz*, April 25. https://www.haaretz.com/israel -news/love-in-the-time-of-racism-the-new-dangerouslow-in-the-campaign-to-stop -interracial-relationships.premium-1.517545.

Mahtani, Minelle. 2014. *Mixed Race Amnesia: Resisting the Romanticization of Multiraciality*. Vancouver: University of British Columbia Press.

Maikey, Haneen. 2017. "From Pinkwashing to Pinkwatching: Palestinian Queer Resistance: An Interview with Haneen Maikey from Pinkwatching Israel." By Nelly Bassily. Medium. https://medium.com/@nellybassily/from-pinkwashing-to-pinkwatchingpalestinian -queer-resistance-26b7e44447e3.

Nahman, Michal. 2013. *Extractions: An Ethnography of Reproductive Tourism*. Hampshire: Palgrave Macmillan.

Nyong'o, Tavia. 2009. *The Amalgamation Waltz: Race, Performance, and the Ruses of Memory*. Minneapolis: University of Minnesota Press.

Parsons, Nigel, and Mark B. Salter. 2008. "Israeli Biopolitics: Closure, Territorialisation and Governmentality in the Occupied Palestinian Territories." *Geopolitics* 13 (4): 701–23.

Puar, Jasbir K. 2017. *The Right to Maim: Debility, Capacity, Disability*. Durham NC: Duke University Press.

Pugliese, Joseph. 2020. *Biopolitics of the More-Than-Human: Forensic Ecologies of Violence*. Durham NC: Duke University Press.

Repo, Jemima. 2013. "The Life Function: The Biopolitics of Sexuality and Race Revisited." *Theory & Event* 16 (3). https://www.muse.jhu.edu/article/520029.

———. 2016. "Thanatopolitics or Biopolitics? Diagnosing the Racial and Sexual Politics of the European Far-Right." *Contemporary Political Theory* 15 (1): 110–18.

Ritchie, Jason. 2015. "Pinkwashing, Homonationalism, and Israel–Palestine: The Conceits of Queer Theory and the Politics of the Ordinary." *Antipode* 47 (3): 616–34.

Said, Edward. 1979. "Zionism from the Standpoint of Its Victims." *Social Text* 1:7–58.

Shalhoub-Kevorkian, Nadera. 2015a. "The Politics of Birth and the Intimacies of Violence against Palestinian Women in Occupied East Jerusalem." *British Journal of Criminology* 55 (6): 1187–206.

———. 2015b. *Security Theology, Surveillance and the Politics of Fear*. Cambridge: Cambridge University Press.

Shragai, Nadav. 2010. *Demography, Geopolitics, and the Future of Israel's Capital: Jerusalem's Proposed Master Plan*. Jerusalem: Jerusalem Center for Public Affairs.

Sperling, Daniel. 2010. "Commanding the 'Be Fruitful and Multiply' Directive: Reproductive Ethics, Law, and Policy in Israel." *Cambridge Quarterly of Healthcare Ethics* 19 (3): 363–71.

Stoler, Ann Laura. 1995. *Race and the Education of Desire: Foucault's History of Sexuality and the Colonial Order of Things*. Durham NC: Duke University Press.

Tawil-Souri, Helga. 2012. "Uneven Borders, Coloured (Im)mobilities: ID cards in Palestine/Israel." *Geopolitics* 17 (1): 153–76.

Vertommen, Sigrid. 2016. "Babies from behind Bars: Stratified Assisted Reproduction in Palestine/Israel." In *Assisted Reproduction across Borders: Feminist Perspectives on Normalizations, Disruptions, and Transmissions*, edited by Merete Lie and Nina Lykke, ch. 15. New York: Routledge.

Weiss, Meira. 2001. "The Immigrating Body and the Body Politic: The 'Yemenite Children Affair' and Body Commodification in Israel." *Body and Society* 7 (2–3): 93–109.

———. 2004. *The Chosen Body: The Politics of the Body in Israeli Society*. Palo Alto CA: Stanford University Press.

Weizman, Eyal. 2007. *Hollow Land: Israel's Architecture of Occupation*. London: Verso.

Wolfe, Patrick. 2001. "Land, Labor, and Difference: Elementary Structures of Race." *American Historical Review* 106 (3): 866–905.

———. 2006. "Settler Colonialism and the Elimination of the Native." *Journal of Genocide Research* 8 (4): 387–409.

Yad L'Achim. 2012. "After 25 Years in Tulkarm, Dina Is Rescued with Her Children." July 12. https://yadlachim.org/after-25-years-in-tulkarm-dina-is-rescued-with-her-children/.

———. 2014a. "After Decades as a Muslim, R. Discovers That She's Jewish." May 28. https://yadlachim.org/after-decades-as-a-muslim-r-discovers-that-shes-jewish/.

———. 2014b. "Yad L'Achim Warns: Assimilation Poses Security Threat." September 8. https://yadlachim.org/yad-lachim-warns-assimilation-poses-security-threat/.

———. 2016. "To Touch the Stones of the Kosel for the First Time." June 23. https://yadlachim.org/to-touch-the-stones-of-the-kosel-for-the-first-time/.

———. 2018. "Youth Cruelly Cut Off from Jewish Mother and Raised in Arab Village, Reunited with His People." November 28. https://yadlachim.org/youth-cruelly-cut-off-from-jewish-mother-and-raised-in-arab-village-reunited-with-his-people/.

———. n.d.a. "Daring Rescues." Accessed March 4, 2023. https://yadlachim.org/daring-rescues/.

———. n.d.b. "Non-Conventional Warfare." Accessed March 4, 2023. https://yadlachim.org/non-conventional-warfare/.

———. n.d.c. "Rescue from Life-Threatening Situations." Accessed March 4, 2023. https://yadlachim.org/departments/anti-assimilation/.

Yiftachel, Oren. 1999. "'Ethnocracy': The Politics of Judaizing Israel/Palestine." *Constellations* 6 (3): 364–90.

Yosef, Raz. 2004. *Beyond the Flesh: Queer Masculinities and Nationalism in Israeli Cinema.* New Brunswick NJ: Rutgers University Press.

Yuval-Davis, Nira. 1989. "National Reproduction and 'the Demographic Race' in Israel." In *Woman-Nation-State*, edited by Nira Yuval-Davis and Floya Anthias, 92–109. London: Palgrave Macmillan.

2   Settler Capitalism and Its Witches

Palestinian Bedouin Women Struggling for
Space and the Commons in the Naqab

Sophie Richter-Devroe

We should transform the Bedouin into an urban proletariat—in industry, services, construction, and agriculture. . . .
Indeed this would be a radical move which means that the
Bedouin would not live on his land with his herds, but
would become an urban person who comes home in the
afternoon and puts his slippers on. His children would
be accustomed to a father who wears trousers, does not
carry a *shabaria* [the traditional Bedouin knife] and does
not search for vermin in public. The children would go
to school with the hair properly combed. This would be
a revolution, but it may be fixed within two generations.
Without coercion but with governmental direction . . . this
phenomenon of the Bedouin will disappear.

—MOSHE DAYAN (*Haaretz*, July 13, 1963)

We have to take all the Bedouin and get them out of the
desert a bit and bring them closer to a normal state from
the perspective of legislation, life expectancy, education
and livelihood. Perhaps we could even deal with the phenomenon of multiple wives to reduce the birthrate and
raise the standard of living.

—YAIR SHAMIR, minister of agriculture (cited in S. Seidler, *Haaretz*,
    September 29, 2014)

Statements on forced modernization, directed at the native population of historic Southern Palestine, a region now commonly known as al-Naqab (or Negev in Hebrew), have a long history among Israeli policy makers.[1] Today the indigenous Naqab Bedouin community consists of more than 280,000 Arab Palestinians who hold Israeli citizenship (Nasasra and Bellis 2020, 398) and predominantly reside in the northern Naqab. During the Nakba, the Palestinian "Catastrophe," in 1948, Israeli forces killed and expelled most Naqab Bedouins in a process of ethnic cleansing (Pappé 2006, 2014). The approximately 11,000 (Abu-Saad 2010, 117) who remained in what became the state of Israel had their lands confiscated, were placed under military law, and forcibly displaced into a segregated enclosure zone, the *siyagh*, where they needed permits to leave (Marx 1967; Falah 1989; Nasasra 2014). From the late 1960s onward, the state adopted a new strategy, which is outlined in Dayan's quote above: under the guise of "modernization" and "urbanization," the state once again expropriated Bedouin lands and forcibly transferred the native population to seven state-planned impoverished and crowded urban townships (Falah 1985, 1989). Today, around half of all Palestinian Bedouins live in these urban enclaves; the other half resides in villages, which, since the Israeli state classifies them as unrecognized or only partially recognized, do not receive state infrastructural support.[2]

In Israeli state discourse and policy, a central modernization logic thus undergirds the governance and control of the Palestinian Naqab Bedouins.[3] This logic maintains that the enclosure of native lands and the transferral of the Bedouin Palestinian people into designated state-planned townships serve to assimilate them into the structures of the modern nation-state and capitalist market. The Bedouins need to become modern citizens and an "urban proletariat," as Moshe Dayan put it, as only then will they cease to exist as the natives of the land. This modernization process is biopolitical: under the guise of improving life, it secures and extends state power and control to all spheres of life through regulating and disciplining individual bodies and whole populations (Foucault 1997). Women's bodies, in particular, are targeted: controlling women's birth rates, for example, as Minister Shamir states, is presented as a step toward progress and raising living standards.[4] The state thus assumes the role of "modernizing" women and their bodies (within the specific frames and limits of its own agenda) so that women's bodies become symbols of the nation's progress and modernity.

This, of course, is the case in all nation-states (see, e.g., Yuval-Davis 1997; Abu-Lughod 1998), but "modernizing women" takes specific forms and meanings in the context of Palestinians in Israel (see Kanaaneh 2002). For the settler colonial state, "modernizing" and "urbanizing" (i.e., spatially confining women) are not only strategies to create docile governable citizens but also ways to advance the settler colonial project of taking over the land and "eliminating the native" (Wolfe 1999, 2006; Salazar Hughes 2020).[5] Although presented in official state discourse as "development" and "modernization" aimed at "freeing" the Bedouins from their "backward" "tribal" norms, the state's policies of urbanization continue the settler colonial project of land expropriation, dispossession, forced transfer, and transformation and elimination of the native population (Yiftachel 2008; Nasasra et al. 2014; Kedar, Amara, and Yiftachel 2018). In the townships, the Bedouins were stripped of their traditional self-subsistent lifestyle of seminomadic pastoralism and transformed into landless, cheap labor for Israeli industry and agriculture. These racialized and gendered settler capitalist strategies of elimination, dispossession, and exploitation thus exercise specific impacts on native Palestinian women and their bodies. Just as the biopolitics of modernization claims to improve women's lives, capitalist transformations, too, grapple with, target, and exploit women's productive and reproductive roles (Federici 2014). The settler capitalist state adjusts and adds to these practices of modernization and capitalist exploitation a set of different gendered strategies of elimination.

In this chapter, I thus argue that behind the guise of "modernization" and "development" in the Bedouin townships lies the biopolitical, exploitative, and erasive project of the Israeli settler capitalist state aimed at, first, enclosing and expropriating the commons and, second, transforming, exploiting, and eliminating the native. I investigate these imbrications of racial capitalism and settler colonialism in the Naqab by studying how one particular constituency—Palestinian Bedouin women from the Nakba generation—are impacted by, cope with, and resist the Israeli settler capitalist project. I thus follow scholarly calls (e.g., Bhandar and Ziadeh 2016; Barakat 2018) to study Israeli settler colonialism—or, as I conceptualize it here, Israeli settler capitalism[6]—not from a structuralist perspective but from the vantage point of native agency, reading Bedouin women's resistance as a "diagnostic of [settler capitalist] power" (Abu-Lughod 1990, 42). Drawing on my ethnographic fieldwork in three Bedouin townships (Rahat, Laqiya, and Shqeeb as-Salam) from 2014 to 2016 and approximately eighty interviews with older women,[7] I show how women from this generation circumvent, challenge, and resist settler colonial and capitalist control over their bodies, lives, and epistemes. By remaining on the margins of the modern settler state and capitalist market system, they maintain and enact their own alternative social, cultural, and political spaces, which often run counter to the logics and channels of so-called modernization and development.

Witches, Enclosure, and the Commons: Theorizing Bedouin Women's Everyday Struggles in the Naqab

Postcolonial feminist scholars have questioned the possibilities of classic liberal feminism, especially in the form of state feminism, to advance and strengthen women's struggles in the Global South. Instead, they have searched for alternative spaces and forms of women's social, political, and economic empowerment away from the liberal modernist trajectory of gender mainstreaming in state- and nation-building.[8] These debates have been further refined to capture the specificities of Palestinian women's struggles in the context of Israeli occupation and settler colonialism (Jad 2018; Shalhoub-Kevorkian 2009; Richter-Devroe 2018).

Here, I propose to rethink this framework further by attending to the gendered dimensions and interlinkages of Israeli settler colonialism and the expansion of capitalist market structures. While the settler colonial paradigm has "made a career" (Veracini 2013b) in writings on Palestine/Israel since the 1990s, it remains crucial to note that Palestinian writers (e.g., Falah 2005; Hilal 1976; Said 1979; Sayegh [1965] 2012; Zureik 1979) have used the framework from early on, as have other critical scholars who used it to understand Zionist policies of land grab and frontier expansionism (Kimmerling 1983), native dispossession (Rodinson 1973), and land and labor exploitation (Shafir 1989, 1996), as well as the settler colonial logic and practice of elimination (Sayigh 2007). While some of this early settler colonial scholarship employed class as an analytical lens, reading the relationship between settler colonizers and the colonized as one dominated by labor relations, and relations to the means of production (e.g., Hilal 1976; Rodinson 1973), it is probably Shafir's work (1989, 1996) that foregrounds questions of land and labor with more depth. Arguing that Israeli settler colonialism depended on economic separatism rather than colonial racialized labor exploitation, Shafir shows how Zionists strove from the beginning to exclude Palestinian labor in their attempts to create a "pure settlement colony." Their aim, Shafir analyzes, was to exploit the resources and land expropriated from the native population, not through native labor exploitation but predominantly through a settler and immigrant labor force (mainly Mizrahim and Russian Jewish).[9]

As Patrick Wolfe (1999, 2006) reminds us, settler colonialism, as an ongoing structure, aims at eliminating the native through territorial dispossession, native expulsion, and erasure. Differently from colonialism, which destroys to exploit the native, Wolfe's (2006, 388) argument that "settler colonialism destroys to replace" captures well the latter's eliminatory nature. Yet, by drawing a sharp line between colonialism and settler colonialism, Wolfe (and others who follow him, such as Veracini 2013a) might neglect to trace how settler colonization in its different stages is also informed by capitalist exploitation (see Coulthard 2014; Desai 2021; Englert 2020). Although Wolfe (1991, 1) makes the important distinction between positive and negative forms of native elimination, he upholds that "settler colonies were not primarily established to extract surplus value from indigenous labor." As such, he prioritizes territorial dispossession at the expense of the different forms of bodily and labor exploitation that natives endure and resist in the settler colony (Coulthard 2014; Desai 2021; Englert 2020; Speed 2017). Settler colonialism and capitalism, as I hope to

RICHTER-DEVROE

show through my analysis of Naqab Bedouin women's engagement with questions of land (ownership) and (female) labor, are not two separate structures in Palestine. Indeed, particularly since the late 1960s onward, Israeli policies toward the native Palestinian population might best be characterized as "settler capitalist."

To better understand particularly the gendered dimensions of the Israeli settler capitalist state, I draw on the work of feminist Marxist scholar Silvia Federici. In *Caliban and the Witch*, Federici (2014) rereads the witch hunts that occurred in medieval Europe during the shift from feudalism to capitalism. Moving beyond the limits of radical and socialist feminist theorizing on women's oppression and agency, Federici studies the enclosure of the commons through the figure of the witch to highlight the central position that women's bodies play in processes of capitalist transformation. The enclosure of the commons aimed not only at "reorder[ing] patterns of land ownership, use, and circulation" but also at "reorganiz[ing] socioeconomic life and demography" (Fields 2010, 66). According to Federici, these processes targeted in particular three aspects: land, labor, and women's bodies. Communal lands were expropriated from the peasantry, and bodies needed to be disciplined and transformed into laborious bodies as a means of production and, in the case of female bodies, reproduction. "The body," Federici writes (2014, 16), "has been for women in capitalist society what the factory has been for male waged workers: the primary ground of their exploitation and resistance, as the female body has been appropriated by the state and men and forced to function as a means for the reproduction and accumulation of labour."

The newly emerging capitalist elites, aligned with a wider political initiative supported also by the church,[10] targeted older women and cast them as "witches," not only because they resisted land confiscations but also because their bodies could no longer serve as labor power or as biological reproducers of the labor force. Consequently, older women were deemed redundant to the developing system and hunted as "witches." That women's bodies function as biological, cultural, and social reproducers of the nation, and thus become core targets of biopolitical control, is well established (e.g., Yuval Davis 1997). Federici's analysis takes this point further by revealing that women's bodies are reduced to reproducers not only of male citizens in and of the nation-state but also of laborers in and of the capitalist market system.

Yet, these same female bodies also are sites of resistance, as captured by Federici in the figure of the witch. She questions the common Enlightenment narrative, which holds that women were accused of witchcraft because of medieval society's "backward" superstitious beliefs. Rather, Federici shows that women were targeted because they challenged the capitalist politics of enclosure. Both in medieval Europe and in later neoliberal restructuring processes and land enclosures in the Global South, women were at the forefront of resistance, protesting the expropriation of their lands and the erasure of their livelihoods and communal cultures. Through their communal practices of reproductive labor (child-rearing and other care work), everyday knowledges of the land, communal ways of subsistence farming and co-living, and different local healing practices (which earned them the title "witches" practicing "magic" [Federici 2014, 174]), women defended, built, and rebuilt their alternative collective spaces away and out of reach from privatized capitalist, (neo-)colonial, and state control. Their commons and commoning practices (Federici 2014, 2019) are spaces of communal resistance where people come together, pool their resources, and create communities, homes, and collective bonds that run counter to the logics and subjectivizing forces of state, neoliberal, and capitalist market structures.[11] Since women's commoning practices do not fit into liberal modernization narratives of development and empowerment, these everyday forms of women's agency remain overlooked in classic approaches to "the political" and to women's activism.

The forms of enclosure analyzed by Federici share with the Israeli settler colonial project a move to reorganize social and property relations *on* and *to* the land (see also Fields 2010, 65). Recuperating the Marxist angle of earlier settler colonial studies (e.g., Hilal 1976) by centering an analysis of enclosure and the commons thus promises to raise relevant questions also for native resistance in Palestine. Applying this framework to the Naqab,

I ask: Can older women in the Naqab resist or negotiate the enclosure of their commons and avert the elimination of their native communal lives as pursued by the Israeli settler capitalist project? How do their everyday commoning practices and knowledges *on* and *of* the land challenge the transformation of their bodies into docile modern citizens and laborious workers? What might women's everyday forms of resistance reveal about the gendered functionings and intersections of capitalism and the Zionist settler state in Palestine?

Aware of the various forms of intersecting discriminations that they face as female Bedouin Arab, Palestinian, Muslim citizens of an older generation in the Israeli state, and given the strict state control and surveillance in the Naqab, the women I interviewed about their lives in the townships tended not to directly articulate their criticisms of Israeli policies. Yet, attending ethnographically to their everyday practices reveals how women from this generation are well aware of the exploitation and discrimination they face and, with this knowledge, are engaged in daily struggles to quietly, subtly, but continuously challenge and circumvent state and market control over their lands, communities, bodies, and intimate lives. In the following discussion, I analyze Naqab Bedouin women's quotidian micro struggles and commoning practices in relation to the three fields identified by Federici: land (enclosures), labor (exploitation), and (women's) bodies.

Land Expropriation, Enclosure, and Im/mobility: "The House Is like a Prison"

> They [the Israeli authorities] do not allow you to add even
> this much space inside your own home. *We are on a map.*
> If you add this much, they would come and destroy it. You
> build something, they come and destroy it.
>
> —AMNEH, author interview, 2016; also cited in Richter-Devroe 2016a

Amneh is an eighty-year-old Nakba survivor.[12] Today she lives in Rahat, the biggest of the seven townships in the Naqab region, built in the 1970s, and now home to about sixty-five thousand people. It is true, as Amneh states, that in Rahat Bedouin residents are "on a map": they were forcibly moved to the townships, dispossessed, and uprooted from their ancestral lands as part of the state's urbanization policies from the late 1960s onward. This ongoing process of land expropriation and spatial control takes institutional (through the Jewish National Fund), legal (through, for example, the Absentee Property Law and the reinterpretation of Ottoman *miri* and *mawat* laws [see Kohlbry 2018; Amara 2013]), and material dimensions (through transforming the landscape, restricting access, creating boundaries of exclusion/inclusion [see Fields 2010, 70]). Core to the settler colonial project (Kedar, Amara, and Yiftachel 2018; Nasasra et al. 2014; Yiftachel 2008), expropriation in this region began during the Nakba and continued through military rule and the enclosures of the commons (i.e., Bedouins' ancestral tribal lands) on which was built communal life in the practices of farming and pastoralism. Later, enclosure and spatial control continued under the guise of modernization in the state's urbanization projects from the 1960s onward when Bedouins were again forcibly removed and transferred into the seven townships. While the Israeli government claimed to provide more efficient services in the urban enclaves—such as housing, roads, clinics, water, electricity, schooling—economic infrastructure and employment opportunities are in fact dramatically lacking.

In the so-called unrecognized villages (i.e., dwellings outside state-planned structures), Bedouin residents receive no infrastructural support (roads, electricity, water), they are threatened with evictions, and their houses are regularly demolished (Abu Saad 2014, 142). The struggle over land is thus ongoing in the Naqab: while Naqab Bedouins constitute 25 percent of the population in the Naqab, they have jurisdiction over less than 3 percent of the land (Abu-Ras 2006; Abu Saad 2014). Unrecognized villages do not exist in official state planning, surveys, and statistics as they are considered illegal. Only once Bedouins are forcibly removed from their lands and placed in the overcrowded townships are they recognized and, as the interviewee Amneh put it, "on a map."

Amneh's statement reflects what many older women I spoke to expressed. Their uprooting from their villages and their transference to the townships were particularly painful and destructive for them, as they, more than the men and more so than the younger generation, lost their previous freedoms and roles in society. Im Faiz, an elderly Bedouin woman whom I met and interviewed in one of the townships in 2016, articulated this feeling well: "The house is like a prison. There is no space. In the open (*bi-l barr*) you can relax, there is freedom." Most women from this generation do not identify with the urban built environment; the built house and, more generally, the urban landscaping of the townships constitute for them a confined space that the state keeps under constant oversight. Living inside, within the four walls of a built house, is unbearable for most. Instead, it is in the open (*bi-l barr*), as Im Faiz and others made clear, where women from this generation feel free.

Women of the Nakba generation, who had grown up in a semi-pastoral agricultural lifestyle on their ancestral lands, feel the loss of mobility and space in the tight and crowded urban enclaves. They had enjoyed a freedom of movement and had played an essential role in agricultural and pastoral activities on their lands (see Abu-Rabia 2014; Richter-Devroe 2016a). All the women I spoke to talked extensively about the very active lives they had lived before being uprooted and displaced from their lands. They talked about the harvest; the products, such as cheese and yogurts, that they made; the animals they reared; the carpets and embroidery work they mastered; and, more generally, the healthy bodies, social relations, and community life in the *barr* had nurtured. Women played an important and integral role in both the economic and social lives of their communities (Dinero 1997; see also Biernacka, Abu-Rabia-Queder, and Kressel 2018). Although clearly delineated male and female roles existed in the family economy, segregation was, in practice, minimal as both women and men needed to move and work on their lands. The settler colonial transfer of the native population to urban enclaves thus heightened patriarchal control: women lost their previous freedoms, roles, and social status (see also Abu-Rabia-Queder 2019, 82; Richter-Devroe 2016a, 327–29).[13]

Spatial enclosure, by reshaping and delineating boundaries and limits on the land and by immobilizing the displaced, constitutes a first step in a broader process of social and political reordering. Landscape functions as "a mechanism of spatial discipline," but "territorial space [is also] an instrument that helps constitute power in the social order" (Fields 2010, 65). Spatial—and indeed "spacio-cidal" (Hanafi 2009)—politics are core mechanisms through which the Israeli settler colonial state creates its racialized and classed social, political, and economic order not only inside Israel but also in the West Bank, Gaza, and East Jerusalem. By declaring "its own kind of 'monopoly on movement' [the Israeli settler colonial regime] interrupt[s] the movement of people, goods, culture and ideas that had been characteristics of the Levantine region for centuries" (Lloyd and Wolfe 2016, 116). Hierarchies between settlers and natives, colonizers and colonized are thus enforced through spatial politics: while settlers move freely on the land, Palestinian movement is blocked, controlled, and immobilized (see also Parizot 2018; Peteet 2017, 2018; Tawil-Souri 2012; Weizman 2007) with particular gendered impacts (Griffiths and Repo 2020; Hammami 2019).

In the Naqab, older Bedouin women were hit hardest by this immobility regime, losing their social status, freedoms, and roles in the community. For them "urbanization" meant not only the loss of their lands, sources of subsistence, and freedom of movement but also their collective identities and communal ways of life—in short, their commons. Women's spaces of social and political involvement shrank dramatically in the urban environment, as gender segregation and oversight increased, and as women were transformed into caretakers and housekeepers (Dinero 1997; Jakubowska 2000; Lewando Hundt 1978). Along with its modernization project, the Israeli state supported the rise of the Islamic movement (as a "softer" alternative to the Palestinian national movement) and sought to further tribal divides in the townships (Yiftachel 2008, 7). More conservative and increasingly religiously defined notions of modesty and piety, confining women further to the newly designated area of the "private sphere," were thus normalized. While younger women's bodies, as Shamir's opening statement illustrates, became prime targets for the state's modernization policies—both as a source of demographic anxiety and as a symbol of progress—older women were cast as redundant to the state and market project of development, remained confined to the house, and were robbed of their previous social, economic, and political roles in society. The process of land expropriation and forced urbanization in the Naqab thus impacted women in a way that bears similarity to the processes of capitalist developments described by Federici (2014). While Federici traces the transformations from a feudal to capitalist society in medieval Europe, forced urbanization and the enclosures of the commons in the Naqab must be placed, however, in the context of the ongoing Israeli settler capitalist project of eliminating the native.

Still, and just as the medieval witches, Bedouin women from the older generation also navigate, re-signify, and reappropriate the colonial spaces of the urban townships, trying to make them their own. Many women from this generation refuse to be housed inside and instead live most of the time outdoors. While men have a more official structure—their *shiqq*, which often is attached to the built house and constructed around a concrete or metal frame—most older women I met have makeshift tents that resemble their original Bedouin tents in their yards next to the built structure of their house. Rather than using wool, they construct them today with plastic and fabric coverings, wood, and corrugated iron. Spending their mornings, afternoons, and evenings there to receive guests, drink tea and coffee, chat, discuss, or sleep, many women told me that it is there, in their tents outside, that they feel they can breathe. Im Nasir, similarly to Im Faiz, stressed the need to have an open view not restricted by walls and fences: "What do I want with a house? A house is closed-up, small. If I'm sitting here [in the tent], I can see the whole world, right? In a house you don't see anything. Here, you see everything" (author interview, 2014). She was sitting in the backyard of her house where she had arranged a small fireplace and was meeting women of the neighborhood for their daily tea and coffee circles. Having opened the side coverings of the tent, she had a view from inside the tent over the open fields at the edges of and beyond the concrete buildings of the township.

1. Makeshift Bedouin tent in the yard, 2015. Courtesy of the author.

In continuing their pre-township lifestyles and commoning practices, many older women also keep livestock—mainly sheep, chicken or turkeys, sometimes camels—even in the towns. If they have space, they also continue small subsistence farming, planting olive trees, peas, beans, other small vegetables, and fruits in the areas around the houses they were moved into. Within the crowded environments of the townships, most women still find and make space in their backyards to continue to bake *saj* bread, to make *laban* and cheese, to spin and weave.

Women also try to leave the townships whenever possible. For some months of the year, during the grazing period, many older women—often, but not always, accompanied by their sons or husbands—take their livestock out of the township and into the fields. This move from summer to winter camps had marked their previous lifestyles and endowed women with freedom of movement on extensive areas of land. By continuing this seminomadic pastoral pattern to the extent possible, women maintain their relationships to the land. I also met many older women who organized return visits, taking their families and communities, in particular the younger generation, to their ancestral lands for picnics or family outings.

While older women are at the forefront of cultivating their families' relationships to their lands, they also communicate their knowledge of the land through songs, oral poetry, and memories (Abu-Rabia 2014, 2016; Richter-Devroe 2016a, 2016b). Through these mediums they remind their kin of the Arabic names of their ancestral lands (thus contesting the state's Judaization of the land through Hebrew naming practices [see Nasasra 2012]), telling them about the lives they lived on the native land, how they demarcated boundaries between different tribal lands, and how they farmed the lands, growing and harvesting different types of barley, wheat, grains, and vegetables. In such everyday practices of commoning, older women continue their previous lifestyles and transmit native knowledges, epistemes, and worldviews to the next generations, reminding them of the lives, histories, and experiences their parents and grandparents lived before their forced removal. In the townships, native spaces are colonized, but older women nevertheless maintain their alternative intimate and affective relationships to the land, space, and community in which they grew up. They refuse the colonization of their identities, socialities, and epistemes. Instead, they imagine, rebuild, and live their native commons, their own material and ideational spaces, within and against the constraints of settler colonial cartographies.

Labor Exploitation and Native Agency: "Now It's All about Money"

In 2015, when I visited Sabha, a Nakba-generation Bedouin woman in Laqiya, the second-largest Bedouin township in the Naqab, she spent much time explaining to me the kind of life she had lived before the Israeli state forcibly removed her people from their ancestral lands and confined them in the urban enclaves. She covered many topics, but Sabha was perhaps most lucid in her understanding and critique of how state and market structures both discipline and restructure social realities in her native community. She developed this critique from her memories of the past:

2. Baking *saj*, 2014. Courtesy of the author.

3. Weaving in a backyard, 2015. Courtesy of the author.

In the old days, there was water from the well. The sheep ate grass in the mountains. . . . Here [in the township] there isn't any. There isn't any land. The government has taken it. . . .

When I remember life before, it was nice. My grandfather [and] my father died, I wish I had died with them. It is hard, life now. I can't stand it. Everything is about money. Grain, water, clothes, educating children, it's all about money. And there isn't any. People say it's better now—I say [to them]: "How? It's hard!"

It's better because there's water, there's electricity, houses, you have televisions—but you have to pay for all of that.

Sabha's critique is pointed: Israel's modernization and urbanization project did not improve Naqab Bedouins' living standards but rather led the community to precarity, pauperization, and dependence on wage work. Although differently than the Palestinian peasantry, the *falaheen*, Palestinian Bedouins had also sustained small-scale agriculture on their lands and trade (see Abu Sitta 2009; Amara 2016; Falah 1985). They thus also underwent the process of "proletarianisation of agrarian communities" (Fields 2010, 71) that is integral to capitalist transformations but also enters the process of settler colonization at different moments.

It is true that Israeli settler colonialism today continues to strive for a "pure settlement colony" (Shafir 1989), maximizing settler and eliminating native presence, and relying predominantly on settler and immigrant labor. Yet, while the early Labor Zionist doctrines of "conquest of labor" and "Hebrew labor" indeed aimed at the exclusion of Palestinians from the labor force (Desai 2021, 10; Englert 2020, 1655; Lockman 2012, 12; Shafir 1989), this shifted and had to be adapted, particularly from the mid-1960s onward. In the West Bank, for example, Israel relied heavily on racialized wage labor exploitation of Palestinian workers after the 1967 occupation (see Clarno 2018; Hilal 1976; Kohlbry 2018), and in the Naqab, too, forced native relocation to the urban enclaves from the late 1960s pushed the process of Bedouin proletarianization for the settler economy. The rigid separation between colonialism as a project of labor exploitation and settler colonialism as focused on native elimination thus cannot capture the ways in which "settler colonies [such as Israel] have a variety of different strategies at their disposal, which can include exploitation, elimination, or both" (Englert 2020, 1654; see also Coulthard 2014; Desai 2021).

Much of Palestinian labor in Israel is informal and underpaid. Official labor force participation of the Naqab Bedouins is estimated at 28 percent, and monthly salaries average at $US1,229 compared to $US2,373 in the Jewish-Israeli population (Abu Saad 2016; see also Abu Bader and Gottlieb 2009). Most of the young men, and few women, who have managed to find employment work in the Israeli industrial sectors, in factories, or in agricultural farms as cheap seasonal labor. The relocation of the SodaStream factory from an illegal Israeli settlement in the West Bank to the Naqab (see Fin and Maidhof 2015) is but one example of how the settler capitalist state relies on the exploitation of native labor in its attempt to expand not only the frontier but also capitalist market structures. Increasingly the Israeli settler capitalist state views natives as a cheap labor force, and land not only as resource for settlement but also for production and capital accumulation. Striving to turn those Naqab Bedouins who remained on the land into a cheap and landless labor force, the state trapped them in a cycle of poverty, dispossession, and labor exploitation in the urban enclave. They were indeed transformed into an "urban proletariat" serving Israeli farms and factories, as Dayan had envisioned in 1963.

For older women, such as Sabha, this capitalist transformation had particularly harsh impacts. Women of the younger generations received schooling in the Israeli system, and few (about 9 percent) entered the labor market (Biernacka, Abu-Rabia-Queder, and Kressel 2018, 65; see also Abu-Bader and Gottlieb 2009), becoming teachers, nurses, or other care-related professionals.[14] Older women, however, did not integrate into the wage labor of the new settler market economy. With life, space, and community increasingly structured by state and market institutions, stranded in the alien environment of the township, and without any source of income, older Bedouin women were left at the fringes of the developing settler capitalist state. Much like the witches—that is, expropriated peasant women in medieval Europe—the older generation in the Naqab, who had very different social and economic relations on their own lands before, began to see wage labor and capitalist consumption not as an "instrument of freedom" but rather "as instruments of enslavement" (Federici 2014, 72).

Sabha's words demonstrate her awareness of the subjectivizing and controlling forces of settler capitalism. When she showed me her sheep in the backyard, she emphasized that she is able to keep only a few, explaining how difficult it is to keep sheep in an urban setting. Taking them for grazing outside the townships has become increasingly complicated; with more and more native land expropriated as state, settler, or military spaces, there is hardly anywhere to go. The state has also levied heavy fines for trespassing and animal grazing, and a large amount of paperwork and payments are needed to register animals. Sabha detailed how now all animals need to be registered: a vet is required to certify their health, and owners must acquire the necessary paperwork and pay for health checks, vaccinations, and other records. "All this costs. . . . They [Israeli state officials] don't want that we have a life, that we have land, or that we have sheep. They want only that we work and eat—nothing more . . . they take the land and the sheep, and want us to be employed. Now everything is with money" (author interview, 2014). Lamenting the loss of her land, sources of subsistence, and freedoms, Sabha contrasts her community's past life as small-scale farmers and pastoralists on their own lands with that of their current reality as landless wage laborers whose social relations derive from capitalist market dynamics of demand, supply, and consumption. She thus develops a sharp critique of how the settler colonial state and its capitalist market structures first violently uproot and dispossess the native population from its commons and then forcibly discipline and restructure its social life in the townships, defining land no longer in terms of life and social relations but as a source of profit (see also Alkhalili 2017, 4–5). Along with this rearrangement of property and relations to the land emerge new social hierarchies between settler owners and dispossessed, proletarianized natives. The process of enclosure, native removal, and transfer is thus also coupled with the dynamics of class formation and relations. With natives uprooted and settlers affixed to place and territory, different patterns of land use, movement, property relations, and ownership, and thus also different social orders, emerge (see also Fields 2010, 71).

Most importantly in the Naqab, natives are transformed into dispossessed, laborious bodies, who, as Sabha puts it eloquently, only "work and eat—nothing more." Those who do not enter the labor market—the majority of Bedouin women—are robbed of their previous active economic social roles in society and turned into unpaid housekeepers, thus constituting the building block of capitalist (re-)productive labor exploitation. This process, of course, is fundamental to capitalist and colonial processes, but it also constitutes a settler colonial technique of "eliminating of the native" (Wolfe 1999, 2006). Settler colonialism, as I expanded above, holds a primary focus on the expropriation of native land, but this also entails an attempt to discipline natives into modern citizens and productive workers. Settler colonial policies aimed at "managing [native] surplus population" include different techniques of elimination: killing, expulsion, and confinement but also assimilation (Lloyd and Wolfe 2016, 111). In Wolfe's (2006, 402) words: "This logic [of elimination] certainly requires the elimination of the owners of that territory, but not in any particular way. . . . Indeed, depending on the historical conjuncture, assimilation can be a more effective mode of elimination than conventional forms of killing, since it does not involve such a disruptive affront to the rule of law that is ideologically central to the cohesion of settler society." Settler policies that isolate individuals from nonnational (e.g., kinship) structures (see Wolfe 2006, 397), confine and immobilize native populations, transfer native communal lands to individual and state settler property, and aim to assimilate the native—all are ways to attack native commons and eliminate native presence on and rights to the land.

Lloyd and Wolfe (2016, 111), however, maintain that Israeli settler colonialism today remains focused on expanding its frontier and thus applies its logic of elimination through policies of native confinement and transferral rather than assimilation. In any case, assimilation, for Wolfe, would not include native integration into the labor market. He states that positive elimination "can include officially encouraged miscegenation, the breaking-down of native title into alienable individual freeholds, native citizenship, child abduction, religious conversion, resocialisation in total institutions such as missions or boarding schools, and a whole range of cognate bio-cultural assimilations" (Wolfe 2006, 388). Relying on "preaccumulation" achieved through "centuries of Eurocolonial history" (Wolfe 2012, 133), the Zionist regime therefore, in his analysis, does not depend on accumulation through native labor exploitation.

Yet, as the case of the Naqab shows, different colonial, capitalist, and settler colonial techniques and temporalities exist in parallel across different contexts in Palestine. As highlighted above, the settler capitalist state has shifted its policies from native expulsion to labor exploitation since the late 1960s. Assimilating natives into the modern settler capitalist state through wage labor by transforming them into modern laborious sources of (re-) production—workers, citizens, and legal subjects—thus also constitutes a technique to erase and eliminate native lives and communities. Late settler colonial capitalism in Israel proceeds not only through expulsion, confinement, and ethnic cleansing to eliminate the native but also through urbanization and modernization by turning natives into a proletarianized landless workforce deprived of their communal lands, livelihoods, and social relations. Such settler capitalist policies of native land expropriation, dispossession, forced resettlement, and proletarianization also always constitute an attack—and attempted settler colonization—of the native commons.

Although it might be in particular older women who feel the loss of their commons most in the new urban environments, their positionality on the margins of a society forced to transition also endows them with social power. Marginality, as Federici (2014) captures through the figure of the witch, also constitutes a site for resistance. Most women from this generation, as I tried to show here, have not been disciplined into the new subjectivities carved out for them by settler colonial capitalist transformations. They remain outside the labor market and are hardly affected by consumption and wage labor demands; they tend to simply not participate in global capitalist market structures. Instead, they keep their own alternative networks of subsistence farming, production (such as cheese, embroidery, *saj*), and exchange economy.

Women from this generation also continue to engage in traditional healing practices, such as wet cupping and treatments against the evil eye, against children's fear and anxiety, or against infertility. In their practices, they use local plants and herbs and, in connection with and complementary to other Islamic references, mention local shrines and saints. Their healing practices reinforce the community's connection to the land as part of their everyday lives, practices, and knowledges—as a source of community and social relations rather than a resource to be exploited for profit.[15] They also reveal women's alternative relations and conceptions of their bodies that stress connections to their land and community rather than to science and modern medicine (see Richter-Devroe, forthcoming). That such practices remain widespread and that Bedouins from all generations consult traditional healers show older women are able to maintain some of their social roles and status even in the urban enclaves. Women in particular rely on these native knowledges and continue what they have learned from their mothers and grandmothers, be it in the intimate field of healing or child-rearing, in small-scale farming and production, or in seminomadic pastoralism.

Older Bedouin women from the Nakba generation thus not only constantly remind the younger generations that another life is possible on their native lands but also practically maintain and actively rebuild their commons through their everyday practices in the townships.

Conclusion: Embodied Resistance,
Women's Informal Networks, and the Commons

Israeli confiscation and expropriation of communal tribal lands, enclosure, and forced urbanization and modernization policies in the Naqab are set at the intersections of settler colonial and capitalist processes. Settler colonialism in Palestine, as I have argued, relies on the exploitation of native bodies, lives, and labor. A narrow conceptualization of settler colonial elimination, which ignores wage labor as a form of positive elimination and assimilation, cannot therefore adequately capture the ways in which the Israeli settler capitalist project functions in Palestine today. Reading and thinking capitalist restructuring of native societies as a part of, rather than separate to, settler colonialism also reveal specific gendered dynamics. In the Naqab, women's bodies became targets of Israeli settler capitalist control, and older women's bodies were outcast as redundant—a process reminiscent of how capitalist transformations in medieval Europe led to the marginalization and hunting of older women (Federici 2014). Focusing this chapter on older Naqab Bedouins from the Nakba generation, I have argued that, mirroring the medieval witches described by Federici, older Bedouin women have resisted the settler capitalist enclosure of their native commons. I have traced their forms of everyday resistance and commoning in the three interconnected fields of land, labor, and the body.

The expropriation of Bedouin ancestral lands and the forced native transfer to an enclosure zone and, later, urban enclaves at the hands of the Israeli settler colonial state had profound impacts on the native population, particularly so on women. Robbed of their previous lifestyles; social, economic, and political roles; and freedom of movement, these women were confined to the house and private sphere. Yet, even in the urban enclaves, women try to maintain their relations to their native land, space, and community. They continue to cherish their lives outside, visit their ancestral lands when and if possible, practice traditional healing, keep livestock, and engage in small subsistence farming and exchange economy. Most never entered the labor force, and they hardly participate in consumerist practices. Their encounters with the state, its institutions, and its bureaucracy are minimal: most are illiterate, never went to school or ran for political office, and hardly interact with nongovernmental organizations and other developmental/modernizing organizations. Just as capitalist market structures have not transformed them into laborious means of production, the state's biopolitical regime has not managed to mechanize, medicalize, and discipline their bodies through its institutions (Foucault 1973, 1979). It is their position on the margins of settler state and capitalist market structures that allows older women (more so than men and more so than the younger generation) to maintain their independent spaces and defend their commons.

That women from this generation are at the forefront of critical counter-practices should remind us not to limit the search for feminist struggles to the younger generations, to liberal and developmental trajectories of empowerment, or to the modernization logics and spaces provided by the state and the market. Indeed, tracing and analyzing women's everyday forms of commoning in the Naqab reveal that the so-called old or traditional is not necessarily "unfree," "backward," or "patriarchal" but can in fact offer important social, economic, and political spaces for women and their struggles. This political work, however, takes place in informal ways; it is not a clear-cut resistance against modernization or the settler colonial state or the capitalist market. Rather, in today's commons in the Naqab, women need to engage in creative politics to survive and circumvent the omnipresent, intrusive, and violent policies of late settler colonial capitalism. Their commoning practices are neither confrontational nor clearly articulated as a feminist strategy. Rather, they seem to just happen as women practice them in a somewhat understated, silent, and mundane manner.

Older women's bodies are certainly heavily scarred by the dispossession, displacement, and proletarianization that their community was forced to undergo as a result of the state's settler capitalist modernization project. But their position on the margins of that system also means that they have not internalized its racialized, classed, and gendered logics. Women retain a native understanding of the relations between the body, the community, and the land in and through their own local epistemes and everyday practices. Dayan predicted that "within two generations" the Bedouins would disappear, but Bedouin women from the Nakba generation have worked against that. Not only do they circumvent and evade the settler state's and market's disciplining mechanisms, but they also actively build, maintain, and transmit their native commons to future generations. In doing so, they uphold important sources of women's social, political, and economic power in the community and resist the "elimination of the native." They have not been disciplined into docile, cheap, laborious bodies and good modern citizens of the Israeli settler colonial capitalist state.

Notes

1. I use the term "Naqab" throughout because it is the one used by members from the community. For a detailed discussion on terminology, see Ratcliffe et al. 2014.

2. There are thirty-seven unrecognized villages in the Naqab, and eleven remain partially recognized. They do not receive state support. See Kedar, Amara, and Yiftachel 2018, 11. There is also ample advocacy literature on the ongoing displacements and house demolitions in the unrecognized villages. See, among others, Adalah 2010, 2011.

3. This modernization discourse and policy, which merge demographic concerns with policies of land grab and surveillance, undergird the governance and control not only of the Naqab Bedouins but of all Palestinians inside Israel (see Kanaaneh 2002; Sa'di 2011, 2014).

4. It is important to note that while Israeli state discourse frames polygamy as a "traditional," "backward" cultural Bedouin practice, its actual policies are ambivalent and might indeed be encouraging, rather than combating, the practice (see, e.g., Abu Rabia 2011; Bolous 2021). This seeming contradiction is core to the state's modernization project as it answers to demographic concerns while simultaneously casting Bedouins as backward.

5. Space here does not allow for a review of the growing literature on settler colonialism in Palestine. For overview papers and special editions, see Jabary-Salamanca et al. 2012; Svirsky 2014; Veracini 2015; Lloyd and Wolfe 2016; Amoruso, Pappé, and Richter-Devroe 2019.

6. While an analysis of racialized labor exploitation, native dispossession, and class has been integrated (and indeed foregrounded) in scholarship on Israeli settler colonialism (e.g., Desai 2021; Englert, 2020; Hilal 1976; Rodinson 1973; Shafir 1989, 1996), to my knowledge the term "settler capitalism" has not been used in the context of Israel. I borrow it here from Speed (2017), who uses the term in the context of Latin America.

7. I thank the women who agreed to be interviewed for this project and everyone who offered their generous help and hospitality during my fieldwork in the Naqab, especially my host family. I have anonymized all names of interviewees to ensure their protection. This research project was funded through an Arts and Humanities Research Council (AHRC) Early Career Fellowship (2014–16) titled "Gender and Settler Colonialism: Women's Oral Histories in the Naqab." I thank the AHRC for its financial support. I am also very grateful to Mikko Joronen and Mark Griffiths for their insightful comments and feedback on earlier drafts. All mistakes are mine.

8. See, among others, Rai 1996; Jayawardena 1986; Kandiyoti 1992; and the edited volumes by Abu-Lughod (1998) and Kandiyoti (1991) for the context of the Middle East.

9. See also Lockman's (2012) critique of Shafir's (1989) analysis, which highlights the role of violence and coercion in the Zionist pursuit of the "pure settlement" approach.

10. Federici understands the witch hunts as a "major *political* initiative" to which the church lent its "metaphysical and ideological scaffold" (2014, 168). She thus recognizes the ideological role of the church but identifies the economic, social, and political transformations from feudalism to capitalism as root causes for the medieval witch hunts.

11. The notion of the commons has a long tradition in Marxist writings on enclosure. Luxemburg (2003), for example, showed how capitalist exploitation needed to confiscate communal lands and break up what she termed the "natural economy" to turn land into a resource for capital accumulation. Some decades later, Harvey (2003) shows how neoliberal "accumulation by dispossession" attacks the commons in various ways.

12. All names are changed to protect the research participants' anonymity. All interviews were conducted in Arabic by me, and translations are mine. Sometimes translations are approximate as not all contextual idioms in Naqab Bedouin dialect can be translated in a literal way into English.

13. There is rich feminist scholarship that traces the intersections between patriarchy and (Israeli) settler colonization and occupation. This work shows how different Israeli policies—those related to militarization and violence (Shalhoub-Kevorkian 2009; Nashashibi 2006), spousal visa policies and regulations (Griffiths and Joronen 2019), "modernization" and demographic politics (Kanaaneh 2002), and spatial control/immobilization (Richter-Devroe 2018, 109–15)—strengthen patriarchal control over Palestinian women.

14. Women's "integration" into the labor market, although presented by the state as a form of modernization and development, is in fact a part of native labor exploitation serving capitalist expansion. Even those few Bedouin women who made it into highly skilled jobs suffer from "declassing" (Abu Rabia-Queder 2019). Similarly, women's high unemployment rates are sustained through structural racialized discrimination aimed at maintaining settler class sovereignty, because unpaid (i.e., exploited) female domestic and reproductive labor enables (underpaid and thus also exploited) male wage employment. As such, both women's exploited productive labor and their unemployment and transformation from active social and economic contributors to unpaid "modern" housekeepers function as core pillars for capitalist expansion and profiteering (see Federici 1995; Mies 2014).

15. For more on land as relation, rather than resource of profit, in Palestine, see Alkhalili 2017 and Quiquivix 2013.

References

Abu-Bader, S., and D. Gottlieb. 2009. *Poverty, Education and Employment in the Arab-Bedouin Society: A Comparative View*. Jerusalem: Van Leer Institute.

Abu-Lughod, Lila. 1990. "The Romance of Resistance: Tracing Transformations of Power Through Bedouin Women." *American Ethnologist* 17:41–55.

———, ed. 1998. *Remaking Women: Feminism and Modernity in the Middle East*. Princeton: Princeton University Press.

Abu Rabia, R. 2011. "Redefining Polygamy among the Palestinian Bedouins in Israel: Colonialism, Patriarchy, and Resistance." *Journal of Gender, Social Policy & the Law* 19 (2).

Abu-Rabia, S. 2014. "Land, Identity and History: New Discourse on the Nakba of Bedouin Arabs in the Naqab." In Nasasra et al., *Naqab Bedouin and Colonialism*.

———. 2016. "Memory, Belonging and Resistance: The Struggle over Place among the Bedouin-Arabs of the Naqab/Negev." In *Remembering, Forgetting and City Builders*, edited by T. Fenster and H. Yacobi. London: Routledge.

Abu-Rabia-Queder, S. 2019. "The Biopolitics of Declassing Palestinian Professional Women in a Settler-Colonial Context." *Current Sociology* 67 (1): 141–58.

Abu-Rabia-Queder, S., A. Morris, and H. Ryan. 2019. "The Economy of Survival: Bedouin Women in Unrecognized Villages." *Journal of Arid Environments* 149:80–88.

Abu-Ras, T. 2006. "Land Disputes in Israel: The Case of the Bedouin of the Naqab." *Adalah's Newsletter* 24 (April). http://www.adalah.org/newsletter/eng/apr06/ar2.pdf.

Abu-Saad, I. 2010. "Arabs of the Naqab: Past, Present and Future Challenges." Beer-Sheva: Negev Centre for Regional Development, Ben-Gurion University of the Negev. [In Arabic.]

———. 2014. "State–Directed 'Development' as a Tool for Dispossessing the Indigenous Palestinian Bedouin-Arabs in the Naqab." In *Decolonizing the Palestinian Economy: De–Development and Beyond*, edited by Mandy Turner and Omar Shweiki, 142. London: Palgrave Macmillan.

Abu-Saad, K. 2016. "Indigenous Data Matter: Spotlight on Negev Bedouin Arabs." *The Lancet* 388, no. 10055 (October 22). https://www.thelancet.com/journals/lancet/article/PIIS0140-6736(16)31866-9/references.

Abu Sitta, S. 2009. "The Denied Inheritance: Palestinian Land Ownership in Beer Sheba." Paper presented to the International Fact-Finding Mission. Beer Sheba: Regional Council for Unrecognized Villages of Negev.

Adalah. 2010. "As Requested by the Prime Minister's Office: The National Council for Planning and Building, in an Exceptional Move, Cancels Its Decision to Recognize Two Arab Bedouin Villages in the Naqab (Negev)." Haifa: Adalah—the Legal Center for Arab Minority Rights in Israel, November 22. http://www.adalah.org/en/content/view/7080.

———. 2011. "Nomads against Their Will: The Attempted Expulsion of the Arab Bedouin in the Naqab: The Example of Atir-Umm al-Hieran." Haifa: Adalah—the Legal Center for Arab Minority Rights in Israel. http://www.adalah.org/en/content/view/7405.

Alkhalili, N. 2017. "Enclosures from Below: The Mushaa' in Contemporary Palestine." *Antipode* 49 (5): 4–5.

Amara, Ahmad. 2013. "The Negev Land Question: Between Denial and Recognition." *Journal of Palestine Studies* 42 (4): 27–47.

———. 2016. "Beyond Stereotypes of Bedouins as 'Nomads' and 'Savages': Rethinking the Bedouin in Ottoman Southern Palestine, 1875–1900." *Journal of Holy Land and Palestine Studies* 15 (1): 59–77.

Amoruso, F., I. Pappé, and S. Richter-Devroe, eds. 2019. "Knowledge, Power and the 'Settler Colonial Turn' in Palestine." *Interventions: International Journal of Postcolonial Studies* 21 (4).

Barakat, Rana. 2018. "Writing/Righting Palestine Studies: Settler Colonialism, Indigenous Sovereignty and Resisting the Ghost(s) of History." *Settler Colonial Studies* 8 (3): 349–63.

Bhandar, B., and R. Ziadah. 2016. "Acts and Omissions: Framing Settler Colonialism in Palestine Studies." *Jadaliyya*, January 14. https://www.jadaliyya.com/Details/32857.

Biernacka, A., A. Abu-Rabia-Queder, and G. Kressel. 2018. "The Connective Strategies of Bedouin Women Entrepreneurs in the Negev." *Journal of Arid Environments* 149 (2): 62–72.

Bolous, S. 2021. "National Interests versus Women's Rights: The Case of Polygamy among the Bedouin Community in Israel." *Women & Criminal Justice* 31 (1): 53–76.

Clarno, A. 2018. "Neoliberal Colonization in the West Bank." *Social Problems* 65 (3): 323–41.

Coulthard, G. 2014. *Red Skin, White Masks: Rejecting the Colonial Politics of Recognition.* Minneapolis: University of Minnesota Press.

Desai, Chandni. 2021. "Disrupting Settler-Colonial Capitalism: Indigenous Intifadas and Resurgent Solidarity from Turtle Island to Palestine." *Journal of Palestine Studies* 50 (2). https://doi.org/10.1080/0377919X.2021.1909376.

Dinero, S. 1997. "Female Role Change and Male Response in the Post-Nomadic Urban Environment: The Case of the Israeli Negev Bedouin." *Journal of Comparative Family Studies* 28.

Englert, Sai. 2020. "Settlers, Workers, and the Logic of Accumulation by Dispossession." *Antipode* 52 (6): 1647–66.

Falah, G. 1985. "How Israel Controls the Bedouin in Israel." *Journal of Palestine Studies* 14 (2): 35–51.

———. 1989. "Israeli State Policy toward Bedouin Sedentarization in the Negev." *Journal of Palestine Studies* 18 (2): 71–91.

———. 2005. "The Geopolitics of 'Enclavisation' and the Demise of a Two-State Solution to the Israeli-Palestinian Conflict." *Third World Quarterly* 26 (8): 1341–72.

Federici, S. 1995. "Wages against Housework." In *The Politics of Housework*, edited by Ellen Malos. Cheltenham: New Clarion Press.

———. 2014. *Caliban and the Witch: Women, the Body and Primitive Accumulation.* Brooklyn: Atonomedia.

———. 2019. *Re-enchanting the World: Feminism and the Politics of the Commons.* Oakland CA: PM Press/Kairos.

Fields, G. 2010. "Landscaping Palestine: Reflections of Enclosure in a Historical Mirror." *International Journal of Middle East Studies* 42 (1).

Fin, M., and C. Maidhof. 2015. "Seltzer Colonialism." *Middle East Report Online* (MERIP), March 17. https://merip.org/2015/03/seltzer-colonialism/.

Foucault, M. 1973. *The Birth of the Clinic: An Archeology of Medical Perception*. New York: Vintage Books.

———. 1997. "The Birth of Biopolitics." In *Ethics, Subjectivity, and Truth*, edited by P. Rabinow, 73–79. New York: New Press.

Griffiths, M., and M. Joronen. 2019. "Marriage under Occupation: Israel's Spousal Visa Restrictions in the West Bank." *Gender, Place & Culture* 26 (2): 153–72.

Griffiths, M., and M. Repo. 2020. "Women's Lives beyond the Checkpoint in Palestine." *Antipode* 52 (4).

Hammami, R. 2019. "Destabilizing Mastery and the Machine: Palestinian Agency and Gendered Embodiment at Israeli Military Checkpoints." *Current Anthropology* 60 (19): 87–97.

Hanafi, S. 2009. "Spacio-cide: Colonial Politics, Invisibility and Rezoning in Palestinian Territory." *Contemporary Arab Affairs* 2 (1).

Harvey, D. 2003. *The New Imperialism*. Oxford: Oxford University Press.

Hilal, J. 1976. "Imperialism and Settler-Colonialism in West Asia: Israel and the Arab Palestinian Struggle." *Utafiti* 1 (1): 51–70.

Jabary-Salamanca, O., M. Qato, K. Rabie, and S. Samour. 2012. "Past Is Present: Settler Colonialism in Palestine." *Settler Colonial Studies* 2 (1).

Jad, I. 2018. *Palestinian Women's Activism: Nationalism, Secularism, Islamism*. Syracuse: Syracuse University Press.

Jakubowska, L. 2000. "Finding Ways to Make a Living." *Nomadic Peoples* 4 (2): 94–105.

Jayawardena, K. 1986. *Feminism and Nationalism in the Third World*. London: Zed Books.

Kanaaneh, R. 2002. *Birthing the Nation: Strategies of Palestinian Women in Israel*. Oakland: University of California Press.

Kandiyoti, D., ed. 1991. "Introduction." In *Women, Islam and the State*. Philadelphia: Temple University Press.

———. 1992. "Identity and Its Discontents: Women and the Nation." *Millennium* 20 (3): 429–43.

Kedar, A., A. Amara, and O. Yiftachel. 2018. *Emptied Lands: A Legal Geography of Bedouin Rights in the Negev*. Stanford: Stanford University Press.

Kimmerling, B. 1983. *Zionism and Territory: The Socio-territorial Dimensions of Zionist Politics*. Berkeley: University of California Press.

Kohlbry, P. 2018. "Owning the Homeland: Property, Markets, and Land Defense in the West Bank." *Journal of Palestine Studies* 47 (4): 30–45.

Lewando Hundt, G. 1978. "Women's Power and Settlement: The Effect of Settlement on the Position of Negev Bedouin Women." MA thesis, University of Edinburgh.

Lloyd, D., and P. Wolfe. 2016. "Settler Colonial Logics and the Neoliberal Regime." *Settler Colonial Studies* 6 (2): 109–18.

Lockman, Z. 2012. "Land, Labor and the Logic of Zionism: A Critical Engagement with Gershon Shafir." *Settler Colonial Studies* 2 (1): 9–38.

Luxemburg, R. 2003. *The Accumulation of Capital*. New York: Routledge.

Marx, E. 1967. *The Bedouin of the Negev*. Manchester: Manchester University Press.

Masalha, N. 2005. *Catastrophe Remembered: Palestine, Israel and the Internal Refugees: Essays in Memory of Edward W. Said*. London: Zed Books.

Mies, M. 2014. *Patriarchy and Accumulation on a World Scale: Women in the International Division of Labour*. 3rd ed. London: Zed Books.

Nasasra, M. 2012. "The Ongoing Judaisation of the Naqab and the Struggle for Recognising the Indigenous Rights of the Arab Bedouin People." *Settler Colonial Studies* 2 (1): 81–107.

———. 2014. "The Politics of Non-cooperation and Lobbying: The Naqab Bedouin and Israeli Military Rule, 1948–67." In Nasasra et al., *Naqab Bedouin and Colonialism*.

Nasasra, M., and E. Bellis. 2020. "The Role of Bedouin Youth and Women in Resistance to the Israeli Prawer Plans in the Naqab." *Middle East Critique* 4:395–419.

Nasasra, M., S. Richter-Devroe, S. Abu-Rabia-Queder, and R. Ratcliffe, eds. 2014. *The Naqab Bedouin and Colonialism: New Perspectives*. London: Routledge.

Nashashibi, R. 2006. "Violence against Women: The Analogy of Occupation and Rape— the Case of the Palestinian People." In *Gender in Conflicts: Palestine-Israel-Germany*, edited by Ulrike Auga and Christina von Braun, 183–90. Berlin: LIT Verlag.

Pappé, I. 2006. *The Ethnic Cleansing of Palestine*. Oxford: Oneworld.

———. 2014. "The Forgotten Victims of the Palestine Ethnic Cleansing." In Nasasra et al., *Naqab Bedouin and Colonialism*.

Parizot, C. 2018. "Viscous Spatialities: The Spaces of the Israeli Permit Regime of Access and Movement." *South Atlantic Quarterly* 117 (1): 21–42.

Peteet, J. 2017. *Space and Mobility in Palestine*. Bloomington: Indiana University Press.

———. 2018. "Closure's Temporality: The Cultural Politics of Time and Waiting." *South Atlantic Quarterly* 117 (1): 43–64.

Quiquivix, Linda. 2013. "When the Carob Tree Was the Border: On Autonomy and Palestinian Practices of Figuring It Out." *Capitalism Nature Socialism* 24 (3): 170–89. https://doi.org/10.1080/10455752.2013.815242.

Rai, S. 1996. "Women and the State in the Third World: Some Issues for Debate." In *Women and the State: International Perspectives*, edited by S. Rai and G. Lievesley. London: Taylor and Francis.

Ratcliffe, R., M. Nasasra, S. Abu-Rabia-Queder, and S. Abu-Rabia-Queder. 2014. "Introduction." In Nasasra et al., *Naqab Bedouin and Colonialism*.

Richter-Devroe, S. 2016a. "Biography, Life History and Orality: A Naqab Bedouin Woman's Narrative of Displacement, Expulsion and Escape in Historic Southern Palestine, 1930–1970." *Journal of Women of the Middle East and the Islamic World* 14 (3): 310–41.

———. 2016b. "Oral Traditions of Naqab Bedouin Women: Challenging Colonial Representations through Embodied Performance." *Journal of Holy Land and Palestine Studies* 15 (1): 31–57.

———. 2018. *Women's Political Activism in Palestine: Peacebuilding, Resistance, and Survival.* Chicago: University of Illinois Press.

———. Forthcoming. "*Tibb 'Arabi*: Palestinian Bedouin Women's Healing Practices in and against the Israeli Settler-Colonial Regime."

Rodinson, Maxime. 1973. *Israel: A Colonial-Settler State?* New York: Monad Press.

Sa'di, Ahmad H. 2011. "Ominous Designs: Israel's Strategies and Tactics of Controlling the Palestinians during the First Two Decades." In *Surveillance and Control in Israel/Palestine*, edited by Elia Zureik, David Lyon, and Yasmeen Abu–Laban, 83–98. London: Routledge.

———. 2014. *Thorough Surveillance: The Genesis of Israeli Policies of Population: Management, Surveillance and Political Control towards the Palestinian Minority.* Manchester: Manchester University Press.

Said, Edward. 1979. *The Question of Palestine.* London: Routledge.

Salazar Hughes, S. 2020. "Unbounded Territoriality: Territorial Control, Settler Colonialism, and Israel/Palestine." *Settler Colonial Studies* 10 (2): 216–33.

Sayegh, Fayez A. 2012. "Zionist Colonialism in Palestine (1965)." *Settler Colonial Studies* 2 (1): 206–25. https://researchbank.swinburne.edu.au/file/30c016d4-7dd5-454d-bba2-358a164cc3ec/1/PDF%20%28Settler%20Colonial%20Studies%202_1%20-%20Full%20issue%29.pdf.

Sayigh, R. 2007. *The Palestinians: From Peasants to Revolutionaries.* London: Zed Books.

Seidler, S. 2014. "Minister: Israel Looking at Ways to Lower Bedouin Birthrate." *Haaretz*, September 29. https://www.haaretz.com/.premium-israel-wants-to-lower-bedouin-birthrate-1.5308477.

Shafir, G. 1989. *Land, Labor, and the Origins of the Israeli-Palestinian Conflict, 1882–1914.* Cambridge: Cambridge University Press.

———. 1996. "Zionism and Colonialism: A Comparative Approach." In *Israel in Comparative Perspective: Challenging the Conventional Wisdom*, edited by Michael Barnett. New York: State University of New York Press.

Shalhoub-Kevorkian, N. 2009. *Militarization and Violence against Women in Conflict Zones in the Middle East: A Palestinian Case Study.* Cambridge: Cambridge University Press.

Speed, S. 2017. "Structures of Settler Capitalism in Abya Yala." *American Quarterly* 69 (4): 783–90.

Svirsky, M., ed. 2014. "Collaborative Struggles in Australia and Israel-Palestine." *Settler Colonial Studies* 4 (4).

Tawil-Souri, H. 2012. "Uneven Borders, Coloured (Im)mobilities: ID Cards in Palestine/Israel." *Geopolitics* 17 (1):153–76.

Veracini, L. 2010. *Settler Colonialism: A Theoretical Overview*. London: Palgrave Mac-Millan.

———. 2013a. "The Other Shift: Settler Colonialism, Israel and The Occupation." *Journal of Palestine Studies* 42 (2): 26–42.

———. 2013b. "'Settler Colonialism': Career of a Concept." *Journal of Imperial and Commonwealth History* 41 (2).

———, ed. 2015. "What Can Settler Colonial Studies Offer to an Interpretation of the Conflict in Israel-Palestine?" Special Issue: Settler Colonialism and Israel-Palestine. *Settler Colonial Studies* 5 (3): 268–71.

Weizman, E. 2007. *Hollow Land: Israel's Architecture of Occupation*. London: Verso.

Wolfe, Patrick. 1999. *Settler Colonialism and the Transformation of Anthropology: The Politics and Poetics of an Ethnographic Event*. London: Cassell.

———. 2006. "Settler Colonialism and the Elimination of the Native." *Journal of Genocide Research* 8 (4): 387–404.

———. 2012. "Purchase by Other Means: The Palestine *Nakba* and Zionism's Conquest of Economics." *Settler Colonial Studies* 2 (1): 133–71.

Yiftachel, O. 2008. "Epilogue: Studying Naqab/Negev Bedouins—Toward a Colonial Paradigm?" *HAGAR Studies in Culture, Polity and Identities* 8 (2): 83–108.

Yuval-Davis, N. 1997. *Gender and Nation*. London: Sage.

Zureik, E. 1979. *Palestinians in Israel: A Study of Internal Colonialism*. London: Routledge and Kegan Paul.

3   Encountering the Israeli War Machine

Imminent (In)security, Vortical
Violence, Rhizomatic Sumud

Wassim Ghantous

At the center of Israel's occupation of the Palestinian territories (oPt) lie
ongoing demographic and territorial processes aimed at the *elimination* of
the native Palestinians—that is, their dispossession and replacement (see
Jabary-Salamanca et al. 2012; Sayegh 2012; Wolfe 2006). While the *logic of
elimination* serves as a "compass" that directs Israel's regime of control in
the oPt, the ways in which elimination is effectuated have taken different
forms. Over the last two decades, Israeli eliminatory mechanisms have multiplied and intensified significantly, producing a multilayered, complex, and
diffuse colonial regime via a multitude of colonial actors, institutions, and
technologies. Today, Israeli military mechanisms of control—for example,
walls, checkpoints, the "permit regime," daily policing activities, surveillance systems—are bolstered by vigilante and policing roles enacted by
civilian settler groups and hybrid security actors operating across the oPt
(see Berda 2017; Gazit 2015; Levy 2021; Makdisi 2008; Maoz 2020; Peteet
2017; Humanitarian Policy and Conflict Research 2008). Israel's colonial
regime thus functions via ranging modalities of power produced by state
and non-state actors and by different combinations between them. In fact,
the growing roles played by non-state actors, together with transformations
within the logics of Israeli military operations, shift Israel's colonial power
away from systemized rules and principles; instead, it becomes ever more
elusive, volatile, and pervasive (see Ghantous 2020; Ophir, Givioni, and
Hanafi 2009).

These transformations and intensifications in the dynamics of power are conjoined with new spatiotemporal vocabularies that modulate the distribution of violence in Palestinian spaces and on Palestinian bodies. This is evident in scholarly works that speak of Israeli violence in markedly polycentric and topological terms such as "war of maneuver" and "swarming maneuver" (Weizman 2006; 2007, 105–8) or that track its dynamic unfolding as an economy of violence oscillating between intense and meticulous "slow violence" and periodical "spectacular violence" (Bhungalia 2018; see also Azoulay and Ophir 2009). Relatedly, such violence can also be conceptualized in qualified form—for instance, as the "slow wounding" (Joronen 2021) and "maiming" (Puar 2017) of Palestinian bodies, or as the maintaining of terrorizing climates in Palestinian living spaces (Shalhoub-Kevorkian 2015) and engendering exacerbated affective states of uncertainty and fear (Griffiths 2017; Zureik 2016). Even amid such colonial force, however, Palestinians continually develop different modes of *sumud* (steadfastness) that confront, negotiate, and decelerate Israeli power as the means to remain in their (home-)land (see Alkhalili 2017; Hammami 2015; Joronen and Griffiths 2019; Meari 2014; Ryan 2015).

This chapter examines such complex and interlocking dynamics—of multiple colonial actors, controlling mechanisms, and resistances—as modes of a particular assemblage that philosophers Gilles Deleuze and Félix Guattari (2010) term the "War Machine." Engaging in the conceptual depth of the War Machine, this chapter sheds light on spatiotemporal shifts underlying Israeli eliminatory power and their projections onto the native Palestinians, as well as Palestinians' efforts to evade them. Based on empirical accounts of Palestinians' lives in rural areas of the West Bank and Israeli soldiers' firsthand testimonies published by the nongovernmental organization (NGO) Breaking the Silence (2012, 2017), the chapter brings new conceptual insight into the functioning of contemporary Israeli settler colonialism as a War Machine.[1] Specifically, the first section provides a purview of Deleuze and Guattari's theorizations on politics and war-making, and situates the Palestine-Israel "model" within contemporary global processes of (in)security and wars. The second section draws a conceptualization of the

Israeli War Machine to address the increasing elusiveness, pervasiveness, and unpredictability of Israeli eliminatory power as it plays out across a public-hybrid-civilian colonial continuum. Following this, the third section examines the violent projections of such colonial machinery by invoking the concepts of *vortical violence* and *imminent (in)security*. A fourth section identifies a particular mode of Palestinian maneuvering of such violence—*rhizomatic sumud*.

Overall, the chapter suggests novel ways to (re)think the formation, unfolding, and evasion of contemporary Israeli colonial power and offers a prelude to particular forms of encounters with colonial violence—namely, Palestinians' encountering a colonial War Machine and their "rhizomatic" struggle to evade it.

Locating Palestine-Israel in the Age of War Machines

A key thesis in Deleuze and Guattari's writing on the War Machine is built through a historical account of states appropriating War Machines—that is, mercenaries, conscripted citizens, or civil society—as a means to launch relatively controlled and delineated wars. A central point, which provides insight into the case at hand, is that starting from the second half of the twentieth century, the War Machine began appropriating the State; thus, wars and warlike relations become immanent processes (Deleuze and Guattari 2010, 93–103). For Deleuze and Guattari, this shift, which has its origins in the totality of the Cold War, and the transformation into finance capitalism and the intensification of investments in the war economy, is also ultimately spatiotemporal one.[2] Unlike state wars that operated along clearly defined plans and rules (e.g., strategies, chain of command), regulated arrangement and movement (e.g., rear, front, attack, defense, etc.), systemized violence, and the enclosing of space—for example, the roads, supply chains, and trenches exemplary of the First World War—in the age of War Machines, warfare becomes an everyday commodity, an economy of violence that is driven by quick profits and conducted by variable combinations of public and private, and local and international, actors. In this stage, warfare becomes an affective and immanent force that operates through speed—a movement of violence that occupies space-time and constantly permeates new domains. This change is hence defined by a shift from the "striated space" in which movement of warfare is measured, is regulated, and transmits between defined points to that of the "smooth space," which is characterized by speed, or the swift alteration of unimpeded movement.[3]

The relevance of this thesis gained momentum among critical scholarly works interrogating developments of the post-9/11 era of the "war on terror." This is evident in the work of Achille Mbembe (2003, 30–34), who depicts wars of globalization as initiated by the public and private actors that constitute War Machines and have the capability to rapidly divide and recombine, depending on possibilities of capital accumulation, and whose operations unfold through light and mobile attacks launched from unpredictable places. For Ian Buchanan (2006), contemporary (imperial) wars have become unceasing processes that often inflict tactical and limited violence (the exemplary drone attacks) aimed at preserving domination while refraining from vast and costly full-scale wars. In a similar line of thinking, Brian Massumi (2010, 2015a) claims that contemporary wars have become increasingly affective and ontological, and are conducted via a logic of preemption. A central aspect of preemptive wars is their operation on the affective (pre-individuated) domain of (enemy) populations and states to modulate the very emerging conditions of the "threats" they may come to constitute (Massumi 2010). The idea of ontological wars ("ontopower"), thus, is to sustain a "simmering" level of war that operates immanently on the pre-subjectifying moment of its targets to foment their submission and deter future acts of resistance.

In this contemporary form, warfare emerges from manifold processes of convergence—for example, that of internal police and external military groups that merge into networks of "global policing" (Bigo 2008); of private and public actors into "global security assemblages" (Abrahamsen and Williams 2009; see also Bachmann, Bell, and Holmqvist 2016); and of times of war and times of peace toward a state of "everywhere war" (Gregory 2011), "unending war" (Duffield 2007), and "immanent security" (Bratich 2006). Within different convergences between these spatiotemporal states of warfare and (in)security, everyday life becomes infused with fear and uncertainty, whose degrees of intensity vary depending on geopolitical contexts and variable political subjectivities (of race/ethnicity, class, political orientations, etc.) (Bigo 2008; Massumi 1993; Murakami Wood 2017). Indeed, the continuous permeation of warfare (or warlike relations) into different aspects of everyday life has instigated new spatiotemporal articulations and experiences of (in)security.

The Palestine-Israel setting, however, is not only embedded in past and present continuities and expansions of global processes of colonialism, capitalism, and the war economy but also perceived as incarnating a more accomplished, extreme, and accelerated context of violence (Deleuze 1978; Halper 2015; Machold 2018; Mbembe 2003; Medien 2019; Weizman 2007). Seen in this light, the Israeli War Machine, reflected in its relations of enmity and (in)security, as well as its technologies of pacification and spatial control, comes to resemble an intensified (and intensifying) formation of (Western-liberal) worldwide machinery in the age of the war on terrorism. However, what precisely is the Israeli War Machine? What is its constitution? What politics inform it? And what modes of (in)security, violence, and control does it visit on Palestinians? To answer these broad questions, the following sections analyze the Israeli War Machine as it takes shape in rural Palestinian villages in the West Bank.

Reconceptualizing the Israeli War Machine

In recent years, there has been renewed interest in the work of Deleuze and Guattari for studying different facets of Israeli colonization and Palestinian resistance and their links to global political processes. In particular, the concept of the War Machine and its derivative spatiotemporal conceptions of, prominently, *speed*, *smooth space*, and *rhizomes* are useful to identify modes of Palestinian de-colonial resistance and sumud practices as they play out in political and cultural realms (see Abujidi 2014; Al-Shaikh 2009; Ayyash 2018; Svirsky 2015, 2017), while other work has employed these conceptions for probing contemporary formations of Israeli colonization and the violence it produces against Palestinians (see Plasse-Couture 2013;

Weizman 2006). This section expands these latter engagements by suggesting a reconceptualization of the contemporary Israeli War Machine as it operates in rural areas of the West Bank.

In his work on the shifting military paradigm during the Second Intifada (2000–2005), Eyal Weizman (2006) shows how the Israeli army began appropriating and operationalizing the spatiotemporal aspects of the War Machine as exemplified in the military maneuver of "swarming." This maneuver breaks with more traditional forms of combat by allowing an army (i.e., the Israel Defense Forces) to adopt a more flexible organizational mode that grants it capabilities to launch speedy, illusive, and unpredictable attacks inside urban (i.e., Palestinian) centers. Swarming entails that the army replaces traditional forms of "outside" attack by infiltrating enemy space and moving from the "inside out in all directions simultaneously"; it dismisses centralized and top-down chains of command and communications by adopting a polycentric form of organization; and prescribed plans give way to relational "toolboxes" designed to adapt to varying scenarios and whose operationalization is made according to developments in the field (Weizman 2006, 12). In the work of François-Xavier Plasse-Coutour (2013), however, the concept of the War Machine is attributed to the vigilante role played by Israeli settlers as an affective ethno-religious aggressive force that enacts economically efficient forms of violence against Palestinians, whom the Israeli army then captures and governs to modulate the violence produced by Israeli settlers to an "acceptable" level. By governing the insecurity, danger, and risk produced by this Settler War Machine, the Israeli army seeks to establish an "equilibrium" that is both politically and economically rewarding—for example, with land appropriation, establishment of settlements, resource plunder, stabilization of real estate prices, and cost-efficient policing (Plasse-Couture 2013, 450).

I take this further by tracking the Israeli War Machine as it consists in multiple processes within and between military, civilian settler, and hybrid security actors. In my examination of Palestinian villagers' everyday encounters with colonial control and violence, similar to Plasse-Couture (2013), I identify an initial War Machine originating from the heterogeneous and flexible body of "the settlers"—for instance, settler groups, settler security actors, and settler NGOs. In these encounters with a Settler War Machine, a particularly intense mode of violence is unleashed such as the "price-tag" attacks that target *anything* Palestinian: bodies, homes, trees, groves, infrastructure, water tanks, and so forth.[4] During fieldwork in an area around Hebron in the southern part of the West Bank, a man named Khaled from Susiya described these attacks as "pure terror [that aims to] terrorize us Palestinians. It is a call to eliminate us." Khaled further explained that price-tag attacks, often carried out in secret or at night by disguised settlers, are not delineated to a particular geographical space but to "attack and vandalize whatever comes their way, in our groves and inside our villages and homes" (author interview, 2019).

Such intense violence marks a peak in the economy of violence produced by the Settler War Machine and is accompanied by other instances where settlers effect more chronic, persistent forms of violence. This includes settlers taking on policing and security roles and blocking Palestinian movement via threats and physical violence or by calling the army and civilian security coordinators (CSCs) in settlements. The CSCs are hybrid security agents who are residents of settlements and appointed by councils. They are, at the same time, agents of the army and granted vast policing and security responsibilities to operate in and around settlements.[5] For Palestinians I spoke to during my fieldwork, the CSCs are depicted as vociferous in their commitment to expel Palestinians from their lands. As Dirar from Kafr Qaddum in the Qalqilya Governorate (in the northern West Bank) put it, "They [the CSCs and settlers] have one rule only, and their rule is that they don't want to see an Arab in their sight" (author interview, 2017). The CSC is not perceived merely as one constituent of the category "settlers" but as one who is central to it. "The CSC is the one in control of 99% of the things that happen in the area, he is the one preventing us from going to our lands," as Elias from Susiya put it. He continued, "Of course the CSC has more authority than an ordinary settler, but they are always together and back each other up, then comes the army, and its role is to execute the orders given by them" (author interview, 2017). Indeed, the CSCs do not only draw on settler privilege and force but also utilize their authority to facilitate their violent operations, help cover them up, and at times even lead them (see also Hareuveni 2014; Kanoich 2018).

Figured this way, the Settler War Machine is primarily constituted of civilian and hybrid colonial actors who form an ethno-religious colonial force driven by an intense relation of enmity and urgency for Palestinian elimination—that is, to "redeem" the "Land of Israel" via a process of native dispossession (see Muhareb 2012; Shalhoub-Kevorkian 2015). Driven by this affective force, the Settler War Machine is understood to acquire an exaggerated and magnified sense of (in)security that works according to an inversion of power relations whereby settlers become "native victims" and Palestinians are seen as "colonial aggressors" (see Perugini and Gordon 2015). Consequently, ordinary activities by Palestinian villagers such as accessing lands for cultivation or grazing and constructing a house or planting a tree come to constitute *imminent security threats*, as "infiltrations" into the "Land of Israel" or as acts of "terrorism" directed at harming the settler body. In this specific colonial encounter, the Settler War Machine instigates an intense sense of insecurity that captures the speed and violence of the *hunted animal* (to use Deleuze and Guattari's analogy [2010, 66]), producing an economy of violence that does not rest until the "threat" is removed—specifically in this case, until the corporeal removal of Palestinian bodies, properties, or built structures. Such settler violence, therefore, is neither aimed at dismantling a specified threat nor bound to a defined geographical space but rather indiscriminately targets Palestinian bodies and landscapes with varying intensities of violence wherever they exist (their mere existence is the threat).

Working in concert are other processes that transfuse the Israeli military institution into a War Machine, ones that are taking place both on the *molar* (macropolitical) and the *molecular* (micropolitical) levels.[6] On the molecular level, changes are reflected in the increasing deviation of everyday Israeli army operations from the striated spaces that traditionally orient state-military activity—for example, clearly assigned plans and defined tasks, rules of engagement and chain of command, precise designation of geographical boundaries, and so forth—to being gradually "smoothed out" through their routine interactions with the Settler War Machine. This is particularly evident in the almost automatic compliance of soldiers stationed in settlements with the Settler War Machine's magnified (in) security that calls for the expulsion of any Palestinian body they see in the surrounding areas. As Elias put it, the soldiers' "role is to execute the orders" (author interview, 2017). When it comes to csc-soldier relations, the soldiers' subjugation to the cscs is not only based on Palestinians' impressions but also is evident in many soldiers' testimonies. For instance, this one assertively states, "Every force that enters the settlement answers to the Civilian Security Coordinator: the civilian guards and us as soldiers on Settlement Defense Duty, the settlement's Civilian Emergency Response Team for when there's an incident—we're all subject to him" (Breaking the Silence 2017, 31).

In this way, and significantly, soldiers' everyday security activities in the settlements unfold increasingly within the unbounded smooth space of the Settler War Machine, joining its magnified (in)security and the solutions it demands as for achieving security—or "security" insofar as it means the expulsion of Palestinians. Another Israeli soldier's testimony reads: "What we were really interested in were the roads. Molotov Cocktails on roads, stones [hurled at] roads. The hermetic guarding of the settlements—I felt it wasn't the army's objective; that it was the objective of the Civilian Security Coordinator and the settlers" (Breaking the Silence 2017, 44–45). This arrangement clearly indicates the shift in which the army's measurable defensive-leaning security considerations (e.g., securing roads) are constantly losing their boundaries in favor of the speed of the affective and intolerant offensive-leaning security impetus of the Settler War Machine that intends to "hermetically" seal Palestinian lands. This shift from *security measures* to *security impetus* is paralleled in shifts in the modes of violence that the army engages in every day, as evidenced by the many Palestinians who recount that soldier violence *used to be* more predictable given that soldiers would give warnings prior to taking action. In recent years, however, soldiers' violence is often unpredictable and operates outside the striated spaces of army operations. This is particularly evident in situations that start with settlers' attempts to ward Palestinian farmers from their lands and where the soldiers' presence at these incidents often results in their joining the settlers' violence. Waleed, a farmer from Burin (in the Nablus District), explained that "settlers used to attack rapidly and leave rapidly or sometimes even run away when they saw the army approaching. Today, they throw stones at the farmers, the army arrives and joins them, shooting gas canisters, rubber and live bullets at us" (author interview, 2018). This shift, and to use Deleuze and Guattari's (2010, 66) analogy once again, projects a divergence from the systemized violence of *the hunter* that "arrests the movement of the wild animal" and operates a "blow-by-blow violence," and a sliding into durable and unlimited violence of the *hunted animal*. Moreover, this subsumption of soldiers into the affective force of the Settler War Machine has reached new levels in recent years whereby soldiers are increasingly involved in executing settler-style price-tag attacks inside Palestinian villages, in some cases with their commanders' consent and approval (see, e.g., Kubovich 2020; Shezaf 2020).

On the molar level, projections of the War Machine within the Israeli army play out in the two main processes of *security outsourcing* and *military reconfigurations*. The first relates to the army's increasing transferring security tasks to private and hybrid security actors operating in the West Bank, as is the case with the cscs. The Israeli army delegates policing powers to the cscs who are themselves settlers but who are not part of the army's chain of command or its supervisory, regulatory, or accountability mechanisms (see Breaking the Silence 2017; Hareuveni 2014). This lack of regulation (or striation) creates an organizational void through which the cscs de facto extend their sphere of influence, further enhancing the force of the Settler War Machine and, in a crucial reversal, absorbing the army into it. A second and complementary process is in the reconfiguration of the military doctrines directing the army's routine policing activities in rural Palestinian areas and is best exemplified in the army's "demonstration of presence" military approach, which is part of the broader "searing of consciousnesses" doctrine.[7] According to this doctrine, the entire Palestinian population is perceived as a potential terroristic threat that necessitates a constant army presence: "violent patrols," "harassing activity," and "disruption of normalcy," to use common parlance among Israeli military staff (Breaking the Silence 2012, 29; see also Huss 2019). This approach results in army troops routinely roaming Palestinian villages and conducting random night searches of houses, arbitrary stops and searches in streets, erratic and sudden closures of areas and roads, and all manner of actions that trigger clashes with Palestinian residents and precipitate further violence—the detention, injuring, and killing of Palestinian "rioters," for instance. In this way, vast numbers of Palestinian communities are constantly subject to a spectrum of violence—intimidation, humiliation, harassment, imprisonment, surveillance, and physical harm—that is intended to sear the consciousness so as to impel submission. The routinization of these practices thus produces a form of policing that operates on the pre-subjectifying or affective registers of Palestinian bodies by subjecting them to a continuous but sometimes background violence that intensifies disproportionally when met with any sort of resistance. Such an affective power aims to make Palestinians embody submission and refrain from future resistance to colonial domination and expansion, suggesting a preemptive and future-facing operation par excellence, or an *ontopower* (Massumi 2015a).

In sum, the transfiguration—*and subsummation*—of the Israeli army into a War Machine is effectuated through two broad processes that take place simultaneously on molar and molecular levels. First, the Settler War Machine's force emanates from "below," carrying soldiers' everyday military activities along its affective, smooth, and speedy eliminatory force; and, second, the Israeli army smooths out its own operations through military reconfigurations and security outsourcing, an "inward-out" process of becoming a War Machine. Importantly, however, these processes indicate a different direction of the relationship governing the Israeli state and the War Machine, one in which the Israeli army is no longer *appropriating* the War Machine—as in Weizman's (2006) account of "swarming maneuvers"—nor *capturing* and *governing* the Settler War Machine, as in Plasse-Couture's (2013); instead, conversely and increasingly, the state is *appropriated by it.* In this reversed relation of appropriation, the Israeli state (military) is no longer *external* to the War Machine but is consumed by it, forming an overall *Israeli War Machine* that cuts across the public-hybrid-civilian colonial continuum.

Vortical Violence, Imminent (In)security

The economy of violence produced through the Israeli War Machine discussed so far can be seen to assume a "machinic" or a "rhizomatic" mode of organization—that is, via symbiotic connections between heterogonous bodies—whereby different colonial actors, in different combinations, come to (co-)produce variable offshoots of violence and control. The speed of these violent offshoots, the variable intensities they assume, and their unboundedness to a particular geographical space come to form what I term here a "vortical (motion of) violence." In vortexes, violence (lurking or actualized) assumes a dissipative motion that fills and delimits space, like a moving "cloud" or a "swarm," and that solidifies along axes composed of anything signifying Palestinian-ness (bodies and landscapes) with variable densities of violence. In practice, and as has been shown earlier, vortical violence is produced and sustained across a suite of violent offshoots: price-tag attacks against Palestinian bodies, villages, infrastructures, and groves; ordinary coercion and violence such as beatings, threats, expulsions, and blocking of movement; and routine surveillance, arrests, and home and body searches, among others. For Palestinian villagers, however, the increasing difficulty to predict the direction from which violence is initiated as well as the place and time at which it will manifest (inside the village or the fields, during the day or night, etc.) can produce profound affective states of insecurity and uncertainty (see also Ghantous 2020; Griffiths and Joronen 2021; Shalhoub-Kevorkian 2015; Zureik 2016).

The affective power of the Israeli War Machine and its production of immanent vortexes of violence is evident in Palestinian villages in different parts of the West Bank. A primary effect relates to the severe restriction on Palestinian villagers to pursue agricultural work, a primary source of income. This is mainly exemplified in the fact that a large proportion of villagers—including many I have interviewed—are no longer able to access their agricultural lands except during short and infrequent "coordination periods" (one to two weeks per year).[8] It should be emphasized in this regard that Palestinians are not *officially* prevented from accessing their lands as no official military orders (at least not the majority of them) clearly mark their lands as "closed areas"; thus, there is no "striation" (see also Joronen 2021). Rather, the villagers' embodiment of the fear and uncertainty of the smoothness and speed of vortical violence ensures they refrain from accessing their lands. As Ali, a farmer from Burin, asserted, "We don't know what areas we shouldn't enter and in any case we don't dare going there anymore, it's too dangerous and we keep on being nervous all the time" (author interview, 2018). His friend Munther added, "We know which lands we shouldn't enter through our experiences of violence and expulsion, today, these are vast areas of agricultural lands" (author interview, 2018). However, the few farmers who still attempt to access their lands do so intermittently and as quickly as possible for fear of being attacked: "You feel psychological unease. You know that at a certain point they will pop up from somewhere and you will have to face them [settlers, soldiers, the csc]. . . . When I'm walking there, I keep looking to all sides, up and down, everywhere" (Kareem, author interview, Kafr Qaddum, 2019).

This intense fear and insecurity experienced by Palestinian villagers is tied to the ways in which the Israeli War Machine constantly modulates them as "security threats," "infiltrators," or "trespassers"—*imminent threats* to be neutralized, expelled, detained, attacked, dispossessed. But this pertains not only to Palestinian bodies but also to any tool or device they carry, causing them to undergo a similar security elevation to its absolute antagonizing end. For example, when in their lands, the villagers' very ordinary act of using mobile phones becomes a delicate operation, particularly if they are used for taking photos or video recording, as this behavior could be construed by any of the colonial actors as gathering intelligence materials for a part of some future lethal plan against the settlement and its settlers (see Hareuveni 2014, 40). A similar fear of such magnified state of (in)security is reflected in the main agricultural tool used by villagers—scissors. Any tool bigger or sharper than a pair of scissors could be swiftly transformed by the War Machine's imagination into a weapon. "You can get accused easily if you have any sharp tools with you. A pair of scissors is our main tool there, as it is the least likely to be perceived as a weapon. Even if you have a small vegetable knife, the csc or soldiers could accuse you of wanting to kill a settler or whatever" (Mahmoud, author interview, Kafr Qaddum, 2017).

Imminent (in)security thus refers to the automatic impulse of (magnified) insecurity activated by the Israeli War Machine when encountering any Palestinian body (property or tool) it perceives as an actual or potential threat that should be preemptively "neutralized" through security measures. As such, imminent (in)security suggests the affective impulse that presupposes and instigates vortical violence. Concomitantly, such an affective antagonizing force enmeshes Palestinians' bodies in a state of *imminent insecurity*, an embodiment of intense states of fear and uncertainty from a violence that is constantly hovering and is about to solidify at any moment, yet its direction and magnitude is difficult to predict. Given that, Palestinians' bodies and landscapes become sites engulfed with an intensification of the three spatiotemporal states of everywhere war (Gregory 2011), unending war (Duffield 2007), and immanent war (Bratich 2006), suggesting a state of "*imminent* (in)security" that simultaneously compresses temporality, fills space, and fluctuates within it. The terms "everywhere," "unending," and "immanent" portray *extensive* spatiotemporal states of (in)security and war, whereas "*imminent* (in)security" is *intensive* and permeates all spheres of life at every moment. This imminent (in)security and its vortical unfolding run parallel to a wider idea of rural Palestinian areas as subject to a "terrorizing climate" that infiltrates Palestinians' most intimate spaces (villages and homes) with an aim to maintain a "sense of being haunted and uprooted" (Shalhoub-Kevorkian 2015, 22). While such a depiction indicates that Israeli colonization is becoming significantly more pervasive and forceful, this is not to suggest that Palestinians are fully subsumed by it, as the next section shows.

Rhizomatic Sumud: Evading the Vortex through the *Talou'*

As is widely documented, Palestinians have been active in confronting, negotiating, and decelerating Israeli technologies of domination and eliminatory functions in what Palestinians term "sumud"—a steadfastness that plays out in political, cultural, and physical realms as a means to continue their presence in their (home)land (see Alkhalili 2017; Joronen and Griffiths 2019; Meari 2014; Ryan 2015). To further existing notions of sumud, in this final section I outline a preliminary account of a specific form of Palestinian refusal that coexists *spatiotemporally* with the Israeli War Machine discussed so far—one that I term, after Deleuze and Guattari, "rhizomatic sumud." To exemplify this, I use a shepherding tactic common to rural areas of the West Bank, the *talou'* (lookout),[9] which is designed to facilitate relatively safe conditions for sheep grazing that minimizes food costs and, by extension, enhances Palestinian steadfastness.

While both shepherding and farming are primary economic activities for Palestinian villages—and thus crucial for remaining steadfast—villagers seem to invest more in developing shepherding activities and less so in farming (which they invest in intensively during coordination periods). One explanation for this differentiation can be traced to the distinct modes of work inherent to each. Unlike farming, a relatively static and sedentary activity (as in striated space), shepherding is an inherently mobile activity that requires constant movement through vast terrains (as in smooth space). Therefore, farming renders Palestinians an easy target for the War Machine to identify and attack, whereas shepherding seems to have an advantage in evading vortical violence via the opening of a time gap between spotting and attacking in which locations change. The role of the talou', or the lookout who is stationed on a mountaintop to observe the surrounding area and the shepherds, thus expands this advantage into a collective shepherding tactic that increases the capability and safety of herding activities. In cases where any of the colonial actors seem to be making their way to approach the shepherds, the lookouts immediately call and navigate the shepherds to change their location. Riad, a shepherd from the Southern

Hebron area, explained, "If I see a police or army jeep coming from the eastern side, I tell [the other shepherds] and they leave from the western side, and the army keeps spinning around them but never catches them. All of this is done through the phone. We are locals and our knowledge of the area is very precise, so we know how to move and navigate around it quickly" (author interview, 2018). The role of the talou' is not simply to observe and navigate; in cases where the navigation process fails to help the shepherds evade vortical violence, they turn their focus to protecting the endangered shepherds by mobilizing as many people as possible (including international/Israeli activists, lawyers, and human rights NGOs) to approach the area of the encounter and defend against possible violence and arrests. "They all come to help out en masse, including the boys, the girls, the women, and the elderly, they all come," Elias from the Southern Hebron area claimed (author interview, 2018).

The collectivity of Palestinian rural communities and the strong bonds they retain with each other suggest a counter-affective mode of being that operates to overcome the state of imminent insecurity in two main ways. First, it helps break the boundaries of fear that prevent them from accessing their lands in the first place, and, second, their collective mobilization is aimed at protecting shepherds against colonial violence when it occurs. In spatiotemporal terms, Palestinian communities' shepherding activities as exemplified in the talou' are seen to assume a rhizomatic mode of organization and unfolding, one that operates through speed—as the swift alteration of movement—and creates "a map that is always detachable, connectable, reversible, modifiable, and has multiple entryways and exits" (Deleuze and Guattari 1987, 21). By adapting a collective and flexible mode of organization, deploying simple countersurveillance and communication methods, and utilizing topographical conditions and local knowledge, Palestinian communities manage to enhance the *speed* of their shepherding activities so as to evade vortical violence and, hence, to increase their capacities to make a living and remain steadfast in their villages and lands.

While this is just a brief example, rhizomatic sumud suggests an important corrective where symbiotic affective bonds take on a flexible shape that advances the innate understanding that the speed of the colonial machinery can be evaded through the (counter-)speed of shepherding, thus producing a mirroring of motion with an opposing politics: speed for sumud versus speed for elimination. This perspective on sumud overlaps with and extends what Nurhan Abujidi (2014) terms "rhizomatic resistance," a conceptual base capable of accommodating the heterogeneity, adaptability, and connectedness of Palestinian resistance acts. As exemplified above, the notion of rhizomatic sumud describes a mode of sumud whose dynamism and adaptability take on particular affective and spatiotemporal manifestations. In other words, rhizomatic sumud pays attention not only to sumud as a dynamic and adaptable "resilient resistance" (Abujidi 2014; Ryan 2015) and to the political-affective subjectivities constituting it (Meari 2014) but also to the ways in which it unfolds in space-time. At the same time, and albeit specifically situated here, rhizomatic sumud conceives the colonial encounter beyond the realms of discourse and narrative—that is, in its "living" formation as it is materially expressed and (per)formed, and is spatiotemporally unfolding.

Conclusion

This chapter has shown how Israel's colonial regime has come to possess an intense affective force inhabited by an extreme relation of enmity conjoined with an urgency for Palestinian elimination and replacement. In such a relation, the Israeli War Machine reverses power relations and magnifies them in a way that portrays Palestinian bodies and landscapes as imminent security threats (i.e., "colonizers," "infiltrators," "terrorists"), rendering them targets of a mode of violence that is speedy, unpredictable, and geographically unbounded—vortical violence. My analysis thus suggests a particular form of Palestinian encounter with colonial violence, one in which violence and control intensify and expand beyond the time and place of actual physical encounters with colonial bodies. More accurately, the encounter is instilled in the affective registers of Palestinian bodies and in their landscapes (villages, homes, fields) in a form of constant and imminent insecurity, a fear and uncertainty of a violence that is about to erupt anywhere and at any time, a spectral and haunting violence.

However, one should be reminded that the rise of the Israeli War Machine is an outcome of the increasingly intensified conditions of its appropriation by the Israeli state over the years—that is, the intensification of the *Zionist idea* of ethnic/racial ("Jewishness") and territorial exclusivity over all of historic Palestine (the "Land of Israel") and of its accompanied war economy and culture (Kimmerling 2005; Pappé 2014; Said 1994; Shalhoub-Kevorkian 2015). As I claim here, however, at this stage of reversed appropriation, Israeli logic of elimination at the rural frontier becomes less a *logic* (an *idea* or *ideology)* that operates through calculated policies, laws, and the enclosing of territory (as in "striated space") and more of a mode of elimination that is increasingly *affective*, a "thinking-feeling" operation (Massumi 2015b, 91) caught by the speed of the smooth space, as a force of violence and destruction that perpetually unfolds in real time along varying intensities. This shift complements and furthers the idea that Israeli colonization is increasingly operating outside rationalized rules and principles of calculation, transforming into "a pure and simple war machine that is indistinguishably directed against civilians and non-civilians alike" (Ophir, Givoni, and Hanafi 2009, 18, 22). Crucial to this transformation is not a mere blurring of the lines between the public, the hybrid, and the civilian but rather their increasing infusion into an overall Israeli War Machine with intensified eliminatory capacities to colonize—yet ones that simultaneously indicate insistent life-affirming *lines of flight* for the colonized.

Notes

1. The empirical materials were generated through ethnographic methods, interviews, and focus group meetings in the Palestinian villages of Kafr Qaddum, Susiya, and Burin between 2016 and 2019. For safety and privacy considerations, interviewees' names were replaced with fictional ones.
2. Regarding investment in the military-industrial complex as well as the various physical and mental investments in citizenry as war makers and victims of war, see Deleuze and Guattari 2010, 100.
3. The seeming opposition between striated space and smooth space exists only conceptually, as in practice they always appear in varying hybrid compositions. In relation

to contemporary warfare, however, Deleuze and Guattari perceive smooth space as a dominating space that is constantly and swiftly disentangling (or deterritorializing) striated spaces.

4. For more on settlers' price-tag violence, see Muhareb 2012.

5. The role of CSCs is part of the broader "regional defense" military doctrine that predated the Israeli state and was formalized afterward in 1961, and it assumes frontline communities to form ancillary defense functions within the overall military system. In 1971 this doctrine was assigned to oPt settlements and since then was amended several times, most importantly in 1992, when the CSCs were granted powers analogous to those of police officers. See Hareuveni 2014.

6. For more on the concepts of the molar and the molecular, see Deleuze and Guattari's (1987) chapter "Micropolitics and Segmentarity."

7. This doctrine was revealed in testimonies of Israeli (ex-)soldiers conveyed to Breaking the Silence (2012).

8. For more on coordination periods and their impacts on Palestinian agricultural production, see Ghantous 2020, 156–62.

9. While this phenomenon is widespread in many rural areas of the West Bank, the term "the talou'" has been evoked in certain areas only.

References

Abrahamsen, Rita, and Michael C. Williams. 2009. "Security beyond the State: Global Security Assemblages in International Politics." *International Political Sociology* 3:1–17.

Abujidi, Nurhan. 2014. *Urbicide in Palestine: Spaces of Oppression and Resilience*. Routledge Studies in Middle Eastern Politics 63. London: Routledge.

Alkhalili, Nura. 2017. "Between Sumud and Submission: Palestinian Popular Practices on the Land in the Edge Areas of Jerusalem." PhD diss., Lund University.

Al-Shaikh, Abdu-Rahim. 2009. "Palestine: The Nomadic Condition." *Third Text* 23 (6): 763–78.

Ayyash, Mark Muhannad. 2018. "An Assemblage of Decoloniality? Palestinian Fellahin Resistance and the Space-Place Relation." *Studies in Social Justice* 12 (1): 21–37.

Azoulay, Ariella, and Adi Ophir. 2009. "The Order of Violence." In *The Power of Inclusive Exclusion*, edited by Adi Ophir, Michal Givoni, and Sari Hanafi, 99–140. New York: Zone Books.

Bachmann, Jan, Colleen Bell, and Caroline Holmqvist. 2016. *War, Police and Assemblages of Intervention*. London: Routledge.

Berda, Yael. 2017. *Living Emergency: Israel's Permit Regime in the Occupied West Bank*. Palo Alto CA: Stanford University Press.

Bhungalia, Lisa. 2018. "Governing Banishment: Settler Colonialism, Territory, and Life in an Economy of Death." In *Handbook on the Geographies of Power*, edited by Mat Coleman and John Agnew, 313–31. Cheltenham-Northampton: Edward Elgar Publishing.

Bigo, Didier. 2008. "Globalized (In)security: The Field and the Ban-Opticon." In *Terror Insecurity and Liberty: Illiberal Practices of Liberal Regimes after 9/11*, edited by Didier Bigo and Anastassia Tsoukala, 10–48. London: Routledge.

Bratich, Jack. 2006. "Public Secrecy and Immanent Security." *Cultural Studies* 20 (4–5): 493–511.

Breaking the Silence. 2012. *Our Harsh Logic: Israeli Soldiers' Testimonies from the Occupied Territories, 2000–2010*. New York: Henry Holt.

——. 2017. "The High Command: Settler Influence on IDF Conduct in the West Bank." https://www.breakingthesilence.org.il/inside/wp-content/uploads/2017/01/The-High -Command-Shovrim-Shtika-Report-January-2017.pdf.

Buchanan, Ian. 2006. "Treatise on Militarism." In *Deleuze and the Contemporary World*, edited by Ian Buchanan and Adrian Parr, 21–41. Edinburgh: Edinburgh University Press.

Deleuze, Gilles. 1978. "The Troublemakers." *Discourse* 20 (3): 23–24.

Deleuze, Gilles, and Félix Guattari. 1987. *A Thousand Plateaus: Capitalism and Schizophrenia*. Translated by Brian Massumi. Minneapolis: University of Minnesota Press.

——. 2010. *Nomadology: The War Machine*. Seattle WA: Wormwood Distribution.

Duffield, Mark. 2007. *Development, Security and Unending War: Governing the World of Peoples*. Malden MA: Polity.

Gazit, Nir. 2015. "State-Sponsored Vigilantism: Jewish Settlers' Violence in the Occupied Palestinian Territories." *Sociology* 49 (3): 438–54.

Ghantous, Wassim. 2020. "Settler-Colonial Assemblages and the Making of the Israeli Frontier: Palestinian Experiences of (In)security, Surveillance and Carceral Geographies." PhD diss., University of Gothenburg.

Gregory, Derek. 2011. "The Everywhere War." *Geographical Journal* 177 (3): 238–50.

Griffiths, Mark. 2017. "Hope in Hebron: The Political Affects of Activism in a Strangled City." *Antipode* 49 (3): 617–35.

Griffiths, Mark, and Mikko Joronen. 2021. "Governmentalizing Palestinian Futures: Uncertainty, Anticipation, Possibility." *Geografiska Annaler: Series B, Human Geography* 103:1–15.

Halper, Jeff. 2015. *War against the People: Israel, the Palestinians and Global Pacification*. London: Pluto Press.

Hammami, Rema. 2015. "On (Not) Suffering at the Checkpoint: Palestinian Narrative Strategies of Surviving Israel's Carceral Geography." *Borderlands* 14 (1): 1–17.

Hareuveni, Eyal. 2014. "The Lawless Zone: The Transfer of Policing and Security Powers to the Civilian Security Coordinators in the Settlements and Outposts." Yesh Din, September 17. https://www.yesh-din.org/en/the-lawless-zone-the-transfer-of-policing -and-security-to-the-civilian-security-coordinators-in-the-settlements-and-outposts/.

Humanitarian Policy and Conflict Research. 2008. "Private Security Companies in the Occupied Palestinian Territory (OPT): An International Humanitarian Law Perspective." Harvard Humanitarian Initiative Policy Brief, March. Cambridge MA: Harvard University.

Huss, Michal. 2019. "Mapping the Occupation: Performativity and the Precarious Israeli Identity." *Geopolitics* 24 (3): 756–70.

Jabary-Salamanca, Omar J., Mezna Qato, Kareem Rabie, and Sobhi Samour. 2012. "Past Is Present: Settler Colonialism in Palestine." *Settler Colonial Studies* 2 (1): 1–8.

Joronen, Mikko. 2021. "Unspectacular Spaces of Slow Wounding in Palestine." *Transactions of the Institute of British Geographers* (July). https://doi.org/10.111/tran.12473.

Joronen, Mikko, and Mark Griffiths. 2019. "The Affective Politics of Precarity: Home Demolitions in Occupied Palestine." *Environment and Planning D: Society and Space* 37 (3): 561–76.

Kanoich, Yonatan. 2018. "Yitzhar—a Case Study: Settler Violence as a Vehicle for Taking over Palestinian Land with State and Military Backing." Yesh Din, August. https://s3-eu-west-1.amazonaws.com/files.yesh-din.org/2018+yitzhar+case+study/YeshDin+-+Yitzhar+-+Eng.pdf.

Kimmerling, Baruch. 2005. *The Invention and Decline of Israeliness.* Berkeley: University of California Press.

Kubovich, Yaniv. 2020. "Israeli Soldiers Committed Hate Crime against Palestinians to Avenge Friends' Death. Their Commanders Covered It Up." *Haaretz*, March 6. https://www.haaretz.com/israel-news/.premium-israeli-soldiers-committed-hate-crime-against-palestinians-then-it-was-covered-up-1.8889788.

Levy, Yagil. 2021. "The Israeli Policing Army—the Gray Arm of Annexation." *British Journal of Middle Eastern Studies* (September): 1–21.

Machold, Rhys. 2018. "Reconsidering the Laboratory Thesis: Palestine/Israel and the Geopolitics of Representation." *Political Geography* 65 (July): 88–97.

Makdisi, Saree. 2008. *Palestine Inside Out: An Everyday Occupation.* New York: W. W. Norton.

Maoz, Eilat. 2020. *Living Law: Police and Sovereignty in an Occupation Regime.* Tel Aviv: Van Leer Institute Press and Hakibbutz Hameuchad Publishing House.

Massumi, Brian, ed. 1993. *The Politics of Everyday Fear.* Minneapolis: University of Minnesota Press.

——. 2010. "Perception Attack: Brief on War Time." *Theory & Event* 13 (3).

——. 2015a. *Ontopower: War, Powers, and the State of Perception.* Durham NC: Duke University Press.

——. 2015b. *Politics of Affect.* Malden MA: Polity.

May, Todd. 2007. "Deleuze and the Tale of Two Intifadas." In *Deleuzian Encounters: Studies in Contemporary Social Issues,* edited by Anna Hickey-Moody and Peta Malins, 212–20. New York: Palgrave Macmillan.

Mbembe, Achille. 2003. "Necropolitics." *Public Culture* 15 (1): 11–40.

Meari, Lena. 2014. "Sumud: A Palestinian Philosophy of Confrontation in Colonial Prisons." *South Atlantic Quarterly* 113 (3): 547–78.

Medien, Kathryn. 2019. "Palestine in Deleuze." *Theory, Culture & Society* 36 (5): 49–70.

Muhareb, Mahmoud. 2012. *Policy Analysis: The Price Tag Organization and the Price Tag Paid by Palestinians.* Doha: Arab Center for Research & Policy Studies.

Murakami Wood, David. 2017. "The Global Turn to Authoritarianism and After." *Surveillance and Society* 15 (3/4): 357–70.

Ophir, Adi, Michal Givoni, and Sari Hanafi, eds. 2009. *The Power of Inclusive Exclusion: Anatomy of Israeli Rule in the Occupied Palestinian Territories.* New York: Zone Books.

Pappé, Ilan. 2014. *The Idea of Israel: A History of Power and Knowledge.* London: Verso.

Perugini, Nicola, and Neve Gordon. 2015. *The Human Right to Dominate.* Oxford: Oxford University Press.

Peteet, Julie Marie. 2017. *Space and Mobility in Palestine.* Public Cultures of the Middle East and North Africa. Bloomington: Indiana University Press.

Plasse-Couture, François-Xavier. 2013. "Effective Abandonment: The Neoliberal Economy of Violence in Israel and the Occupied Territories." *Security Dialogue* 44 (5–6): 449–66.

Puar, Jasbir K. 2017. *The Right to Maim: Debility, Capacity, Disability.* Durham NC: Duke University Press.

Ryan, Caitlin. 2015. "Everyday Resilience as Resistance: Palestinian Women Practicing Sumud." *International Political Sociology* 9 (4): 299–315.

Said, Edward W. 1994. *The Politics of Dispossession: The Struggle for Palestinian Self-Determination, 1969–1994.* New York: Pantheon Books.

Sayegh, Fayez. 2012. "Zionist Colonialism in Palestine (1965)." *Settler Colonial Studies* 2 (1): 206–25.

Shalhoub-Kevorkian, Nadera. 2015. *Security Theology, Surveillance and the Politics of Fear.* Cambridge: Cambridge University Press.

Shezaf, Hagar. 2020. "Israeli Soldiers Filmed Slashing Tires, Throwing Tear Gas at Palestinian Home." *Haaretz*, May 31. https://www.haaretz.com/israel-news/.premium-israeli -soldiers-filmed-slashing-tires-throwing-tear-gas-at-palestinian-home-1.8885510.

Svirsky, Marcelo. 2015. "BDS as a Mediator." *Concentric: Literary and Cultural Studies* 41 (2): 45–74.

———. 2017. "Resistance Is a Structure Not an Event." *Settler Colonial Studies* 7 (1): 19–39.

Weizman, Eyal. 2006. "Walking through Walls: Soldiers as Architects in the Israeli-Palestinian Conflict." *Radical Philosophy* 136 (March/April).

———. 2007. *Hollow Land: Israel's Architecture of Occupation.* London: Verso.

Wolfe, Patrick. 2006. "Settler Colonialism and the Elimination of the Native." *Journal of Genocide Research* 8 (4): 387–409.

Zureik, Elia. 2016. "Strategies of Surveillance: The Israeli Gaze." *Institute for Palestine Studies* 6:12.

4 The Regavim Show

Settler Colonialism, Simulacra, and Mirroring

Mark Griffiths

Regavim is an Israeli nongovernmental organization (NGO) that was established in 2006 to fight the "quiet occupation" of land by Palestinians in the West Bank and East Jerusalem. In its skewed rhetoric, it is the "*Arab settlements* in Judea and Samaria" that occupy and colonize land, slowly "destroying" and "expelling," and it is the *settlers* whose human rights are threatened in Palestine: "The Jewish People is [*sic*] being robbed of the Land of Israel."[1] There is substance beyond the rhetoric: Regavim's appeal has attracted significant donations that fund legal challenges to Palestinian building and dwelling in the West Bank and Israel, and its effectiveness has won it close relations with municipal councils, including contractual and consultancy work (Berger 2018; Peace Now 2016). Mobilizing these resources, Regavim, for example, has petitioned for the demolition of Palestinian schools in Beit Sira and Khan Al-Ahmar (Dudai 2017) and houses in "unrecognized" villages in the southern West Bank (e.g., in Khirbet Susya; see Ghantous 2019). It is also continuously developing its capacities of surveillance, using drones, aerial photography, and geographic information system (GIS) technology, to map and monitor Palestinians' construction activities and passing that information to the Israeli Civil Administration (Joronen and Griffiths 2019).[2] According to Regavim's published accounts, its funding for 2018–19 was ILS9,968,952 (approximately $2,870,000), and it has twenty-eight employees plus eight salaried board members on its payroll. Between 2006 and 2016, it spearheaded a right-wing movement that brought sixty-three cases to the Israeli courts, and it brought a further thirty-eight between 2018 and 2019, each arguing for the cessation of Palestinians' construction activities or the demolition of Palestinians' homes and communal structures (Regavim 2018a, 2018b, 2019).

A major part of Regavim's success is owed to something of a contiguous relationship to the Israeli state. Regavim is present among law and policy makers, for instance, providing "expertise" to the government on the legal status of Israeli settlements (Perugini and Gordon 2015, 125) and receiving substantial funding from central and local governments.[3] Regavim simultaneously acts as a critic of the state—specifically, of its judiciary and Supreme Court—for a perceived bias against Israeli settlers in the West Bank (Dudai 2017) and seeks to speed up the legal processes connected to Palestinian removal (Ghantous and Joronen 2022). Its press releases on "achievements" are replete with exposés—for example, "Israel pays millions to Bedouin in massive protection racket"—and claims to hold state agencies to account for their inattentiveness to "illegal" Palestinian building activities. As a principal strategy toward these "achievements," Regavim adopts the language of human rights discourse to argue for justice—or, to reference one of its campaigns, against "the perversion of justice" (Regavim 2010)—in the context of settler oppression at the hands of the Israeli courts and Palestinians. This inversion has drawn scholarly critique around the notions of "mimicry" (Dudai 2017) and "mirroring" (Perugini and Gordon 2015; Perugini and Rabie 2012; Rabie 2021) that is defined by a deployment—via appropriation and repurposing—of established human rights approaches to advance colonialism in Palestine. Regavim has thus emerged as an effective colonial actor that maneuvers between being an accomplice *and* an adversary of the state, and instrumentalizes a human rights discourse of justice precisely to deny the rights of the less powerful.

In this chapter, I critically examine the ways that power functions in Regavim's English-language public-facing discourse (e.g., annual reports, website, and social media) and its operations on the ground, specifically in the South Hebron Hills area of the West Bank. Drawing on both publicity materials and fieldwork, I make three discrete critical contributions to understanding power relations in this space. First, I argue that state–

GRIFFITHS

non-state relations are secondary to the perception of a broader field of power that is precedent to the state. From this perspective, the relationship between the state of Israel and Regavim is less an "adversarial collaboration" (Dudai 2017, 881) or one of "osmosis" (Perugini and Rabie 2012, 47) than what Michel Foucault (2015, 230) might have termed a "general disciplinary system," analysis of which draws a crucial focus: it does not matter who effects the demolition of a home but rather that it is demolished; it does not matter who monitors but rather that there is surveillance; and the matter of *who* eliminates is tangential to the issue of elimination itself and the force behind it. In this way, the contradiction presented by Regavim's role of accomplice and adversary is undone: both positions are pragmatic for the advancement of Israel's settler colonial project. In analyzing further the field of power in which Regavim operates, next I consider the crucial issue of its portrayal of Palestinians as "settlers" embarking on a "silent conquest." I contend that this representational practice can be productively understood as a postmodern hyperreality in which the proliferation of images and texts effects a "liquidation of all referentials" (Baudrillard 1994, 2). Third, and finally, the discussion moves to cases where Palestinians adapt settler tactics for their own ends, thus complicating the notion of mirroring as it is currently understood in this context. Accordingly, I reread mirroring as less a two-way closed system than as a continuing effect in which Palestinian actors "reflect" different strategies for the purposes of anticolonial struggle.

The discussion is formed of two main sections. The first presents an account of Regavim's activities with a specific focus on the South Hebron Hills and Um-Al-Khair, a village where I have conducted fieldwork and whose prominent activists have kindly shared information with me for this research. The intention is to give a detailed context for Regavim's actions over recent years and to incorporate Palestinians' accounts and actions. The second section explicates three conceptualizations of the ways that power functions in the encounter with Regavim: as a preceding force of which powerful actors are a product, as a postmodern proliferation of signs without referent, and as a mutable form that is continually reflected and repurposed. A concluding section outlines the wider significance of these conceptualizations for the study of colonial power in the context of Palestine and beyond.

Regavim in the South Hebron Hills and Um-Al-Khair

The South Hebron Hills is part of the Hebron Governorate at the southern tip of the West Bank. The area is formed by the city of Yatta (population of about sixty-five thousand) and its peripheries, known as Masafer Yatta, which is part of Area C under the Oslo Accords and is thus under Israeli military and administrative control. More than four thousand Palestinians—most of them Bedouins—live in about thirty villages in the area, a complex political geography comprising rezoning, segregated infrastructure, and settlement development. Infrastructural connections are denied to the majority of the villages in the South Hebron Hills owing to a refusal by the Israeli Civil Administration (ICA) to recognize them as "social and geographical entities," a situation that is exacerbated by military roadblocks and repeated confiscations of communal facilities such as solar panels and wells.[4] Further complicating the political geography is the presence of more than twenty Israeli settlements in the area—for example, Carmel (population of about 437), Susiya (1,339), and Maʾon (595)—that each have master plans to expand under the administration of the Har Hevron Regional Council, a municipality of Israel formed almost entirely within the West Bank. There are, in addition, a number of settlement outposts (e.g., Mitzpe Yair, Havat Maʾon, Avigail) whose longevity indicates the region's associations with extremist settlers—or "the colony's shock troops," as Rema Hammami (2016, 171) has termed them—whose violence is largely unchecked by the Israeli authorities (Shenhav-Goldberg 2019).[5] According to the United Nations Office for the Coordination of Humanitarian Affairs, since 2008 Palestinians in the South Hebron Hills have sustained 222 serious injuries due to "settler-related incidents," though underreporting means the actual figure is significantly higher.[6] In the same period, at least thirteen Palestinians have died as a result of settler violence. Palestinians in the South Hebron Hills are thus faced with a constant and pronounced threat of dispossession and removal that issues not solely from state apparatuses but also from the activities of settlers.

It is in this context that Regavim operates in the South Hebron Hills, though its meting out of violence proceeds in a markedly different register. Regavim presents a more measured facade as an "independent professional research institute & policy planning think tank," per its website, regavim.org, and claims its staff does not use physical violence. "Regavim is different, they're so kind when they talk to you, not like *normal* settlers, they speak in a gentle and smart way—then you realise you're in a video on their website," as one resident of Um-Al-Khair put it (fieldwork interview, 2019). Settler violence takes on a different register in this respect: it is enacted via a range of advocacy and legal activities that precipitates the denied right of shelter and services to Palestinians. These activities forward a position that the Israeli settlers are threatened by a "land seizure" where Palestinians lead a "'construction race' aimed at creating *facts on the ground* in areas slated for Israeli sovereignty" (Regavim 2020, emphasis added). The attention to "facts on the ground" in this chapter centers on Um-Al-Khair (population of about 150), a Bedouin village approximately twenty-five kilometers to the east of Yatta that is surrounded on two sides by the expanding settlement of Carmel. Since 2011 the Israeli military has demolished twenty-five of Um-Al-Khair's residential structures, and all but two of the village's remaining structures have been served with a demolition order, a prospect that greatly affects the lives of its residents (Joronen and Griffiths 2019). As in most villages in the area, the community keeps meticulous records of events and legal dealings with the close-by settlement and Israeli authorities. The details of Regavim's activities in Um-Al-Khair are drawn from these records as well as four years' research and collaboration with activists in the village and its surroundings.

The first known involvement of Regavim in Um-Al-Khair came in October 2014 when the village's *taboon*—an outdoor clay oven—was demolished for a third time. The oven provided bread for the community and was thus both a vital facility for sustenance and a space of particular social and economic value. As one resident made clear at the time: "This oven

[was] 50 years old. . . . My grandmother used it to bake bread, so did my mother. . . . This is the source of our livelihood. We don't have electricity. This is the only way for us to make bread" (Al Jazeera 2016). While on previous occasions the oven was rebuilt, this time the settlement of Carmel sought an order from the Peace Court in Jerusalem citing health problems arising from the smoke emitted from the oven's coals and demanding a compensatory payment of ILS20,000 ($6,000) from residents of Um-Al-Khair. One resident recounted, "It was a joint case with Regavim and the Settlement Council against us—we weren't sure they were *leading* the case—but they were part of the [legal action] for the first time [in Um-Al-Khair]" (fieldwork interview, 2019). For the community, this new actor was perceived chiefly as "just one more" part of the settler movement's work with state authorities to ease the expansion of Carmel, whose 318-dunam spread southward was approved by the ICA in June 2013 (Applied Research Institute–Jerusalem 2016). The court ruled that compensation was not payable but that the oven should be demolished; the order was executed in November 2014. In the years since, bread has been purchased in Yatta, and the oven remains a ruin in the center of the lower part of the village.

As Regavim's prominence in the region grew—especially in the nearby village of Khirbet Susya (B'tselem 2015)—people in Um-Al-Khair began to document surveillance practices such as photographing and videoing that were notable for being carried out by neither local settlers nor ICA officials. A spokesperson of Um-Al-Khair recalled, "Once I was in the valley [below the village] and this guy was taking photos of water wells and our grazing lands, when he saw me he asked, 'How was your trip recently?'" The photographer was from Regavim and apparently had acquired knowledge of the village and its community via social media. "He knew about my travelling and family and was completely calm while on our land; he took more photos and went away." After sporadic such encounters, people then noticed a car that regularly parked between buildings in Carmel from which a drone would emerge and hover over Um-Al-Khair. "It started to come every few weeks . . . [and] we understood quite quickly that they were taking photos to see if we build or repair structures" (fieldwork interview,

2019). Regavim's Drones Unit was established in the mid-2010s to make surveillance a remote practice. According to Yishai Chamu, head of the Drones Unit, "Instead of having to enter villages . . . with all the entailed dangers, we can now stand outside in some hidden spot, send up the drone, and receive a high-quality photo from the air" (*Israel National News* 2016a). The drones mark a confluence of state and civil knowledge where private citizens draw on their military know-how as "field workers" to compile case files of "violations" and present them to the courts (see, e.g., Baker 2016). "From this point," the Um-Al-Khair spokesperson explained (fieldwork interview, 2019), "everything changed, they could see *everything.*"

The new technological capacities of Regavim enabled a more direct impact on Um-Al-Khair. As part of the European Union (EU)–funded assistance and development programs for Palestinians (see EEAS 2019), six heavy tarpaulin structures were erected in 2012 that Um-Al-Khair residents used as a crèche, meeting space, and community center. As with the taboon, they were important for communal and social activities. After regular drone visits in early 2016, four Regavim representatives arrived in person in July to photograph the structures, claiming that "the EU cannot invest in this village, it's illegal to build here." Once again, the photographers did not pose an immediate violent threat but were officiously conducting an overt practice of surveillance, repeating the phrases "you cannot build on this land, these structures are illegal." The procedure in such circumstances is to inform the police, the Israeli authority that is charged with protecting *all* Area C residents. On doing so, as the event was retold, the response came: "We gave the [car's] plate number and the police replied, 'Ah, don't worry we know that car, it's a safe car, let them be.' . . . [Obviously] Regavim had some kind of special permission [from the ICA/police] to be here." In the days afterward, toward the end of July 2016, the same car was seen again, this time "hidden between settlement houses [in Carmel]" from where more drone photography was captured. The next car to appear came in early August, "a white Toyota SUV with ICA staff who began to film *officially*"—the word "officially" was emphasized to convey an idea that Regavim's footage was something of a first draft—and two days later on August 7, 2016, the Israeli minister of justice Ayelet Shaked stopped in Carmel during a tour of the South Hebron Hills "to meet with the Council of the Settlements and Regavim."[7] "The very next day . . . in the early morning the bulldozers arrived and they demolished these four caravans [tarpaulins] donated by the EU . . . it was a *political demolition organised by Regavim* because they say that we stole from the state and that *we are the thieves, the settlers*."[8]

The second direct targeting of Um-Al-Khair by Regavim came in March 2018, when it filed a petition to the Supreme Court for the evacuation of the village, along with that of two others—Khashm Al-Daraj and Arab Al-Najadeh. In the area, "they attached petitions to the school and mosque . . . they put them all around and they took photos for social media" (fieldwork interview, 2019). The petition amounted to twenty-five pages detailing sixty articles against Palestinian residents based on an argument that "the area where the three neighbourhoods are located is state land . . . which is under Israeli administration and security control" (*Middle East Monitor* 2018). In a formal sense, the case was unsuccessful: "They sent a copy to the Supreme Court and in the end they rejected the claim . . . it was a big failure but they just started to attack the judges, the court and even the government of Israel" (fieldwork interview, 2019). Unsurprisingly, the very circulation of the petition contributed to the already-documented levels of "fears and anxieties about the future loss of home" in Um-Al-Khair (Joronen and Griffiths 2019, 571). In other ways, therefore, Regavim's case achieved the objectives of psychologically targeting Palestinians and positioning itself as a pioneer of (settler) human rights. Toward this latter objective, as one Um-Al-Khair resident keenly noted, the court's rejection was inconsequential: "You know why they do this? They want to have a show, they want more videos, they want to get more support from these churches in the US and in the Western countries to show off how Regavim is working, doing reports and so on, *it's for a show*" (fieldwork interview, 2019).

Regavim remains active in the South Hebron Hills and across Palestine/ Israel, providing surveillance capacities, legal know-how, and policy influence. The effect is that, in the words of Um-Al-Khair activist and author

Awdah Hathaleen, "before Regavim, may[be] our homes would be demol-ished every couple of years. Now our homes are demolished once a year. Because of all the petitions, they file . . . people are now only living their life in the courtrooms rather than with their children. We spend [more] time talking with lawyers than we do our family members" (quoted in Anderson 2019). From this perspective, Regavim is a distinct element of the settler project that effects violence at the colonial frontiers by accelerating state procedures of dispossession and removal via the courtroom. At the same time, Regavim is often indistinguishable from an array of actors—the police, IDF, government ministers, settlers, Aliyah groups, pro-Israel "adventure" tourists, and so forth—that constitute Um-Al-Khair's colonial encounter. As is commonly articulated in the village, Regavim is "just one more part of the occupation . . . it's an occupation that wants us to disappear, Regavim is just a new part of that" (fieldwork interview, 2019).

Conceptualizing Power:
State-Civil Society, Hyperreality, Resistance

As documented so far, Regavim's work on the ground in Um-Al-Khair pro-gressed through close relations with state authorities toward the ruination of important communal facilities and an elevation in the general level of threat in the village. In this section, I discuss further Regavim's activities to explore the function of power (1) as a broader and preceding field of which actors such as the state and Regavim are both symptomatic and constitutive, (2) as a postmodern proliferation of signs without referent, and (3) as a contestable form that is continually reflected and repurposed.

While there is little doubt that Regavim has become a more prominent part of Um-Al-Khair's encounter with Israeli occupation, the views of its residents oscillate: on the one hand, Regavim is an autonomous exertion of newly acquired powers that intensify the processes of colonialism; on the other, the organization is "just another" formation among an always dynamic but consistent assemblage of colonial forces. At the heart of the question of power in this respect is the position of Regavim vis-à-vis the Israeli state, especially in regard to its seemingly contradictory ability to act as both the state's adversary and its accomplice. At first take, the issue is compelling for the multiple exchanges in terms of military expertise and of cooperation in the Knesset and with regional representatives of the ICA and police. In Um-Al-Khair, this exchange was most productive in the case of the EU-funded tarpaulin structures, whose destruction was described as "a political demolition organised by Regavim." Indeed, the specific case of the destroyed tarpaulins reveals something of the power relations within Regavim's capacity to effect demolition in this way: Regavim triggered a series of events that culminated in a visit by the minister of justice to Carmel settlement and the demolition that quickly followed. The meeting in Carmel in fact included a press conference in which Minister Shaked reported, "We were shown the illegal building Palestinians are doing in Area C, including those built with foreign funds" and undertook to "deal with this" (*Israel National News* 2016b). The following day's demolitions, in part, fulfilled this promise and were claimed by Regavim (2016) as a significant victory: "Together with the Har Hebron Regional Council we influenced the Civil Administration . . . we welcome the determination of the Civil Administration for implementing a clear injunction of law and order . . . and taking down illegal construction."

This influence runs deep in the ways that members and activists hold public office and work to further Regavim's objectives "from the inside." For instance, a co-founder of Regavim, Bezalel Smotrich, was elected to the Knesset in 2015 as a member of the Yamina alliance and (as of early 2022) serves as the minister of finance. In the same year, the Ministry of Justice ordered that all high court positions regarding outposts and settlements be brought before Amir Fisher, a lawyer who is closely associated with Regavim and has acted as an "external consultant to the Ministry's directorate on 'settlement' affairs" (Hovel 2017). Regavim wields its influence also by taking various "expert" roles in government—for instance, advising the Knesset Foreign Affairs and Defense Committee; providing expertise for the Levy Commission, which compiled a report on the legality of Israeli settlements for Benjamin Netanyahu's administration (Perugini and Gordon 2015, 125); assuming an amicus curiae position in the Supreme

Court that allows access to confidential legal information (Ghantous 2019, 209); and hosting tours for Knesset members in the South Hebron Hills (Regavim 2021). Simultaneously, Regavim prides itself on holding the government to account in the instances where settler colonial processes are stymied. The organization's website is replete with tabloid-style reporting: "Israel Pays Millions to Bedouin in Massive Protection Racket" and "It's a Fact: Israel's Supreme Court Discriminates against Right-Wing Petitions" (Regavim 2019b; the second report is no longer available at the Regavim site). Furthermore, the website has also framed "what we are up against" as something of a raison d'être for the organization, citing "the hesitant Israeli leadership and the bound hands of the enforcement authorities" as a call to action (Hicks 2020).

In short, Regavim has positioned itself as a key producer of state information on Palestinians in the West Bank ("Arabs in Judea and Samaria") and as an enforcer of Zionist land policies where they are not implemented with sufficient force by the state. The boundaries between state and non-state actors in this dynamic are not merely *blurred* but *dissolved* as each is oriented to common ends (e.g., elimination) via shared means (e.g., surveillance and demolition). On the attendant relationship between civil society and the state, Nicola Perugini and Kareem Rabie (2012, 47–48) draw on the metaphor of osmosis in observing that Regavim and the ICA are "symbiotically and reciprocally related in their ideologies and political agendas," while elsewhere, writing with Neve Gordon, Perugini (2015, 114) has directly addressed the presence of Regavim activists in government as "an overlapping of actors . . . based on shared political objectives" — namely, "the preservation of the state's settler nature." Furthermore, Ron Dudai's (2017, 867) survey of right-wing organizations in Israel identifies Regavim as part of a wider trend of using "human rights as a disguise for pro-state propaganda." Common to each of these critical examinations is a commitment to understanding the ways that power passes between the state and civil society in the form of collusion and contestation between two (or more) actors who *hold*, *exert*, and *exchange* power.[9] This is useful insofar as identifying actors' roles in progressing Israel's settler colonial project, but there is a crucial assumption that those actors preexist the power relations and that the back-and-forth between the state and civil society is a struggle between two autonomous (if aligned) bearers of power. The question thus remains of an earlier entry point into analysis where power is conceived of as a preceding force, of which different actors—the state included—are merely symptomatic.

From this perspective, there is something deeper in the roots of the frequently expressed conviction in Um-Al-Khair that "they're all the same, ICA, Regavim, IDF, the police—they just want our land" (fieldwork interview, 2019). In this formulation, the state and Regavim are undifferentiated expressions of colonialism; thus, the question of power is not analogous to an understanding of state–non-state relations but is instead re-angled toward a preceding and transcending field of power in which a range of actors operate. For Foucault (2007, 119), attending to this primary scene is crucial: "If we want to avoid the circularity that refers the analysis of relations of power from one institution to another, it is by grasping them at the point where they constitute techniques with operative value in multiple processes." A first step toward locating this point, it follows, might (re)figure the state and other actors as "terminal forms" of the "multiplicity of force relations" (Foucault 1978, 92) that are oriented to—and constitutive of— techniques with operative value in the processes of, in this specific case, settler colonialism: the dispossession ("they want our land") and elimination ("they want us to disappear") of the native (Wolfe 2006). A response to the question of power relations *between* actors might therefore position toward Foucault's (2015, 230–31) reflection on the example of the state and family: "Really, it matters little whether the family reproduces the State or the other way round. The family and the State function in relation to each other, by relying on each other, possibly confronting each other, in a system of power that . . . may be characterised as disciplinary in a homogeneous way, that is to say [where] the disciplinary system is the general form in which power is inserted, whether located in a State apparatus or diffused in a general system." Opened out this way, the function of power in Regavim's operations on the ground is indicative and derivative of a more general "disciplinary system" that transcends it and its accomplices and adversaries. In other words, at the level of encounter, the mechanics of relations between actors are quite insignificant: it matters not *who* monitors or *who* effects demolition but that surveillance and demolitions occurs; and the question of *who* eliminates and collaborates is peripheral to the issue of elimination itself and the force behind it. In this sense, the state (ICA, police, IDF, etc.) and non-state actors (e.g., Regavim) emerge as a homogeneous amalgam that constitutes, without remainder, the settler colonialism encountered by Palestinians in the South Hebron Hills and beyond.

A second prevalent function of power issues from Regavim's representational practices in which Palestinians are "settlers," the occupation is Palestinian, and the oppressed are "Israeli residents of Judea and Samaria." This worldview is circulated in different registers to diverse audiences across various channels—from the pithy styles of Twitter and Facebook to longer-form blog posts, newspaper op-eds, and annual reports—whose reach is extensive. Regavim's 2019 annual report boasts of engaging more than ten million people via these platforms with "46,000 active followers who react, comment and share hundreds of our posts . . . [and] over 1,150,000 views on our Facebook pages and hundreds of thousands more on other media outlets" (Regavim 2019a). It makes further claims of its reach:

> In 2019, Regavim made its first trip to the European Parliament in Brussels. . . . We met with 16 MEPs [members of the European Parliament] in their parliamentary offices, including members of the Finance Committee, the Israel Delegation, the Budget Oversight Committee . . . and presented what proved to be eye-opening facts about the EU's financial and non-financial support for illegal activity in Judea and Samaria, the EU's one-sided support for the unilateral establishment of a Palestinian state in the heart of Israel . . . we have already begun to see positive results: Formal information requests demanding transparency and analysis of expenditures and their outcomes have been submitted to the European Council by MEPs who met with us—an important development which we hope is the first step toward our goal. (Regavim 2019a)

Regavim's message thus flows from the most superficial channels of social media to sustained dialogue with powerful policy makers. The significance of its representational practices is thus realized: the extensively disseminated trope of Arab "silent conquest" functions as an economy of signs whose reach and every act of self-perpetuation (via reposts and shares) incrementally weaken the relation between sign and referent—or the "liquidation of all referentials," as Jean Baudrillard put it (1994, 2)—to constitute a realm of "hyperreality."

Baudrillard's diagnosis of the postmodern hyperreal offers an instructive frame toward understanding the power of Regavim's rhetoric for the explication that the function of signs is drawn less from a role of placeholder for an external reality than through a self-referential and self-perpetuating exchange of images that becomes constitutive of all that is intelligible. In the terms set out by Baudrillard, Regavim's (re-)casting of Palestinians as "settlers" in exactly the image of Israeli settlers—for example, "innocent-looking civilians" as a proxy for military soldiers (Regavim n.d.b)—gains purchase in an information-loaded network of social media posts, online reports, and donor appeals that propagate and reenforce a narrative of "Arab settler conquest." The reproduction of this image via the circulatory reposting mechanisms of internet media becomes for Regavim's supporters and donors a simulated reality—a simulacrum, or "a real without origin or reality" (Baudrillard 1994, 1)—that subsumes or "precedes" all other matrices of intelligibility.

The value of attending to simulacra affords valuable interpretive insights into the operations of Regavim. Moving the analytical perspective to the level of signs enables an account of how Regavim animates a virtual world that mobilizes a familiar Orientalist vision of "terroristic Arabs" violently seizing Judeo-Christian land (e.g., Allen 2019, 154–58) that, for Regavim and its supporters, is so persistent and so endlessly reinforced that it becomes the *sole* system of reference that precedes without trace, a simulacrum in which "not only has the world disappeared but the very question of its existence can no longer be posed" (Baudrillard 1996, 5). It follows that not only can inversions (e.g., Palestinian = settler) *not* be doubted but also *there can be no indication that there was ever anything to invert*: the crucial strategy of establishing "facts on the ground"—despite its long association with Zionism (see El-Haj 2001)—is now a main *Palestinian* tactic and always was. First, then, bringing the question of power and Regavim into contact with writing on postmodern cleavages between sign and signified enables some comprehension of not so much the absence of "truth" in representation (i.e., lies and manipulation) but rather the effective replacement of "reality" by the virtual to form a hyperreality that not only replicates but, for a significant number of powerful advocates, policy makers, and donors, also *replaces and remakes* conditions on the ground.

Substance to this claim is added by attending to the hyperreal, where the *remaking* of conditions relates to a political dimension of simulacra— specifically the notion that, Baudrillard (1994, 2) writes, representation "no longer needs to be rational, because it no longer measures itself against either an ideal or negative instance. It is no longer anything but *operational*" (emphasis added). The question of the *operationality* of the hyperreal is a pertinent one in the case of Regavim precisely because its financial resources (and thus its on-the-ground capacities) are boosted by overseas donors whose image of "the cause" in places such as the South Hebron Hills is formed entirely from Regavim's representational practices and that of consonant other pro-Israel sources. Baudrillard (1994, 23) further writes that "power itself has for a long time produced nothing but the signs of its resemblance . . . [and] at the same time, another figure of power comes into play: that of the collective demand for *signs* of power—a holy union that is reconstructed around its disappearance" (original emphasis). Such a union can be envisaged here of Regavim and its physically remote donors entering an exchange where funds are pledged to produce more material that re-presents its mission against the "silent conquest" of "Arab settlers." The operationality of Regavim's hyperreal is perceptible here: images proliferate to generate capital that materializes on the ground not only in the violence of petitions and demolitions but also in the production of more visual materials for circulation. At this point the earlier interview extract bears repeating: "You know why they do this? . . . They want more videos,

... more support from [donors] ... to show off how Regavim is working ... *it's for a show*." In this sense, artifice is positioned less as a means than an end of Regavim's activities; the success of this or that petition is secondary to the message it platforms and the support it generates. With every report and petition, and every claim of its "successes," the "Regavim *show*" becomes a simulation of power "disconnected from its ends and its objectives, and dedicated to the *effects of power* and mass simulation" (Baudrillard 1994, 22, original emphasis).

A third consideration of power has to do with the notion of mirroring, a metaphor used to conceptualize the ways that right-wing organizations such as Regavim deploy techniques that are long established in the field of human rights. In many ways, the very existence of Regavim emerges from a reflection: its monitoring activities replicate, from a diametrically opposed position, the Peace Now initiative of "Settlement Watch," whose objective is to "track and analyze developments in the settlements. Through research, analysis, and exposure of settlement developments, Peace Now works to prevent settlement expansion and stop illegal settlement activity" (Peace Now n.d.). Regavim's (n.d.a) objectives, as we have seen, are precisely the same: "Gathering data ... conducting field surveys ... producing and publishing public reports [on] building violations and the illegal takeover of state lands." Brought to light here are not only the reversals that form the bases of simulacra but also the adoption of techniques that are long established in the field of human rights organizations. One well-documented and illustrative example is the use of "copy-and-paste" petitions that take the petitions of human rights lawyers against Israeli settlement activities and straightforwardly substitute the place names for Palestinian dwellings (Perugini and Gordon 2015, 114; Rabie 2021, 258). Writing around the theme of "a regime of mirrorness," Perugini and Rabie (2012, 49) explicate this litigation strategy practiced by Regavim: "What the pro-Palestinian NGOs call Israeli or Jewish settlements become *Palestinian* settlements; what is 'illegal Jewish construction' becomes 'illegal *Palestinian* construction' ... [and so forth]" (emphasis added). The overwriting of petitions in this way repurposes the tools of the *colonized* for the ends of the *colonizer* in denying the human rights of Palestinians whose homes and amenities are subject to demolition. Thus, Regavim's mirroring is indicative of an adept and reflexive actor that re-purposes tools to troubling effect: "Human rights become a weapon for further indigenous displacement" (Perugini and Gordon 2015, 116). In this interpretation, however, it is notable that the capacity to "reflect" is credited only to the colonizer and that the potential for Palestinians to adopt similar strategies is seemingly foreclosed or left unacknowledged. At a conceptual level, this corrective returns to Foucault's (1978, 95–96) understanding of power and the constant assertion throughout his work that "where there is power, there is resistance." More specifically, "power is not monolithic. It is never entirely controlled from a certain point of view by a certain number of people. At every moment it is in play in little singular struggles, with local reversals, regional defeats and victories, provisional revenges" (Foucault 2015, 228).

Returning to the South Hebron Hills to attend to such "local reversals" indicates that in fact strategies of Palestinian activism do engage in repurposing (or "reflecting") the very tools used by settlers and Regavim. A group of English-speaking Palestinian Bedouins have begun to challenge Regavim's narratives by disseminating firsthand experiences of demolitions past—"I remember being too scared . . . the fear froze me. I couldn't do anything, not even ask what had happened" (al-Hathalean 2017)—and the constant threat of more occurring in the future: "I am afraid . . . [further demolitions] will be catastrophic for the community . . . I want to stay here" (Living Archive 2017). While these efforts might seem quite routine acts of self-exposition in an age of social media, they are also a coordinated move to increase an online presence in recognition that resistance to Regavim involves also wresting control of a narrative to gain outside support. To this end, there is evidence of some success: a 2019 Regavim fund-raising event in London hosted by the group UK Lawyers for Israel was protested by "UK Palestinians, Jews and their supporters" who were, in part, informed by the testimony of the activist and author Awdah Hathaleen from Um-Al-Khair (see Anderson 2019). The connections and achievement here should not be understated; it is quite remarkable that a Bedouin Palestinian's account of demolition-threatened life in a desert village shaped the agendas of London activists with the material result of a blockaded event and its reduced attendance (*Jewish News* 2019). In terms of international visibility, this is not a one-off case, and different people from Um-Al-Khair now regularly feature in international media (e.g., Al Jazeera 2016; *Le Monde* 2013; *New York Times* 2019) and are invited to give talks across Palestine and overseas (*Michigan Daily* 2019).

Stepping up its online presence, in 2019 the community of Um-Al-Khair, under the name "Good Shepherd Collective," launched a public information program via a professional website and social media channels. The collective also purchased a drone to monitor settler construction in the South Hebron Hills and to produce aerial imagery for its advocacy materials. The campaign has so far involved field research to compile a large body of data from around the West Bank that forms the basis of a call to overseas donors to defund Regavim. It argues,

> The Central Fund of Israel and Israel Independence Fund enable Regavim's work by funneling US taxpayers' dollars through tax-exempt donations. This happens through the two organizations' charitable status in the United States and their fiscal sponsorship of Regavim. However, for grants to overseas entities, US Treasury and IRS [Internal Revenue Service] *regulations require* the US grantor to make an "equivalency determination" to determine if the foreign entity is functionally the same as a US nonprofit. In other words, the recipient—the sponsored organization overseas—must fulfill the same requirements as non-profits in the United States. These *guidelines require* that tax-exempt donations "*lessen neighborhood tensions; eliminating prejudice and discrimination; defending human and civil rights secured by law*." (Kilani 2020, original emphasis)

Pointing out that Regavim does not fulfill these criteria, it further states that Regavim's work "runs contrary to the spirit of the laws governing charitable organizations" (Kilani 2020); therefore, its eligibility for tax-exempt donations should be revoked. The online front of the campaign also includes plans for a "mirror website" that will direct potential visitors to Regavim's official website (regavim.org) to an alternative that presents evidence designed to disrupt the circulation of donor-targeted material. This particular strategy not only is a mirror in itself but also reappropriates a settler tactic of digital activism, such as the case of the mirror site www.rawabi .co.il (of www.rawabi.ps) that was used to disseminate misinformation about the new Palestinian town of Rawabi close to Ramallah (see Rabie 2021, 226).

In these ways, the community of Um-Al-Khair has become the center of a campaign to reduce Regavim's funding by directing flows of information from the West Bank (firsthand testimony, fieldworkers, drones) to potentially powerful advocates and donors while also appealing to solidaristic activists such as those who protest overseas fund-raising events. In important ways, therefore, the residents of Um-Al-Khair adapt their practices of resistance by taking on Regavim in the same game and showing symmetry both on a practical level in its information-gathering methods and on a technical level in its dissemination and ability to tap into (and disrupt) sources of donor capital. The ensuing and necessary reconceptualization posits mirroring as less a two-way closed system than a continuing effect in which Palestinian actors *also* mirror different strategies for the purposes of anticolonial struggle.

Conclusions

In this chapter I have provided a detailed account of Regavim's activities in Palestine with the objective of examining the ways that power functions in its public-facing discourse and its operations on the ground, specifically in the village of Um-Al-Khair near Hebron. Regavim, as I have shown, is an effective actor in the colonization of Palestine that reconciles contradictory positions: as an accomplice-adversary of the state, as an advocate for the human rights of colonizers, and as a propagator of narratives about Palestinian "settler/oppressors." The question of power is thus a multifaceted one that addresses state–non-state relations, representational practices, and the always-present potential for countering. In response, the chapter's analytical work has sought to make three discrete contributions to understanding power in the colonial encounter with Regavim: as a preceding force of which powerful actors are a product, as a postmodern proliferation of signs without referent, and as a mutable form that is continually reflected and re-purposed.

Each of these analytical insights might further different areas of inquiry on Palestine. The analytical positioning of power as a precedent to the state is useful to the end of analyzing the increasingly complex array of actors that further the settler colonial project in Palestine. If we limit analysis to the state, or even retain the state as a locus of examination, then we risk losing sight of the unitary forces that thread through the settler drive to requisition land, whether this is expressed more subtly (e.g., in the incremental rulings of the Supreme Court) or most fervently, such as in the case of Regavim and politically aligned actors (e.g., Elad, Lehava, Hilltop Youth) working at Israel's colonial frontiers. Where most pronounced, these actors simultaneously call for a dismantling of the "secular Israeli State" yet advance the settlerism that is the root of its foundation and expansion. Accounting for power in this way does not replace the more nodal examinations of relations as "osmosis" but presents a complement that can undo the conundrum of why extreme settler organizations enter into contested relations with the state and its functions. The turn to postmodernist perspectives on representation is somewhat unusual in the study of Palestine/Israel, but as I hope to have convinced, the political stakes of the hyperreal are high: the production of Regavim's rhetoric grows its capacities—in terms of funding, technology, legitimacy—to target Palestinian communities and further proliferate its message in the circulatory exchange of images, capital, and violence. The critique is not then purely of esthetics but of the operational function that connects the representational to materiality. As I have finally documented and examined, this connection precisely fuels emerging strategies of resistance. The refiguring of the notion of mirroring presents a slight but vital corrective to the analysis of colonizers as dynamic actors who repurpose and reappropriate, and extends these capacities to the practices of anticolonial resistance. Aside from the important political and ethical imperative to remain sensitive to countering, questions of power are always already caught up in questions of in/capacity (see Griffiths 2022; Joronen and Griffiths 2022), and resistance can often take novel forms such as that of the residents of Um-Al-Khair whose increased visibility gradually builds international support.

As for the case in hand, Regavim is by now an established organization whose multimillion-dollar budget and involvement in hundreds of ongoing legal cases against Palestinians make it an urgent object of further study to provide knowledge of its operations. We might ask: What techniques of surveillance is Regavim developing? What precisely are its avenues to law- and policy-making bodies? What are Regavim's networks of self-publicity? Who donates and with what information? How effective are emergent forms of resistance? Answering these and other questions will build the knowledge necessary for understanding a dynamic contemporary front of Israel's occupation of Palestine.

Notes

1. All quotes are from regavim.org, emphases added. "Judea and Samaria" is the term used by settlers to refer to the West Bank.
2. The Israeli Civil Administration is Israel's governing body in the West Bank and is part of the Defense Ministry of Israel.
3. Regavim declared funding of ILS890,000 (approximately $260,000) in "support from local authorities" for the financial year 2018–19.
4. For continually updated information, see B'tselem, the Israeli Information Center for Human Rights in the Occupied Territories, https://www.btselem.org/topic/south_hebron_hills.
5. Outposts are illegal even under Israeli law but are rarely removed.
6. For up-to-date statistics, see the United Nations Office for the Coordination of Humanitarian Affairs, https://www.ochaopt.org/data/casualties.
7. On Shaked's relationship with Regavim, see Magid 2019.
8. See guybo111, "Demolitions in Umm El Kheir 9.8.2016," YouTube, https://www.youtube.com/watch?v=qtoR-Nz3Nks&feature=youtu.be.
9. One important exception is the accomplished doctoral work of Wassim Ghantous (2019), who moves beyond state–non-state dichotomies by conceptualizing state-

settler relations as immanent processes of legal activism (see also Ghantous and Joronen 2022).

References

Al-Hathaleen, Awdah. 2017. "My Village Is under Threat. I'm Not Giving up Hope." *+972 Magazine*, July 16. https://www.972mag.com/my-village-is-under-threat-but-im-not -giving-up-hope-just-yet/.

Al Jazeera. 2016. "Surge in Demolitions Leaves More Palestinians Homeless." April 12. https://www.aljazeera.com/news/2016/04/12/surge-in-demolitions-leaves-more -palestinians-homeless/.

Allen, Lori. 2019. "Subaltern Critique and the History of Palestine." In *A Time for Critique*, edited by Didier Fassin and Bernard Harcourt, 153–73. New York: Columbia University Press.

Anderson, Tom. 2019. "UK Palestinians, Jews and Their Supporters Join Together to Protest against a Visit by a Right-Wing Israeli Charity." Canary Worker's Co-op, December 3. https://www.thecanary.co/global/world-analysis/2019/12/03/uk-palestinians -jews-and-their-supporters-join-together-to-protest-against-a-visit-by-a-right-wing -israeli-charity/.

Applied Research Institute–Jerusalem. 2016. "Israel Extends Plans for New Settler Homes in the Occupied West Bank." Poica: Eye on Palestine, January 27. http://poica.org /2016/01/israel-extends-plans-for-new-settler-homes-in-the-occupied-west-bank/.

Baker, Luke. 2016. "With Demolitions, Israel Tightens Squeeze on West Bank Palestinians." Reuters, April 7. https://www.reuters.com/article/us-israel-palestinians-demolitions -idUSKCN0X41TA.

Baudrillard, Jean. 1994. *Simulacra and Simulation*. Ann Arbor: University of Michigan Press.

———. 1996. *The Perfect Crime*. London: Verso.

Berger, Yotam. 2018. "How Israeli Taxpayers Are Funding a Right-Wing NGO Dedicated to Getting Palestinians Evicted." *Haaretz*, January 19. https://www.haaretz.com/israel-news /israeli-right-wing-ngo-regavim-gets-millions-of-shekels-in-public-fund-1.5744933.

B'tselem. 2015. "Palestinian Village Khirbet Susiya under Imminent Threat of Demolition and Expulsion." May 7. https://www.btselem.org/press_releases/20150507_khirbet _susiya_facing_expulsion.

Dudai, Ron. 2017. "Entryism, Mimicry and Victimhood Work: The Adoption of Human Rights Discourse by Right-Wing Groups in Israel." *International Journal of Human Rights* 21 (7): 866–88.

EEAS (European External Action Service). 2019. "Development Programmes (East Jerusalem, Area C, Water, Civil Society)." January 1. https://eeas.europa.eu/delegations

/palestine-occupied-palestinian-territory-west-bank-and-gaza-strip/65569
/development-programmes-east-jerusalem-area-c-water-civil-society_en.

El-Haj, Nadia Abu. 2001. *Facts on the Ground: Archaeological Practice and Territorial Self-Fashioning in Israeli Society*. Chicago: University of Chicago Press.

Foucault, Michel. 1978. *The History of Sexuality*. Vol. 1, *The Will to Knowledge*. London: Penguin.

———. 2007. *Security, Territory, Population: Lectures at the College de France, 1977–1978*. Basingstoke: Palgrave Macmillan.

———. 2015. *The Punitive Society: Lectures at the College de France, 1972–1973*. Basingstoke: Palgrave Macmillan.

Ghantous, Wassim. 2019. "Settler-Colonial Assemblages and the Making of the Israeli Frontier: Palestinian Experiences of (In)security, Surveillance and Carceral Geographies." PhD diss., University of Gothenburg.

Ghantous, Wassim, and Joronen, Mikko. 2022. "Dromoelimination: Accelerating Settler Colonialism in Palestine." *Environment and Planning D: Society and Space* 40 (3): 393–412.

Griffiths, Mark. 2022. "Thanato-Geographies of Palestine and the Possibility of Politics." *Environment and Planning C: Politics and Space* 40 (8). https://doi.org/10.1177/23996544221099461.

Hammami, Rema. 2016. "Precarious Politics: The Activism of 'Bodies That Count' (Aligning with Those That Don't) in Palestine's Colonial Frontier." In *Vulnerability in Resistance*, edited by Judith Butler, Zeynep Gambetti, and Leticia Sabsay, 167–90. Durham NC: Duke University Press.

Hicks, Donna. 2020. "A New Voice from the Grassroots of the South Hebron Hills." Episcopal Peace Fellowship, January 8. https://epfnational.org/pin/a-new-voice-from-the-grassroots-of-the-south-hebron-hills/.

Hovel, Revital. 2017. "Israeli Justice Minister Using External Consultant to Dictate State's Positions on Settlements." *Haaretz*, October 22. https://www.haaretz.com/misc/article-print-page/.premium-justice-minister-intervening-in-state-s-positions-on-settlements-1.5459398.

Israel National News. 2016a. "Saving the Land of Israel via Drone." December 6. https://www.israelnationalnews.com/News/News.aspx/221293.

———. 2016b. "Shaked: The Possibility of Copying Amona Is Being Examined." August 8. https://www.inn.co.il/news/327806. [In Hebrew.]

Jewish News. 2019. "British Jews Blockade Israeli 'Lawfare' Group Talk in London." December 2. https://jewishnews.timesofisrael.com/jews-block-regavim-uk-talk/.

Joronen, Mikko. 2016. "'Death Comes Knocking on the Roof': Thanatopolitics of Ethical Killing during Operation Protective Edge in Gaza." *Antipode* 48 (2): 336–54.

Joronen, Mikko, and Mark Griffiths. 2019. "The Affective Politics of Precarity: Home Demolitions in Occupied Palestine." *Environment and Planning D: Society and Space* 37 (3): 561–76.

———. 2022. "Ungovernability and Ungovernable Life in Palestine." *Political Geography* 98:1–10.

Kilani, Lara. 2020. "Israel Confiscates School in Susiya." Good Shepherd Collective, February 20. https://goodshepherdcollective.org/2020/03/23/update-2-20-2020/.

Le Monde. 2013. "Avec ces Israéliens qui défendent les Palestiniens." https://www.taayush .org/wp-content/uploads/2013/11/TAAYOUSH.pdf. [In French.]

Living Archive. 2017. "Umm Al-Khair: Introduction: The Questions Were Just Too Big So I Started to Lie to Her." http://living-archive.org/village/um-el-khair/?lang=en.

Magid, Jacob. 2019. "Shaked Demands Half of Potential United Right Slate as Merger Talks Heat Up." *Times of Israel*, July 22. https://www.timesofisrael.com/shaked-demands -half-of-potential-united-right-slate-as-merger-talks-heat-up/.

Michigan Daily. 2019. "Palestinian Activist, Artist Shares Experience with Jewish Students." March 22. https://www.michigandaily.com/section/campus-life/palestinian-activist -artist-shares-experience-jewish-students.

Middle East Monitor. 2018. "Israeli Settlers Call for Evacuating Palestinian Neighbour-hoods in Hebron." March 20. https://www.middleeastmonitor.com/20180320-israeli -settlers-call-for-evacuating-palestinian-neighbourhoods-in-hebron/.

New York Times. 2019. "Birthright Trips, a Rite of Passage for Many Jews, Are Now a Target of Protests." June 11. https://www.nytimes.com/2019/06/11/us/israel-birthright -jews-protests.html.

Peace Now. 2016. "Report on Right-Wing Funding." https://peacenow.org.il/en/whos -funding-the-right-wing-organizations-in-israel.

———. n.d. "Who We Are." Accessed June 2021. https://peacenow.org.il/en/about-us /who-are-we.

Perugini, Nicola, and Kareem Rabie. 2012. "The Human Right to the Colony." In *Shifting Borders: European Perspectives on Creolisation*, edited by Tommaso Sbriccoli and Stefano Jacoviello, 35–56. Newcastle: Cambridge Scholars Publishing.

Perugini, Nicola, and Neve Gordon. 2015. *The Human Right to Dominate*. Oxford: Oxford University Press.

Rabie, Kareem. 2021. *Palestine Is Throwing a Party and the Whole World Is Invited*. Durham NC: Duke University Press.

Regavim. 2010. *The Perversion of Justice*. [Currently unavailable.]

———. 2016. "Um Kheir—Stop the EU's Meddling." Facebook, August 25. https://www .facebook.com/regavimeng/posts/1189835144408444:0.

———. 2018a. *Annual Report*. https://www.regavim.org/wp-content/uploads/2019/01 /Regavim2018-Annual-Report-digital-view-2.pdf.

———. 2018b. *Measure for Measure 2018: An Index of Judicial Parity*. https://www.regavim .org/wp-content/uploads/2018/06/RegavimMadidEng2806-4.pdf.

———. 2019a. *Annual Report*. https://www.regavim.org/wp-content/uploads/2019/12 /Regavim-Annual-Report-English-2019.pdf.

———. 2019b. "Israel Pays Millions to Bedouin in Massive Protection Racket under Guise of 'School Security.'" September 23. https://www.regavim.org/israel-pays-millions-to -bedouin-in-massive-protection-racket-under-guise-of-school-security/.

———. 2020. "Knesset Foreign Affairs and Defense Committee Convenes for Hearing on 'The Battle for Area C.'" *Jewish News Syndicate*, July 29. https://www.jns.org/wire /today-wednesday-knesset-foreign-affairs-and-defense-committee-hearing-on-the -battle-for-area-c/.

———. 2021. "Tour in the Negev for Knesset Land of Israel Caucus." July 22. https://www .regavim.org/field-tour-in-the-negev-for-knesset-land-of-israel-caucus/.

———. n.d.a. "Activities." Accessed June 2021. https://www.regavim.org/activities/ (no longer available).

———. n.d.b. "What We Are Up Against: The Silent Conquest." Accessed June 2021. https://www.regavim.org/what-we-are-up-against-ii-the-silent-conquest/ (no longer available).

Shenhav-Goldberg, Rachel. 2019. "In the Hebron Hills, the Settlers Are the Lords and the IDF Does Their Bidding." +972 *Magazine*, November 12. https://www.972mag .com/idf-hebron-settlers/.

Wolfe, Patrick. 2006. "Settler Colonialism and the Elimination of the Native." *Journal of Genocide Research* 8 (4): 387–409.

5   Staying with the Failures
Iron Dome and Zionist Security "Innovation"

Rhys Machold

In July 2012 I interviewed Amos Golan, a retired Israeli army lieutenant colonel who served as a fighter and commander in elite Israeli police and Israel Defense Forces (IDF) units. Postretirement, Golan became the chief executive officer of Silver Shadow Advanced Security Systems Ltd., a firm that develops, manufactures, and exports small arms and security technologies. He is best known for inventing the Corner Shot, a technology that when paired with a pistol enables military and police units to shoot around corners. Golan's career path embodies the ways that Israel's "experience" with settler colonial dispossession has been fused with the country's status as the "start-up nation," an idea that is captured and popularized by a best-selling book by the same title (Senor and Singer 2009). As Joe Getzoff (2020, 811) elaborates, "Start-up nation" has emerged as a "metonym for Israel, recasting the state as a model of successful, unique, entrepreneurial and technological activity." Getzoff (2020, 813) persuasively argues that the "start-up discourse" represents a "traveling narrative about Israel's supposed economic and scientific exceptionalism" that seeks "to identify Israel as a perfect model for economic success by celebrating the state's unique cultural entrepreneurialism premised on military conscription and training."

I was interested in speaking with Golan because of his position within Israel's political economy of security "innovation." When we spoke in the Silver Shadow board room in Tel Aviv, Golan regaled me with stories about how his experience as a fighter and commander in special units spawned his curiosity in finding new "solutions" to "operational problems" in the battlefield and how he translated this ethos into a transnational corporate enterprise. While Golan said a number of disturbing things, what stood out as constant were the ideological proclivities of his claims. He described his career through core start-up nation tropes but also insisted that I receive a Zionist history lesson as the cost of access to his life story. His account covered the horrors of the Holocaust and the origins of the Israeli state, praising the vision of Vladimir Jabotinsky, a key Zionist ideologue, admirer of Benito Mussolini's, and architect of Palestine's ethnic cleansing (see Massad 2006, 5). In elaborating the enduring prescience of Jabotinsky's uncompromising vision of building an "Iron Wall" against Palestinians, Golan cited the Kippat Barzel (Iron Dome)—the Israeli antimissile defense system—lauding it as an "amazing" achievement unseen anywhere else in the world.[1]

That Golan referenced Iron Dome as the culmination of Jabotinsky's vision and *the* exemplar of Israeli security excellence is neither surprising nor incidental. If start-up nation has become a metonym for Israel, Iron Dome has become a shorthand for Israel's standing as a global security "innovator." As Ian Slesinger (2022, 439) notes, Iron Dome has emerged as "an attention-grabbing bright object," representing perhaps even "the most famous Israeli invention" (Norton and Hever 2018). The specific roles that Iron Dome plays in Israeli start-up discourse, however, are as strange as they are familiar. As I show below, the system has faced a range of technical challenges, with key figures in the scientific community, global weapons industries, and military circles questioning whether it performs as advertised (Talbot 2014). To date, Israeli officials have never provided any scientific data to redress such concerns. And while initially positioned as a lucrative export, Iron Dome has proven hugely costly and difficult to market abroad. In these respects, Iron Dome reflects the centrality of technical and economic failures as defining features of missile defense projects (Peoples 2010; Walt 2000), and we might easily dismiss Iron Dome as yet another example of this history. Yet, Iron Dome continues to enjoy a status in popular culture as an exception to the recurring failures of missile defense projects. In the wake of the Israeli bombardment of Gaza in May 2021, Iron Dome's performance was widely celebrated, with images of its missiles lighting up the night sky being some of the most widely shared on social media. Any residual skepticism about the system's economics and accuracy was shifted into the past tense: "If you've been watching coverage of the latest round of fighting in Gaza and Israel," Anshel Pfeffer enthused in *The Atlantic*, "you won't have escaped the Iron Dome pyrotechnic display, astonishing especially at night as the rockets arching northward from Gaza are picked out of the sky in a litany of mid-air explosions." Pfeffer (2021) continued: "When it was first established more than a decade ago, Iron Dome *had* its skeptics, both in Israel and abroad, but over time, they—and the world—have seen it work. Literally" (emphasis added). The article, appropriately titled "The Costly Success of Israel's Iron Dome," argued that if any such concerns ever had merit, they are now put to rest.

By "staying with" (Haraway 2016) Iron Dome's multiple and persistent failures, this chapter interrogates the meaning of failure in relation to the system. It asks: What is failure? How does it work? How is it connected with Israeli security "innovation"? Through a focus on Iron Dome's failures, I reflect on what Iron Dome represents within the broader Zionist project and its associations with exceptional technological progress and modernity. Following the narratives and controversies surrounding Iron Dome—not only how they have emerged but also how they have been negotiated by interested parties—the chapter analyzes how Iron Dome has been held up as a success through the strategic and repeated dodging and explaining away of its operational failures. Extending thinking on the role of ideational diffusion in the Zionist project, I argue that Iron Dome's centrality within start-up discourse is less novel or surprising than it might first appear. Yet, I further suggest that "staying with" Iron Dome's failures offers important opportunities to destabilize dominant narratives of Zionist violence as progressive, coherent, and instrumental, raising questions about the utility of the paradigm of security innovation. In doing so, this chapter furthers this volume's concern with colonial spaces *in the making* and its core implication—namely, the foregrounding of the incompleteness of colonial projects as well as their potential to be *un*done. More specifically, I show that by *staying with* the failures of Iron Dome—how they emerge and are encountered and negotiated transnationally—can help to challenge prevailing images of settler colonial projects and their security infrastructures as efficient and all encompassing.

The chapter proceeds as follows: I first outline how Israeli security innovation is positioned in literature on the colonization of Palestine and how it might be theorized further. Second, I provide an overview of Iron Dome's background, performance, and surrounding controversies. Third, I examine how its failures have been explained away by Iron Dome's defenders. Finally, I position Iron Dome and its surrounding narratives in relation to the Zionist project and settler colonial formations at large, arguing that a focus on failure offers opportunities to challenge exceptionalist representations of Zionist "innovation."

Questioning Israeli Security Innovation

Scholarly literature on the colonization of Palestine has frequent references to real-world "experimentation" and "innovation" (Weizman 2007; Hajjar 2016; Zureik, Lyon, and Abu-Laban 2011). Often in conjunction with representing Palestine/Israel as a "laboratory," these references are used both to make sense of how Israel has "perfected" its modalities of control, surveillance, and warfare over time through trial and error and to understand Israel's status as a central "location" within (Khalili 2010) or "a model" of global pacification regimes (Halper 2015; Machold 2015). These references to experimentation and innovation have been highly generative in conceptualizing how Israel sustains and progresses its settler colonial project in Palestine (Bresheeth-Zabner 2020; Dana 2020; Erakat 2019; Shalhoub-Kevorkian 2020). Yet, as I have argued elsewhere (Machold 2018), critical accounts of Israeli pacification share considerable common ground with the Zionist start-up discourse. While references to innovation by overcoming failure are common across critical literatures on Israeli security regimes, these discussions often take the meanings of "failure" and "innovation" at face value.

What then is innovation, and how is it connected to failure? As John Patrick Leary (2018) lays out, failure and innovation represent two "keywords" in the language of contemporary capitalism that are closely connected and do particular kinds of work, with "failure" framed as the basis of "innovation." Leary (2018, 92) writes: "Out of failure springs innovation. Failure is innovation's foundation." This celebration of failure as the basis of innovation has become somewhat commonsensical. According to Leary (2018, 119), innovation in its contemporary usage represents "a theological concept which became a theory of commodity production and which has lately become a commodity itself," arguing that innovation is increasingly "understood as the refinement of a technical process." Yet, as Leary (2018, 115, 119) documents, prior to the 1960s, the adjectival use of "innovative" was largely unknown, and he maintains that innovation remains a "strangely contradictory concept," embodying "simultaneously spiritual and technological" qualities dually celebrating the "reaction against bureaucratic malaise and the spirit of anti-orthodox creativity to be cultivated by the same bureaucracy." Antti Tarvainen (2022, 3) further draws attention to the "coloniality of innovation" by centering the key roles of innovation in providing "meaning and significance for violent project[s] of colonization" in Palestine/Israel and elsewhere. Thus, I suggest that engaging with Israeli start-up discourse and its celebration of innovation more critically means taking the term's self-evidence and imbrication with empire seriously while keeping its mythic and "strangely contradictory" qualities close at hand.

In interrogating the failure-innovation nexus further, science and technology studies (STS) are useful for theorizing how knowledges, practices, and technologies become generalized and circulate without attributing their generalization to an inherent superiority (Machold 2018, 94). STS has long grappled with how policies, technologies, and projects "are negotiated and gradually realized as functions of success or failure" instead of treating "success" and "failure" as neutral descriptors (Latour 1996, 184). STS enables us to better grasp how failure becomes a site of political contestation and to rethink the commonsensical failure-innovation nexus as part of ongoing discussions about the "experimental" dimensions of warfare (Hoijtink 2022).

These insights raise broader questions on how to tell stories of capitalism, empire, and infrastructures of violent dispossession. In her illuminating

STS-inspired study of security technologies, Debbie Lisle (2017, 891) recovers evidence of specific missteps in the development of security design as well as "the *failure* of . . . [an] instructive account of failure." Lisle (2017, 906) argues that when interrogating security technologies, "we should not uncritically accept the sanitized stories of failing better; rather, we should . . . explore stories of failing worse in order to see what epistemological, material and political horizons they open up." In a similar vein, Marijn Hoijtink (2022, 336) has insightfully shown that "experimental" war projects "do not need to produce any new knowledge or work successfully to create effects. To the contrary, any demonstrated limitation or vulnerability of these kinds of projects and the technologies they deploy are grounds for further invest-ment and experimentation." Recovering overlooked or suppressed failures through an STS lens offers important "disruptive potential" for opening up new political avenues (Machold 2020, 32) and opportunities to write "dirty histories," which trouble prevailing sanitized narratives of police and military technologies (Lisle 2020). Indeed, one of the most incisive studies of Iron Dome to date has mobilized STS to grapple with the system's tendency to "exceed instrumental functionality . . . in unanticipated ways" (Slesinger 2022, 439).

To extend these insights, I take Donna Haraway's (2016) de-colonial feminist ethos of "staying with the trouble" as a guide. "The trouble" of concern to Haraway (2016, 2) is the "exterminating forces" at the center of planetary ecological crisis. Staying with this trouble, Haraway (2016, 1, 3) argues, requires "learning to be truly present" and finding ways to describe and think beyond the almost "comic faith in technofixes" as rescues to present crises. Haraway further suggests that staying with the trouble means considering *which* stories to tell about planetary crisis and *how* to tell them. Anna Tsing (2015, 17) similarly argues that in thinking about possibilities for life in the ruins of capitalism and empire, we need to better differentiate between the stories we *know* and the stories *we need to know* by cultivating "arts of noticing."

My concern in this chapter—namely, the infrastructures of settler colo-nial dispossession in Palestine—is not explicitly related to Haraway's and

Tsing's respective concerns. Yet, I find their approaches to thinking about and writing against the "exterminating forces" of planetary ecological crisis instructive. Drawing on these insights, I seek to recover and "stay with" the suppressed, overlooked, and forgotten stories of Iron Dome's technical and economic failures as a means of reclaiming the theological dimensions of Israeli security narratives and practices used to racialize, demonize, and dispossess Palestinians (Shalhoub-Kevorkian 2015) and in doing so write "against the hi-tech fantasy" (Tawil-Souri 2012, 170) surrounding Israel's thanato-political infrastructures and their underpinning "entrepreneurial" ethos (Ghantous and Joronen 2022).

The Case of Iron Dome: Marketing, Hype, Failure?

The ostensible purpose of Iron Dome is to intercept "rockets"—that is, low-grade, mostly homemade projectiles launched by Hamas and other militant factions from Gaza (Hever 2018; Finkelstein 2018). As an assemblage of four components working in conjunction (a radar detection unit, a mobile command center, a human operator, and a battery of missile interceptors), Iron Dome was developed by the Israeli Ministry of Defense's Administration for the Development of Weapons and Technological Infrastructure in partnership with Israeli weapons giant Rafael (Slesinger 2022) and Israel Aerospace Industries. U.S.-based Raytheon became a production partner in 2014. First deployed in 2011, Iron Dome gained international renown during Israel's 2012 and 2014 assaults on Gaza, respectively named Operation Pillar of Defense and Operation Protective Edge. Such was Iron Dome's profile that some have suggested that Israeli leaders deliberately launched these operations to "battle test" Iron Dome and showcase it to would-be international buyers (Jaber 2014; Johnson 2015). Whether this is true or not is beside the point; the operations served as real-life test runs for a system that came at enormous expense. A single Iron Dome interceptor rocket costs around $50,000, and each battery that fires these interceptors has a price tag of around $50 million (Ghoshroy 2012). In Operation Pillar of Defense alone, some estimated the cost of operating the system was between $25 million and $30 million, largely subsidized by U.S. military aid

(Ghoshroy 2012). Since 2011 the United States has provided a total of $1.56 billion to Israel to support the system (Yousif 2021), over and above the $3.8 billion the United States gives to Israel annually (Institute for Middle East Understanding 2021).[2]

As part of Israel's extensive *hasbara* (public diplomacy) campaigns that accompanied its recent military assaults on Gaza (Aouragh 2016; Finkelstein 2018; Miéville 2006), Israeli political and military officials have claimed that Iron Dome has been up to 90 percent successful in intercepting projectiles from Gaza. Such claims have been echoed by foreign officials and pundits, and have been repeated as statements of fact in mainstream media, featuring headlines such as "Iron Dome Racks Up 90% Success Rate So Far" (Harel 2014) and "Israel's Iron Dome Missile-Defense System Is an Ironclad Success" (Rubin 2014). This laudatory coverage has also alluded to Iron Dome's purported economic efficiency. As a 2012 *Jerusalem Post* headline puts it: "Iron Dome: Defense at Bargain Prices" (Elis 2012). Indeed, one defense policy analyst suggested its ultimate significance would be determined by its popularity abroad: "The real test of Iron Dome's importance for missile defense is whether other countries end up buying it" (Ross 2013, 16). Much of this reporting has further insinuated that countries including South Korea, Singapore, India, Azerbaijan, Canada, Poland, Romania, Hungary, and the United States have expressed interest in purchasing Iron Dome.

However, a number of scholars and defense experts have cast doubt on these success stories. Criticisms of Iron Dome emerged before Operation Pillar of Defense but became more widespread and pronounced thereafter. Writing in the *Bulletin of the Atomic Scientists*, Subrata Ghoshroy (2012) argued that the system "is . . . not a game changer if one considers its economics." Further noting that the apparent interest by foreign states is frequently "conflated with proof that the system works," he called on Israeli leaders to be more forthcoming with their data. In the years since, a number of prominent U.S. and Israeli weapons scientists went considerably further, systematically challenging Iron Dome's purported efficacy at intercepting Hamas's projectiles (Broad 2013). They have included Richard M. Lloyd, a U.S. weapons expert; Philip E. Coyle III, who previously oversaw the Pentagon's weapons-testing program; Reuven Pedatzur, a former Israeli fighter pilot; Mordechai Shefer, an Israeli Defense Prize winner and aerospace engineering expert; and Theodore Postol of the Massachusetts Institute of Technology (MIT), who famously challenged the technological efficacy of the American Patriot anti-missile defense system during the 1991 Gulf War (Postol 1991; Jeffords 1993).

Though an early supporter of Iron Dome (Talbot 2012), who by his own accounting "drank the Kool-Aid on Iron Dome" (quoted in Koring 2012), Theodore Postol subsequently became one of its most formidable critics. After analyzing videos of the trajectories of Iron Dome interception missiles, he argued that the interception rates of Hamas projectiles are far lower than 90 percent, possibly even close to a zero percent success rate. As he summarized in a 2014 MIT *Technology Review* article: "It is clear that the Iron Dome radar tracking and guidance system is not working" (Postol 2014b). Postol (2014a) also argued that Israeli state officials withheld evidence required to validate their lofty claims, concluding: "The Israeli government is not telling the truth about Iron Dome to its own population, or to the United States, which has provided the Israeli government with the bulk of the funding needed to design and build the much-heralded but apparently ineffective rocket-defense system." Postol further stressed that Israeli officials had shown no sign of trying to address criticisms, arguing that between November 2012 and July 2014 he found no evidence that its interception rates had improved.

Mordechai Shefer has similarly cast doubt on Iron Dome's purported success, even going so far as to call the system an expensive PR stunt. In 2014 he argued that Iron Dome's supposed "interceptions" were simply its own missiles exploding in mid-air: "Iron Dome is a sound and light show that is intercepting only Israeli public opinion, and itself, of course. Actually, all the explosions you see in the sky are self explosions. No Iron Dome missile has ever collided with a single [Hamas] rocket" (cited in *Globes* 2014). Shefer maintains that the widely reported "success" of Iron Dome is a big lie mobilized by Israeli political elites to avoid making peace with Palestinians.

MACHOLD

Other longtime critics of Israel such as Norman Finkelstein have gone even further, concurring with some of other critics' analyses but suggesting that they give Israel undue credit. Whereas Postol has partially attributed low Israeli casualties from Hamas projectiles to the efficacy of Israel's early warning and bomb shelter system, Finkelstein has argued that this alone cannot explain the lack of property damage in Israel from Hamas projectiles historically. He concludes the only plausible explanation is that Hamas likely did not have any substantial arsenal of weapons in the 2014 assault on Gaza and that "the preponderance of these so-called rockets amounted to enhanced fireworks or 'bottle rockets,'" stressing that "Iron Dome probably didn't save many and perhaps not any lives" (Finkelstein 2018, 225, 318). According to Finkelstein, not only is Iron Dome a big lie in the sense that it fails to intercept Hamas projectiles, but also the "rockets" it is ostensibly devised to intercept amount to quite probably little more than glorified fireworks.

Thus, while Iron Dome's success is frequently represented as a settled technical matter, it is anything but. A range of critics have vigorously countered Iron Dome's capabilities. Some of these critics such as Shefer and Pedatzur began speaking publicly around 2010 whereas others (e.g., Postol, Lloyd, Coyle, and Finkelstein) joined later, appearing in media, policy, industry, and scholarly forums. It is also important to note that where Iron Dome has been challenged, it has been primarily on technical grounds. And barring some important disagreements in their diagnoses of Iron Dome, these critics have reached a similar conclusion: Iron Dome is not merely underperforming but represents at best hype and at worst an elaborate ruse. Whatever functions Iron Dome *does* serve, they argue, must be decoupled from its (purported) technological prowess.

Notably, Iron Dome has not proven marketable abroad. I noted above how the system's *overall* success is conflated with its claim to economic efficiency and (allegedly growing) popularity abroad. Yet by 2014, even pro-Israel outlets like the *Jerusalem Post* conceded that foreign governments were proving less than enthusiastic: "Normally, an advanced new weapon system with a battle-proven success rate of 90 percent would have global defense procurement agencies on the phone in minutes. But Israel's Iron Dome rocket interceptor is yet to prove a hit with buyers abroad" (Reuters 2014). A more recent private intelligence report notes that even "Israeli officials admit that [the] Iron Dome system has failed to interest foreign customers" (Intelligence Online 2017). Indeed, the Stockholm International Peace Research Institute's figures show that of all the countries expressing interest in Iron Dome, only the United States went ahead with one order in 2019.[3]

Two underlying limitations thus characterize Iron Dome. First, its capacity to intercept projectiles remains at best highly contested. While expert analyses of its efficacy have made varying assessments, a number of highly credible figures have suggested that this capacity is extremely limited and quite possibly nonexistent. In response, the Israeli state has provided no reliable evidence of Iron Dome's technical capabilities. While this refusal to supply reliable data on its performance makes it impossible to reach a definitive judgment on Iron Dome's technical prowess, its purported 90 percent success rate is simply not credible. Second, in addition to being extraordinarily costly and bankrolled almost entirely by U.S. military aid, Iron Dome has not achieved popularity as an export commodity. While battle testing the system has no doubt worked to build its reputation, its branding as "combat proven" has not translated into sales. In light of these shortcomings, one might imagine that the system would fall out of operational use or that the success stories surrounding it would dissipate. Yet, as I show next, this has not been the case. Iron Dome continues to be deployed alongside Israeli assaults on Gaza, and its self-proclaimed "success" has proven remarkably impervious to critique. With only the exceptions of Finkelstein and Shefer, after 2014 Iron Dome's chief critics became notably silent.[4]

Explaining Away

After 2014, reporting on Iron Dome's technical limitations has all but vanished, and laudatory accounts have multiplied in mainstream news articles, magazines, and books for popular audiences. In a breathless example from

The Weapons Wizards (Katz and Bohbot 2017, 252–53), the authors proclaim: "The development of Iron Dome is a mesmerizing tale that combines all of the characteristics Israelis are famous for—chutzpah, persistence, improvisation and plain old innovation. . . . Iron Dome has achieved stunning success rates. . . . No other country has a system like Iron Dome." Iron Dome's "success" also continues to gain ground in technical and defense policy forums (Bartels 2017; Richemond-Barak and Feinberg 2016), United Nations reports (see Finkelstein 2018, 315), and peer-reviewed articles. One such article by Tel Aviv University history professor Arnon Gutfeld (2017, 944) in *Middle Eastern Studies* celebrates "the success of the Iron Dome in shooting down large amounts of projectiles launched at Israel." Another by Brock University's business professor Michael J. Armstrong (2018b, 129) in the *Journal of Global Security Studies* concludes: "Iron Dome now seems able to provide substantial rocket protection at a lower cost than airstrikes." So how are we to make sense of this? *Where* exactly did controversies surrounding its efficacy go? To answer these questions, I follow the controversies surrounding Iron Dome's efficacy and trace how they were negotiated by the Israeli state and others invested in the success story.

Israeli officials and intellectual defenders have responded directly to some of the previous criticisms. Senior Israeli military figures have been quoted in media articles taking on Shefer and Postol directly (Broad 2013; *Globes* 2014), and a range of scholars and policy analysts have attempted to counter such detractors. Writing in the policy journal *Military and Strategic Affairs*, Yiftah S. Shapir (2013, 83), the director of the Military Balance Project at Tel Aviv University's Institute for National Security Studies, notes that "along with the acclaim earned by the Iron Dome system, there was also not-insignificant criticism from various sources and for various reasons." Others have set out to resolve controversies and "myths" surrounding Iron Dome and establish to what degree it intercepts Hamas "rockets" (Gutfeld 2017). Armstrong (2018b) takes up the controversies surrounding Iron Dome as part of a broader excavation of the "effectiveness and efficiency of Israeli countermeasures as tools for reducing losses inflicted by rocket attacks." However, these authors do not rebut any specific technical criticisms. Instead, they attempt to sidestep the underlying technical basis of the controversies surrounding Iron Dome.

Unsurprisingly, defenders of Iron Dome have sought to discredit the basis of experts' criticisms. For instance, senior Israeli officials dismissed early criticisms as "baseless claims" predicated on "amateur YouTube videos" of (allegedly) questionable accuracy (Broad 2013). Israeli defense scholars have further questioned critics' motives. For instance, Emily Landau and Azriel Bermant (2014) suggest that Postol's challenge to IDF figures on Iron Dome's interception rate is "puzzling" because in the past Postol "has shown a readiness to rely on the conclusions of Israeli defence." According to them, Postol's inconsistencies raise questions about *his* expert credibility.

In defending Iron Dome, some more curiously argue that its true success is not a purely technical or economic matter and that trying to *measure* Iron Dome's performance is misleading. Shapir (2013, 91) posits that "decision making is a complex process that takes into account various types of considerations, the operational consideration being only one of them." Landau and Bermant (2014) decenter a focus on scientific data altogether: while conceding that "precise data on Iron Dome performance from the IDF is still lacking," they argue that "Israelis certainly do not doubt the success of the system." Mirroring this attempt to shift the focus away from clear metrics, Gutfeld (2017, 944) claims that Iron Dome's benefits are "unquantifiable elements in terms of US dollars."

Armstrong (2018b) similarly declares that the controversies surrounding Iron Dome's capabilities and value are misplaced. Citing questionable journalistic sources such as *Jerusalem Post* articles that are held up as evidence of Iron Dome's success, he argues that although operational concerns might have been justified previously, they have been resolved over time. In making this case, he anachronistically cites articles from 2012 (Elis 2012) to refute criticisms made in 2014 (*Globes* 2014). Sidestepping the underlying disagreements entirely, Armstrong argues that military innovation is an inherently slow-moving affair, but in the long term, Iron Dome will inevitably hit its intended targets. Without ever specifying what they are, he alludes to questions of public opinion. In an accompanying *Conversation* article, Armstrong (2018a) stresses that "the Iron Dome debate has been too polarized. The system's initial value may have been largely symbolic. But it later become [sic] very influential."

Some defenders also attempt to explain away its lack of uptake by foreign states. An article in the neoconservative National Interest (Dombrowski, Kelleher, and Auner 2013, 55–56) concedes that "Iron dome [sic] isn't likely to be exported extensively." It explains this, however, not because of Iron Dome's operational inadequacies or extraordinary costs but rather because the system "works best in a threat environment like that of Israel and its particular geography" and its "unique mix of threats." A 2018 Haaretz article similarly argues that "Iron Dome hasn't gotten any export traction because its ability to take down short-range rockets is designed for uniquely Israeli needs" (Amit 2018, emphasis added). In both cases, Israel's security is imagined in a familiar exceptionalist register (Merom 1999; Cheyfitz 2014)—that is, as without parallel and therefore requiring bespoke, and unparalleled, high-tech "solutions."

Indeed, the principal strategy to explain away the claims about Iron Dome's failures has been to dodge critiques while redoubling Zionist ideological tropes. In response to criticisms in 2013, senior Israeli Defense Ministry officials stressed that Israel's security officials were "more than content with the system's impressive results" (Broad 2013). Shapir (2013, 84) emphasizes, "From a technological point of view, the system attained extraordinary success," stressing that "Iron Dome is a unique system with nothing like it in the world." Retired Israeli brigadier general and engineer Daniel Gold—who is often cited as the "father" of Iron Dome—responded to Mordechai Shefer's criticisms as follows: "I won't make personal remarks here. Let him [Shefer] believe what he wants to believe" (Globes 2014). Tellingly, Gold invoked "start-up nation" as his defense of Iron Dome: "We're the startup nation because of things like this, and this [Iron Dome] is much bigger than a startup . . . it works" (Globes 2014).

Israel's efforts to dispel the questions about Iron Dome have also notably focused on mobilizing positive public impressions of the system's exceptional performance and attempting to diffuse such narratives as a means of countering technical and economic criticisms. When pressed by another interviewer to explain why Postol, Shefer, and Lloyd were incorrect, Gold challenged the very idea of measuring Iron Dome's track record on technical grounds. With a peculiar invocation of standpoint epistemology, Gold urged people to trust their real-world experience of the system's "success" instead: "Any layperson can figure out what the truth is. . . . It's too far removed from reality. . . . I don't know . . . I'm not going to get into an argument about technology. It works, I mean, there's nothing to argue about" (Amit 2014). When the interviewer pressed Gold to "prove it," Gold cantankerously responded, "I should prove it? . . . Check it out for yourself and see . . . the system defends very well . . . everything is recorded . . . everything is well researched . . . everything is well known" (Amit 2014).

Despite Iron Dome's extraordinary costs and "hotly contested" interception rates, "the system has been covered positively by the Israeli press and was considered a success" because it precluded any discussion about the structural reasons *why* projectiles are launched from Gaza toward Israel (Hever 2018, 55). Although some of the previously mentioned advocates of Iron Dome have acknowledged certain of its limitations, they have explained them away as little more than "instructive failures" (Lisle 2017) on the road toward success. As the rationalizations of Iron Dome readily allude to, the system serves crucial roles in regulating Jewish Israelis' anxiety about Hamas "rockets" as existential threats to their presence on the land. And mirroring the key imaginative roles that the Patriot missile system performed in the service of U.S. empire during the 1991 U.S.-led Gulf War (Jeffords 1993, 540), one of the most important things that Iron Dome "sells" is the outrageous idea that Israel's posture vis-à-vis Gaza is *defensive* (also see Slesinger 2022, 433).

The spinning of Iron Dome as a success story is not an isolated dynamic; it can be seen in the wider context of Israeli hasbara, the Israeli public diplomacy strategy developed as a self-conscious attempt to blunt Israel's pariah status in global politics (Aouragh 2016). I have shown how Israeli officials and their allies have attenuated critiques of Iron Dome by attacking its critics' credibility, refusing requests for data, and simply repeating that Iron Dome is an exceptional success and the very embodiment of the start-up nation alongside its broader hasbara efforts in recent assaults on Gaza. As Finkelstein (2018, 225) argues, "'Hamas rockets,' 'terror tunnels,' and 'Iron Dome'" have functioned as "meta-props in Israel's *hasbara* (propaganda) campaign." The Iron Dome "success" story has worked in conjunction with these wider strategies to reify the conventional terms of the so-called Israeli-Palestinian conflict. Its usage implies that "Hamas rockets" represent an existential threat that needs to be defended *against*. While critical discussions of hasbara (Aouragh 2016; Miéville 2006) have been highly illuminating, attributing Iron Dome's enduring success to the sheer power of hasbara is incomplete. I suggest that making sense of Iron Dome's success and its broader significance to the colonization of Palestine requires situating it in relation to Zionism's claims to technical achievement, modernity, and innovation while keeping non-instructive conceptions of failure close at hand.

Zionism: Diffusions and Failures

Before proceeding further, I want to clarify the parameters of my argument. While drawing out the peculiarities of how Iron Dome has been fabricated as a success story, I am not suggesting that system's emergence and use are somehow difficult to explain. Regardless of its technical performance and marketability, Iron Dome serves particular political functions for the Israeli state both domestically and internationally. Iron Dome enables Israel to rationalize the idea of technology as a fix to geopolitical cleavage (Hever 2018, 55; Slesinger 2022) and provides a pretext to deepen Israel's core reliance on U.S. military aid. Yet, Iron Dome does not simply illuminate a general faith in commonsense technological fixes characteristic of missile defense (Peoples 2010). As I have argued, what makes Iron Dome notable in these broader histories is its status as an exception to the recurring failures of other missile defense projects. It should be noted that while Postol and other critics significantly discredited the Patriot missile system on scientific grounds, displacing the memory of their "success" in the Gulf War proved more challenging (see Jeffords 1993, 552–53). Nor was the Patriot system ever decommissioned; it was deployed during the 2003 U.S.-led invasion of Iraq (Peoples 2010, 200) and continues to be sold to U.S. allies. For instance, U.S. authorities have recently decided to transfer a single Patriot battery to Ukraine. Nevertheless, missile defense projects are commonly associated with failure in public culture. Moreover, Iron Dome's proponents frequently reference its success in explicit contradistinction to preceding (perceptions of) failure. The fabrication of Iron Dome's success thus requires closer scrutiny of how Zionism works with and through exceptionalist claims, particularly those about technological progress (Saʿdi 1997; Tawil 2015).

In *The Question of Palestine*, Edward Said (1992) foregrounds the centrality of violence, erasure, and silencing in the colonization of Palestine. He notes (1992 [1979], 20–21), "The systematic denial of a substantial native Arab presence in Palestine was accompanied . . . by its destruction, blocking, and confinement in the councils of the world." Said (1992, 21) continues, "In addition, the Zionists were able to diffuse their views and reality of the Palestinian Arabs. A negative project—denial and blocking—entailed an equal and opposite positive project—diffusion. *I am not speaking here about mere propaganda*, which were it to have depended principally upon lies about Palestine, would never have brought Zionism to its realization in Israel. What concerns me a great deal more is the *strength of the process of diffusion* whose main focus was the Zionist colonization of Palestine, *its successes, its feats, its remarkable institutions*" (emphasis added). Said's claims speak to the importance of grasping how the fabrication of Iron Dome's success has played an important role in the broader demonization and racialization of Palestinians as the quintessential terrorist Other. It works not only through lies or assertions of power over life, death, and truth (Miéville 2006) but also through the "diffusion" of an exceptionalist narrative of Zionist violence as technological innovation.

Israel's status as the start-up nation and its position as a global security innovator play key roles in ideological and normative contestations surrounding what Ilan Pappé (2014) calls "the idea of Israel" and how the imperative of diffusion has developed into Israeli strategies of nation branding. A crucial corollary of Pappé's (2014, 13) idea of Israel centers on the fact that ideas can be commodified and marketed, both domestically and internationally, through their *packaging* in narrative form. As he elaborates, Israel is increasingly preoccupied with (re)branding itself abroad to challenge its pariah status. By decentering Israel's associations with war, colonization, and ethnic cleansing, these strategies attempt to (re)brand Israel "as a heaven on earth, a dream come true," and "one of the happiest places on earth because of its high-tech achievement" (Pappé 2014, 484).

Drawing on these insights about the role of diffusion within the Zionist project, I argue that it becomes clear why the Israeli state and its allies are so invested in Iron Dome as *the* quintessential Israeli innovation regardless of its technical capacities or marketability. It also helps explain why leading defenders of Iron Dome default to a strategy of asserting that Iron Dome is successful *because* it is an embodiment of Israeli chutzpah and of the start-up nation. Thus, by following how the controversies surrounding Iron Dome were explained away, we come to recognize how the system's status as a success story and pathbreaking innovation is negotiated and worked out (Latour 1996) not only through asserting settler narratives of futurity, progress, and inevitability (Dunbar-Ortiz 2018; Veracini 2010; Wolfe 1999) but also by *settling* Iron Dome's failures.

However, when we stay with (Haraway 2016) Iron Dome's failures, as I have here, we find not merely evidence of the theological and contradictory nature of Israeli security innovation, as per Leary (2018), but also the limitations of what, following Lisle (2017, 891), we can call an "instructive" conception of failure. Indeed, staying with Iron Dome's failures enables us to poke holes in the prevailing triumphalist stories that surround it. But we also find a possible basis for changing the story in the terms set out by Haraway (2016), from one of "failing better" to one of "failing worse" (Lisle 2017). For instance, we find that the Israeli military and its contractors have provided no evidence of any commitment to improving the system. When Israeli military spokespeople say they are "more than content" with Iron Dome's performance (Broad 2013), there seems to be every reason to take them at their word. Thus, there is no trajectory from failure toward innovation and success but rather a repeated story of recurring and unresolved failures.

Staying with Iron Dome's failures, moreover, enables us to notice the often-overlooked cracks in imperial and colonial forms of power (Tsing 2015). The spinning of Iron Dome as a success is perhaps most striking in its underlying lack of sophistication and credibility. Far from mounting a substantial rebuttal of Iron Dome's critics, many of its defenders' assertions amount to simply repeating that it *is* an exceptional and quintessentially Israeli innovation, regardless of, well, *anything*. Its advocates cite no data, and senior Israeli military personnel seem genuinely surprised that anyone might ask that they *prove* their lofty claims. As one commentator aptly noted of the repeated assurances of Iron Dome's "father," Daniel Gold: "[His] reply amounts to little more than an arrogant 'trust me, pal'" (Amit 2014). While Gold's hubris is striking, so, too, is his response's hollowness. The attempts to explain away Iron Dome's failures are not merely *in*credible but also contradictory. In responding to the system's critics, Iron Dome's advocates explicitly argue—in a mode of thinking that is, in important ways, counterintuitive—that it is unfair and unwise to be too committed to "operational," or technical, metrics of success. Iron Dome's defenders concede that its technical capacities are quite a bit less than "ironclad." But by explicitly arguing that its success cannot be understood in technical terms and that other considerations such as Israeli morale and public opinion should be privileged, they also (tacitly) agree with Theodore Postol and the other prominent critics discussed here that Iron Dome's innovation and success are *exclusively* symbolic.

Thus, through their efforts to shift debates on Iron Dome's success away from technical and economic matters, the system's defenders participate in a kind of "emperor has no clothes" moment, breathlessly repeating "it works, it works" but in doing so betraying their total indifference about *whether* Hamas projectiles are intercepted, how much Iron Dome costs, or whether it will be sold abroad. Thus, staying with the failures enables us to unsettle and rearticulate the meaning of Iron Dome's success in a narrow technical sense; it also gives us opportunities to tell different stories, such as the contested and subjugated histories of settler colonial technologies and their violences (Lisle 2020; Tawil-Souri 2012), that center the theological and contradictory aspects of innovation (Leary 2018) and more actively challenge Zionism's association with the ability to turn its violence into efficiency and profit. In doing so, I build on others' efforts to de-fetishize so-called Israeli innovations by situating them as "elements of a historically situated settler colonial project" (Hughes, Velednitsky, and Green 2022, 496). Indeed, given that start-ups are characterized by recurring failure (Cockayne 2019; Getzoff 2020), perhaps Gold's representation of Iron Dome as the embodiment of a start-up nation is more apt than he realized.

Telling different and non-instructive stories about Iron Dome and Israeli security innovation might compel us to reconsider the critical frame of "cruel innovation" (Dana 2020). The reasons for this are a matter of accuracy and concern political questions about what a scholarly analysis of Zionism might achieve. In relation to Iron Dome, testing it in practice does not seem to have significantly improved the system in operational terms. Referring to it as an innovation thus dangerously replicates Iron Dome's misleading techno-fantasy of progress, a narrative at odds with the system's trajectory. But in light of Said's (1992) attention to the Zionist project's reliance on its successes and feats, there are also good reasons to consider refusing its claims to innovation on polemical grounds. Doing so might deprive Zionism of one of its most powerful nurturing mythologies—that is, its core violence is an unfortunate but necessary part of a broader path toward techno-modernity.

Conclusion

In this chapter I have argued that staying with Iron Dome's multiple and unresolved failures offers important opportunities to rethink the parameters of Israeli security innovation in the Zionist colonization of Palestine. To conclude, I want to reflect on what staying with failures might offer to broader discussions about failure within settler colonial formations. Staying with failures might be a useful analytic as we encounter multiple failures of and within settler colonialism in ways that can deepen our understanding of failure—how it is encountered and negotiated transnationally—as well as its critical weight in the analysis of power and empire.

Settler colonial formations are often theorized as a specific *type* of colonial domination and are defined by their attachments to land and core narratives of futurity, progress, and inevitability (Wolfe 1999; Veracini 2010). Yet, indigenous critiques of settler colonialism draw attention to the potential for critics to reproduce these narratives. Writing in the context of U.S. imperialism and post-coloniality, Jodi Byrd (2011, 20) notes that much critical scholarship effectively "relegate[s] American Indians to the site of the already-doneness." In upending such portrayals, others suggest that incompleteness and failure are definitive of settler colonial formations. Audra Simpson (2016, 1) stresses, "Indigenous political orders are quite simply . . . prior to the project of founding, of settling, and as such continue to point, in their persistence and vigour, to the failure of the settler project to eliminate them." Ann Laura Stoler (2016) argues that this core failure of settler projects challenges us to reconsider the idea of settler colonialism as a specific "type" or fixed set of relations of colonial domination. "Settler colonialism might better be understood not as a unique 'type,'" Stoler (2016, 61) writes, "but as the effect of a failed or protracted contest over appropriation and dispossession." She continues, "Settler colonialism is only ever an imperial process in formation whose security apparatus confirms that it is always at risk of being undone" (61). In other words, the existence of settler polities' security apparatuses reflects the endurance of Indigenous life.

This is certainly true of the Zionist project. Zionist settlers' anxiety over Palestinian persistence has spurned a grotesquely disproportionate security apparatus of which Iron Dome is one particularly extravagant part. Whereas Stoler (2016) situates settler security apparatuses as reflective of broader settler failures to eliminate Indigenous life, what concerns me here are the more minute, mundane, and unresolved failures *within* these security apparatuses. I argue that staying with the failures of settler colonial security projects enables us to break open the edifice of settler projects as being efficient and all encompassing. Tsing (2015, 25) argues that "progress stopped making sense . . . the emperor had no clothes." In light of this, Israel's continued staking of its entire national brand on an arcane vision of a techno utopia makes its claims to inevitability increasingly suspect. Iron Dome might then be seen as a monument to Israel's hubris and Zionism's empty promise of a better world (Machold 2021). And while its reputation as a success seems to endure at a distance, up close, its machinations come into view as incredible, incoherent, and hollow.

Notes

1. Personal interview, August 2012.
2. In September 2021 the U.S. House of Representatives authorized an additional $1 billion to replace missiles used in Israel's bombardment of Gaza earlier in the year.
3. In 2021 another sale to the United States was reported, and some countries beyond the United States have purchased Israeli radar technologies that are part of the Iron Dome system. See Stockholm International Peace Research Institute (SIPRI), "SIPRI Arms Transfers Database," www.sipri.org/databases/armstransfers.
4. Pedatzur died in 2014 in a traffic accident. Postol has been involved in a number of other military controversies but hasn't published anything on Iron Dome since 2014 from what I can tell.

References

Amit, Hagai. 2018. "Behind Congressional Drive to Buy Iron Dome: Money from Raytheon." *Haaretz*, April 26. https://www.haaretz.com/us-news/behind-congressional-drive-to-buy-iron-dome-money-from-raytheon-1.6030800.

Amit, Or. 2014. "Checking under Israel's Iron Dome." Mondoweiss, August 16. https://mondoweiss.net/2014/08/checking-under-israels/.

Aouragh, Miriyam. 2016. "Hasbara 2.0: Israel's Public Diplomacy in the Digital Age." *Middle East Critique* 25 (3): 271–97. https://doi.org/10.1080/19436149.2016.1179432.

Armstrong, Michael J. 2018a. "As Missiles Fly, a Look at Israel's Iron Dome Interceptor." *The Conversation*, April 15. http://theconversation.com/as-missiles-fly-a-look-at-israels-iron-dome-interceptor-94959.

——. 2018b. "The Effectiveness of Rocket Attacks and Defenses in Israel." *Journal of Global Security Studies* 3 (2): 113–32. https://doi.org/10.1093/jogss/ogx028.

Bartels, Elizabeth M. 2017. "Is Iron Dome a Poisoned Chalice? Strategic Risks from Tactical Success." RAND Corporation, November 29. https://www.rand.org/blog/2017/11/is-iron-dome-a-poisoned-chalice-strategic-risks-from.html.

Bresheeth-Zabner, Haim. 2020. *An Army Like No Other: How the Israel Defense Forces Made a Nation*. London: Verso.

Broad, William J. 2013. "Weapons Experts Raise Doubts about Israel's Antimissile System." *New York Times*, March 20. https://www.nytimes.com/2013/03/21/world/middleeast/israels-iron-dome-system-is-at-center-of-debate.html.

Byrd, Jodi A. 2011. *The Transit of Empire: Indigenous Critiques of Colonialism*. Minneapolis: University of Minnesota Press.

Cheyfitz, Eric. 2014. "The Force of Exceptionalist Narratives in the Israeli-Palestinian Conflict." *Journal of the Native American and Indigenous Studies Association* 1 (2): 107–24.

Cockayne, Daniel. 2019. "What Is a Startup Firm? A Methodological and Epistemological Investigation into Research Objects in Economic Geography." *Geoforum* 107 (December): 77–87. https://doi.org/10.1016/j.geoforum.2019.10.009.

Dana, Tariq. 2020. "A Cruel Innovation: Israeli Experiments on Gaza's Great March of Return." *Sociology of Islam* 8 (2): 175–98.

Dombrowski, Peter, Catherine Kelleher, and Eric Auner. 2013. "Demystifying Iron Dome." *National Interest* 126 (July/August): 49–59.

Dunbar-Ortiz, Roxanne. 2018. *Loaded: A Disarming History of the Second Amendment*. San Francisco: City Lights Books.

Elis, Niv. 2012. "Iron Dome: Defense at Bargain Prices." *Jerusalem Post* (blog), March 28. https://www.jpost.com/Blogs/The-Bottom-Line/Iron-Dome-Defense-at-bargain -prices-365908.

Erakat, Noura. 2019. *Justice for Some: Law and the Question of Palestine*. Stanford: Stanford University Press.

Finkelstein, Norman. 2018. *Gaza: An Inquest into Its Martyrdom*. Oakland: University of California Press.

Getzoff, Joseph F. 2020. "Start-up Nationalism: The Rationalities of Neoliberal Zionism." *Environment and Planning D: Society and Space* 38 (5): 811–28. https://doi.org/10.1177 /0263775820911949.

Ghantous, Wassim, and Mikko Joronen. 2022. "Dromoelimination: Accelerating Settler Colonialism in Palestine." *Environment and Planning D: Society and Space* 40 (3): 393–412. https://doi.org/10.1177/02637758221090968.

Ghoshroy, Subrata. 2012. "Iron Dome: Behind the Hoopla, a Familiar Story of Missile-Defense Hype." *Bulletin of the Atomic Scientists* (blog), December 13. https://thebulletin .org/2012/12/iron-dome-behind-the-hoopla-a-familiar-story-of-missile-defense-hype/.

Globes. 2014. "Defense Prize Winner Moti Shefer: Iron Dome Is a Bluff." July 13. https://en .globes.co.il/en/article-defense-prize-winner-shefer-iron-dome-is-a-bluff-1000954085.

Gutfeld, Arnon. 2017. "From 'Star Wars' to 'Iron Dome': US Support of Israel's Missile Defense Systems." *Middle Eastern Studies* 53 (6): 934–48. https://doi.org/10.1080 /00263206.2017.1350844.

Hajjar, Lisa. 2016. "Israel as Innovator in the Mainstreaming of Extreme Violence." *Middle East Report* 279 (Summer). https://merip.org/2016/09/israel-as-innovator-in-the -mainstreaming-of-extreme-violence/.

Halper, Jeff. 2015. *War against the People: Israel, the Palestinians and Global Pacification*. London: Pluto Press.

Haraway, Donna J. 2016. *Staying with the Trouble: Making Kin in the Chthulucene*. Durham NC: Duke University Press.

Harel, Amos. 2014. "Iron Dome Racks Up 90% Success Rate So Far." *Haaretz*, July 9. https://www.haaretz.com/iron-dome-racks-up-90-success-rate-1.5254947.

Hever, Shir. 2018. *The Privatization of Israeli Security*. London: Pluto Press.

Hoijtink, Marijn. 2022. "'Prototype Warfare': Innovation, Optimisation, and the Experimental Way of Warfare." *European Journal of International Security* 7 (3): 322–36. https://doi.org/10.1017/eis.2022.12.

Hughes, Sara Salazar, Stepha Velednitsky, and Amelia Arden Green. 2023. "Greenwashing in Palestine/Israel: Settler Colonialism and Environmental Injustice in the Age of Climate Catastrophe." *Environment and Planning E: Nature and Space* 6 (1): 495–513. https://doi.org/10.1177/25148486211069898.

Institute for Middle East Understanding. 2021. "Explainer: The Controversy over Increased Funding for Iron Dome." September 22. https://imeu.org/article/explainer-the-controversy-over-increased-funding-for-iron-dome.

Intelligence Online. 2017. "Iron Dome, a Technical Success but an Export Failure." December 13. https://www.intelligenceonline.com/government-intelligence/2017/12/13/iron-dome-a-technical-success-but-an-export-failure,108285795-bre.

Jaber, Samer. 2014. "A War to Market the Iron Dome." Al Jazeera, July 29. https://www.aljazeera.com/opinions/2014/7/29/a-war-to-market-the-iron-dome/.

Jeffords, Susan. 1993. "The Patriot System, or Managerial Heroism." In *Cultures of United States Imperialism*, edited by Amy Kaplan and Donald E. Pease, 535–66. Durham NC: Duke University Press.

Johnson, Jimmy. 2015. "The Client State and the U.S. Arms Industry." Mondoweiss, February 14. https://mondoweiss.net/2015/02/client-state-industry/.

Katz, Yaakov, and Amir Bohbot. 2017. *The Weapons Wizards: How Israel Became a High-Tech Military Superpower*. New York: St. Martin's Press.

Khalili, Laleh. 2010. "The Location of Palestine in Global Counterinsurgencies." *International Journal of Middle East Studies* 42 (3): 413–33.

Koring, Paul. 2012. "Success of Israel's Iron Dome Defensive Shield Questioned." *Globe and Mail*, November 29. https://www.theglobeandmail.com/news/world/success-of-israels-iron-dome-defensive-shield-questioned/article5830196/.

Landau, Emily B, and Azriel Bermant. 2014. "Iron Dome Protection: Missile Defense in Israel's Security Concept." In *The Lessons of Operation Protective Edge*, edited by Anat Kurz and Shlomo Brom, 7. Tel Aviv: Institute for National Security Studies. https://www.inss.org.il/publication/the-lessons-of-operation-protective-edge/.

Latour, Bruno. 1996. *Aramis, or, The Love of Technology*. Translated by Catherine Porter. Cambridge MA: Harvard University Press.

Leary, John Patrick. 2018. *Keywords: The New Language of Capitalism*. Chicago: Haymarket Books.

Lisle, Debbie. 2017. "Failing Worse? Science, Security and the Birth of a Border Technology." *European Journal of International Relations* 24 (4): 887–910. https://doi.org/10.1177/1354066117738854.

———. 2020. "Making Safe: The Dirty History of a Bomb Disposal Robot." *Security Dialogue* 51 (2–3): 174–93. https://doi.org/10.1177/0967010619887849.

Machold, Rhys. 2015. "Mobility and the Model: Policy Mobility and the Becoming of Israeli Homeland Security Dominance." *Environment and Planning A* 47 (4): 816–32.

———. 2018. "Reconsidering the Laboratory Thesis: Palestine/Israel and the Geopolitics of Representation." *Political Geography* 65 (July): 88–97. https://doi.org/10.1016/j.polgeo.2018.04.002.

———. 2020. "Policing Reality: Urban Disorder, Failure, and Expert Undoings." *International Political Sociology* 14 (1): 22–39. https://doi.org/10.1093/ips/olz027.

———. 2021. "The Iron Dome System Is a Monument to Israel's Hubris." *Jacobin*, May 28. https://jacobin.com/2021/05/israel-military-iron-dome-system-high-tech-hubris-missile-defense-palestine.

Massad, Joseph A. 2006. *The Persistence of the Palestinian Question: Essays on Zionism and the Palestinians*. New York: Routledge.

Merom, Gil. 1999. "Israel's National Security and the Myth of Exceptionalism." *Political Science Quarterly* 114 (3): 409–34. https://doi.org/10.2307/2658204.

Miéville, China. 2006. "The Lies That Aren't Meant to Deceive Us." *Socialist Review*, November 1. http://socialistreview.org.uk/311/lies-arent-meant-deceive-us.

Norton, Ben, and Shir Hever. 2018. "Israel Turns Gaza into 'Arms Race' Laboratory, While Palestinians Fly Kites (Pt 2/2)." *Real News Network* (blog), June 19. https://therealnews.com/israel-turns-gaza-into-arms-race-laboratory-while-palestinians-fly-kites-pt-2-2.

Pappé, Ilan. 2014. *The Idea of Israel: A History of Power and Knowledge*. Ebook. London: Verso.

Peoples, Columba. 2010. *Justifying Ballistic Missile Defence: Technology, Security and Culture*. Cambridge: Cambridge University Press.

Pfeffer, Anshel. 2021. "The Costly Success of Israel's Iron Dome." *The Atlantic*, May 24. https://www.theatlantic.com/international/archive/2021/05/iron-dome-israel-netanyahu-hamas/618973/.

Postol, Theodore A. 1991. "Lessons of the Gulf War Experience with Patriot." *International Security* 16 (3): 119–71. https://doi.org/10.2307/2539090.

———. 2014a. "The Evidence That Shows Iron Dome Is Not Working." *Bulletin of the Atomic Scientists* (blog), July 19. https://thebulletin.org/2014/07/the-evidence-that-shows-iron-dome-is-not-working/.

———. 2014b. "An Explanation of the Evidence of Weaknesses in the Iron Dome Defense System." *MIT Technology Review*, July 15. https://www.technologyreview.com/s/528991/an-explanation-of-the-evidence-of-weaknesses-in-the-iron-dome-defense-system/.

Reuters. 2014. "Iron Dome, the Star of the Gaza War, Proves a Tough Sell Abroad."
   Jerusalem Post, October 6. https://www.jpost.com/israel-news/iron-dome-the-star
   -of-the-gaza-war-proves-a-tough-sell-abroad-378155.
Richemond-Barak, Daphné, and Ayal Feinberg. 2016. "The Irony of the Iron Dome:
   Intelligent Defense Systems, Law, and Security." *Harvard National Security Journal*
   7:469–525.
Ross, Philip E. 2013. "Score One for Antimissiles." *IEEE Spectrum* 50 (1): 16. https://doi
   .org/10.1109/MSPEC.2013.6395292.
Rubin, Uzi. 2014. "Israel's Iron Dome Missile-Defense System Is an Ironclad Suc-
   cess." *Reuters Blogs* (blog), August 5. https://www.reuters.com/article/rubin
   -missile/column-israels-iron-dome-missile-defense-system-is-an-ironclad-success
   -idINL2N0QC24V20140806.
Saʿdi, Ahmad H. 1997. "Modernization as an Explanatory Discourse of Zionist-Palestinian
   Relations." *British Journal of Middle Eastern Studies* 24 (1): 25–48. https://doi.org/10
   .1080/13530199708705637.
Said, Edward W. 1992. *The Question of Palestine*. London: Vintage.
Senor, Dan, and Saul Singer. 2009. *Start-Up Nation: The Story of Israel's Economic Miracle*.
   Toronto: McClelland & Stewart.
Shalhoub-Kevorkian, Nadera. 2015. *Security Theology, Surveillance and the Politics of
   Fear*. Cambridge: Cambridge University Press.
──── . 2020. "Speaking Life, Speaking Death: Jerusalemite Children Confronting
   Israel's Technologies of Violence." In *The Emerald Handbook of Feminism, Crimi-
   nology and Social Change*, edited by Sandra Walklate, Kate Fitz-Gibbon, JaneMaree
   Maher, and Jude McCulloch, 253–70. Emerald Studies in Criminology, Feminism and
   Social Change. Bingley: Emerald Publishing. https://doi.org/10.1108/978-1-78769-955
   -720201021.
Shapir, Yiftah. 2013. "Lessons from the Iron Dome." *Military and Strategic Affairs* 5 (1).
   https://www.inss.org.il/publication/lessons-from-the-iron-dome/.
Simpson, Audra. 2016. "The State Is a Man: Theresa Spence, Loretta Saunders and the
   Gender of Settler Sovereignty." *Theory & Event* 19 (4). https://muse.jhu.edu/article
   /633280.
Slesinger, Ian. 2022. "A Strange Sky: Security Atmospheres and the Technological Man-
   agement of Geopolitical Conflict in the Case of Israel's Iron Dome." *Geographical
   Journal* 188 (3): 429–43. https://doi.org/10.1111/geoj.12444.
Stoler, Ann Laura. 2016. *Duress: Imperial Durabilities in Our Times*. Durham NC: Duke
   University Press.
Talbot, David. 2012. "Why Israel's 'Iron Dome' Missile-Defense System Actually Works."
   MIT Technology Review, November 26. https://www.technologyreview.com/2012/11/26
   /17839/why-israels-iron-dome-missile-defense-system-actually-works/.

———. 2014. "Israeli Rocket Defense System Is Failing at Crucial Task, Expert Analysts Say." *MIT Technology Review*, July 10. https://www.technologyreview.com/2014/07/10/172100/israeli-rocket-defense-system-is-failing-at-crucial-task-expert-analysts-say/.

Tarvainen, Antti. 2022. "The Modern/Colonial Hell of Innovation Economy: Future as a Return to Colonial Mythologies." *Globalizations*, March 21. https://doi.org/10.1080/14747731.2022.2048460.

Tawil, Yoël. 2015. "A 'Start-Up Nation': On Performance and Creativity in Israel." *Ethnologie Française* 45 (2): 223–33.

Tawil-Souri, Helga. 2012. "Uneven Borders, Coloured (Im)Mobilities: ID Cards in Palestine/Israel." *Geopolitics* 17 (1): 153–76. https://doi.org/10.1080/14650045.2011.562944.

Tsing, Anna Lowenhaupt. 2015. *The Mushroom at the End of the World: On the Possibility of Life in Capitalist Ruins*. Princeton: Princeton University Press.

Veracini, Lorenzo. 2010. *Settler Colonialism: A Theoretical Overview*. Basingstoke: Palgrave Macmillan.

Walt, Stephen M. 2000. "Rush to Failure." *Harvard Magazine*, May 1. https://harvardmagazine.com/2000/05/rush-to-failure-html.

Weizman, Eyal. 2007. *Hollow Land: Israel's Architecture of Occupation*. London: Verso.

Wolfe, Patrick. 1999. *Settler Colonialism and the Transformation of Anthropology: The Politics and Poetics of an Ethnographic Event*. London: Cassell.

Yousif, Elias. 2021. "Factsheet: US Arms Sales and Security Assistance to Israel." *Security Assistance Monitor*, April. https://securityassistance.org/publications/factsheet-us-arms-sales-and-security-assistance-to-israel/.

Zureik, Elia, David Lyon, and Yasmeen Abu-Laban, eds. 2011. *Surveillance and Control in Israel/Palestine: Population, Territory, and Power*. London: Routledge.

6   Neo-Apartheid Jerusalem

Palestine/Israel and the Question of Urban Apartheid

Haim Yacobi and Moriel Ram

In this chapter we explore Jerusalem as an urban regime that we define as the *neo-apartheid city*. We build this notion around ongoing efforts to examine the critical conceptual capacities of the term "apartheid" and its relevance to the dynamic shaping cities today in general (Abu-Lughod 1981; Clarno 2017; Massey and Denton 1993) and in Palestine/Israel in particular (Yacobi 2015; Yiftachel and Yacobi 2005). We suggest that the current urban dynamics of the city of Jerusalem represent a paradigm shift in the way we understand apartheid in general and its localized urban manifestations more specifically.

Our main argument is that apartheid today can be productively understood through an analysis of lived *urban* realities and day-to-day colonial encounters in the city. We develop this argument by examining two critical components of Israel's apartheid regime. First, to understand the character, scope, and operation of this regime—as a lived reality—we need to examine its spatial attributes. As a political project, apartheid regimes operate to produce a cohesive territory under one sovereign rule that creates a hierarchy among the different groupings sharing the same territory. While such a claim can be contested in the context of a national territorial conflict and the two-state solution argument, it gains significant traction when moving to an urban scale—for instance, in Jerusalem. Our second critical component assumes that to investigate the facets of apartheid today (or a neo-apartheid modality, as we suggest), we must acknowledge its multiscalar and "messy" manifestations. More specifically, we propose that one must move *beyond* the level of the state to that of the city to explore the *relational* formation of the neo-apartheid city as a novel regime and to highlight new apparatuses of territorial management and colonization.

In the majority of existing inquiry, unpacking Israel's apartheid focuses on the state level, assuming its existence can be unraveled by analyzing the juridical measures used to control, govern, exclude, or benefit specific ethnic groupings. But what happens when we move *beyond* the level of the state to that of the city (Maylam 1995; Smith 1994; Turok 2014)? What are the conditions that shape apartheid's novel manifestations in the city, and how do they connect to the foundation of state power? In other words, what if instead of looking at the institutions that facilitate apartheid by one unified polity (such as the Jewish state), we think of the state and its institutions as tools within a larger emerging network operating in the city?

Our discussion situates Jerusalem in the context of Israel's occupation of Palestine, understanding Jerusalem within the general framework of Israel as an existing apartheid state. As noted recently (B'tselem 2021), Israel's practice of territorial division, exclusive immigration policy, land dispossession, and denial of Palestinians' rights to political participation qualify it as an apartheid state. In situating the analysis of Israel's apartheid regime within the larger discussion of settler colonialism (Tatour 2021), we present Jerusalem as one modality that fits the paradigm of a neo-apartheid city.

Jerusalem's situation within this paradigm enables us to underscore three main issues. First, Jerusalem should be juxtaposed with other cases of colonial urbanism and division, not just globally (Besteman 2020; Richmond 1994; van Houtum 2010) but also to Palestinian cities within Israel's internationally recognized borders (Monterescu 2017; Weiss 2011; Yacobi 2009) and to the radical *urbicide* (deliberate violence against the city) of Palestinian space in the West Bank (Cesari 2019; Graham 2003; Jabareen 2017) and Gaza Strip (Stanley 2017). In particular, we position our analysis vis-à-vis the massive literature on Jerusalem that, notwithstanding several exceptions (e.g., Bollens 1998), mostly eschews critical evaluation of the conceptual properties of apartheid (Avni et al. 2022; Boano 2016; Dumper 2014). Second, any discussion of apartheid should consider the scalar relations through which this regime's modes of control materialize, operate, and are challenged. Understanding Jerusalem as a neo-apartheid city enables a better vantage point on the messiness of apartheid as a political project, of its relations, and of its dependence on other forces that constitute the settler colonial rationalities dominating and shaping the structure of control in Palestine/Israel. For our discussion, the scalar manifestations of state power that established apartheid in Jerusalem (and Jerusalem as an apartheid city) are also re-formed by the emergence of neoliberal logic, which is an outcome of globalization processes that abate the control of the state over the production of national space and hence encroach on its ability to achieve national-colonial goals and universal welfare (Brown 2019). However, neoliberalism in Jerusalem (in the form of privatization of land, planning, services, housing) both establishes and erodes state power in the city. In other words, scale matters (Delaney 1997; Marston, Jones, and Woodward 2005; Jonas 2006) to the understanding of apartheid as a physical and political structure. Third and finally, for our analysis we suggest considering the *colonial encounters* through which this regime inheres as a lived reality. Hence, our main objective is to situate the formation of Jerusalem within the overall matrix of Israel's governance of Palestinian lives and space, as well as the colonial encounters with the state in the city, and to explore these dynamics through both territorial and scalar lenses. We discuss throughout this chapter how apartheid metabolizes in(to) the city as a statal power structure and how, in turn, this structure gains particular urban characteristics.

Taken together, these issues enable an understanding of apartheid as a multi-scalar regime in which variegated forms of separation and inclusion (legal, governmental, spatial, cultural, social, and economic) shape relationships between national identity and racial categorization, between political freedoms and physical mobilities, and between political power, private capital, and governance.

Notes on Palestine/Israel and the State of Apartheid

> Are you kidding? Apartheid has been here for ages. Ages.
> —ASSAF HAREL, March 2017

The preceding quote, taken from the Israeli comedy show *Good Night with Assaf Harel*, reflects through humor public and academic discussions on the presence of apartheid in Palestine/Israel. Referring to Israel's occupation and colonization of the West Bank as an apartheid regime in the mainstream Israeli media is usually followed by a controversial public debate. However, discussing Israel's politics within such a framework is not at all new in academia (Marshall 1995; Mbembe 2003). Since its establishment in 1948, Israel has constructed a citizenship system in which Jews are entitled to unconditional, full membership no matter their place of birth. In contrast, the level of political membership afforded to Palestinians is always limited and dependent upon their geographic location, whether it is within the Green Line, the West Bank, East Jerusalem, or Gaza. This scalar citizenship is determined also in accordance with an ethno-national identification that distinguishes Palestinians by their ethnicity (Plonski 2018) or faith (McGahern 2011) and accordingly awards or revokes various privileges. Beyond the uneven distribution of citizenship, existing scholarship has pointed out the varied array of oppressive mechanisms, mainly deployed in the territories under occupation, that includes an arbitrary permit regime, administrative detention, land confiscation, checkpoints, outposts, and military incursions. All are used to splinter Palestinian space and bear a close resemblance to those wielded in South African Bantustans (Kovel 2007; Nogueira and Davidson 2012).

Yet, implicitly embedded in Harel's remark is that while Israel's apartheid system has existed since the establishment of the state, the regime's manifestations have tended to elude formal categorization, political recognition, and public acknowledgment. Indeed, the academic discussants of Israel's forms of apartheid agree that its central characteristic is the stealth-like mode in which it operates to construe life in Palestine and Israel. For instance,

Israel's separation regime has been defined as a "creeping apartheid," a dynamic and constantly developing process that operates through planning tools that classify, contain, and manage deeply unequal societies, and are most typically found in basic rights to property, services, and political power (Yiftachel 2001; Yiftachel and Yacobi 2005). The creeping element of apartheid stresses that its undeclared a-structural ordering of politics is a gradual process that develops over time. Saree Makdisi (2018) argues that the Israeli separation regime is less declarative than its South African counterpart and more sophisticated in the ways in which it curtails mixed marriages, controls and allocates material resources, and initiates legislation that benefits the ethnic majority. The sense here—and for a majority of critical scholars—is that Israel has established a de facto apartheid regime that dominates the Palestinian people as a whole by successfully rendering invisible some of the mechanisms that solidify racial hierarchies. The significant contribution of the evolving concept of the apartheid paradigm in Palestine/Israel is in pointing to the routinized, day-to-day practices that solidify different forms of separation that allude to long-established definitions of apartheid. In short, the most important feature of Israel's apartheid is the denial of its own existence. While the separation policy was facilitated by various political constructs (military government inside Israel between 1948 and 1966, martial law and civil administration after 1967 in the occupied Palestinian territories, and the abandonment and blockade of Gaza since 2007), it was never officially formalized (Gordon 2009; Yacobi and Cohen 2007).

This (in)visibility enabled the academic debate over the relevance of the apartheid paradigm to Palestine/Israel. More specifically, the efforts to reject arguments about apartheid have been based on the idea that the apartheid regime was sui generis to South Africa, where it existed between 1948 and 1994. From a legal perspective, some scholars question analyzing Israel as an apartheid state and suggest that apartheid necessitates, first and foremost, an explicit legal construct of regulations and laws that prioritize one racial group over another (Ellis 2019; Sabel 2011). Furthermore, those rejecting a comparison between Palestine/Israel and South Africa draw upon the common understanding of apartheid, based on the definition of the Rome Statute of the International Criminal Court, that refers to an "institutionalized regime of systematic oppression and domination by one racial group over any other racial group or groups and committed with the intention of maintaining that regime." Defenders of Israel's practices in Palestine point precisely to the fact that an official—or "systematic"—separation policy must be formalized to be considered apartheid (Zilbershats 2013; Wilf 2021). In another key argument based on Article 2 of the International Convention on the Suppression and Punishment of the Crime of Apartheid, advocates find the apartheid paradigm does not apply to Israel as it hasn't openly proclaimed a racial separation regime and that at least those Palestinians who hold Israeli citizenship can and do serve as government officials and members of parliament and in the judiciary, including the Supreme Court (Pogrund 2015).

These arguments have, of course, been challenged and critically discussed by many who have explicated the ways in which the law has shaped settler colonial politics and space in Palestine/Israel and that legal formations have advanced Israel's interests (in land, migration, and selective political rights) over those of Palestinians (see, e.g., Clarno 2017; Erakat 2019; Peteet 2016; Turner 2019). Also, Israel's practices of governing, similar to the ones in apartheid-era South Africa, separate one group of people from another in a manner that makes apartheid a useful analytical descriptor (Soske and Jacobs 2015). A key point here is that Israel as a state exclusively favors one ethno-national identity and grouping to the extent that it is, as was recently noted in a statement of the United Nations Economic and Social Commission for Western Asia, "beyond a reasonable doubt that Israel is guilty of policies and practices that constitute the crime of apartheid as legally defined in instruments of international human rights law and principles" (Economic and Social Commission for Western Asia 2017, v). From these perspectives, largely oriented around international law and governance, apartheid is understood as a mode of governing devised and directed by a centralized state. It ends with the elimination of legalized racial discrimination and the transformation of the racial state.

In his analysis of the historiographic discussion on apartheid's rise and fall in South Africa, Saul Dubow (2014, v) notes that the precise meanings of apartheid are "deeply contested . . . for all its familiarity apartheid resists easy definition." Here, we follow Dubow's call to open up the discussion over what we mean by "apartheid": a legal structure, a territorial engineering, an unjust demographic divide, or a combination of these (and other) elements. In short, apartheid can denote not only a historical epoch but also a legal definition and a global reality (see Besteman 2020). The multiple conceptualizations of apartheid thus pose a significant analytical challenge. On the one hand, apartheid can be relevant for a broader critical evaluation of current forms of (colonial) control, most notably in places such as Palestine/Israel. On the other hand, we need to rethink, and perhaps revise, our understanding of apartheid as a form of domination that necessitates and emanates only from state power and has a clear scalar structure where power from a centralized sovereign source projects upon other levels of governance. The imperative here is to think through the messy realities of urban life as they are shaped by—*and shape*—apartheid regimes today. A further key question has to do with whether conventional definitions of apartheid and arguments about a unifying form of "global apartheid" apply to contemporary forms of de facto political separation that may be "institutionalized" in practice rather than in de jure legal statutes. As suggested throughout this chapter, apartheid should be seen beyond legal constructs as a multi-scalar spatial, social, and political reality. Apartheid, we stress, is the outcome of policies, practices, and discourses that enhance separation based on race, ethnicity, and religion.

Notes on Neoliberalism and the Apartheid City

The dominant body of knowledge exploring contemporary configurations of apartheid regimes concentrates on their interactions with neoliberalism and racial capitalism. Scholars studying postapartheid South Africa have charted the increasingly hegemonic nature of neoliberal thought and practice (Hart 2008). They have addressed the economic and material aspects that shaped the apartheid regime and, prior to its inception, the racial segregation of South African society (Parnell and Mabin 1995). David Smith (1994, 3) notes that in South Africa the apartheid regime began to shift toward privatization in the 1980s, thus abandoning its role of housing provider for the urban population. The neoliberalization of postapartheid South Africa cannot be understood without locating it in the process of global capital expansion.

In her analysis of neoliberalism in postapartheid South Africa, Gillian Hart (2008) implores us to understand how neoliberal projects and practices operate on terrains that always exceed them. The material conditions of life and livelihood are, simultaneously, struggles over the meaning of the nation and liberation. Hart suggests that the main analytical and political challenge is to produce concrete concepts that are adequate to the conditions with which they seek to come to grips. She calls on us to understand the multiplicity of neoliberalism as a political project that can transcend class projects, combine different forms of government rationalities, and articulate several ethno-racial narratives. Indeed, mechanisms of segregation and mixing play out differently according to urban spatial structure (Schensul and Heller 2011). In a similar vein, Andy Clarno (2017) has called for an exploration of the segregating dynamics that emerge and persist in post-Oslo Palestine/Israel and postapartheid South Africa. Clarno's comparative analysis of Palestine/Israel and South Africa suggests that contemporary forms of apartheid are inherently connected to neoliberal rationalities operating on the seam line between the private and the public. By marrying the concepts of racial capitalism and settler colonialism, and by comparing postapartheid South Africa to Palestine/Israel after the Oslo Accords, Clarno demonstrates that any reading that regards the change in apartheid policies as a shift from racial domination to a class conflict is flawed. In South Africa, apartheid was not dismantled but simply reconfigured. Similarly, the Oslo Accords, which have set the conditions for the furthering of neoliberal policies in both Palestine and Israel (Haddad 2018; Rabie 2021), did not conclude Israel's domination of Palestinians but rather reorganized the modalities that ensure this domination (Gordon 2009). Thus, racial capitalism and settler colonialism coincide with a specifically *neoliberal* apartheid system of control.

What is missing from the analysis of Hart and Clarno is a more nuanced examination of how moving from the scale of the state to that of the city alternates the forms and means of control that apartheid regimes create as well as the ways in which political resistance to apartheid in the city can take shape. Like Hart, we suggest situating the settler colonial framework within a larger, perhaps global, dynamic of neoliberal logic. Yet, in contrast to scaling upward—that is, in "relational comparison" to capitalism at a global scale (see, e.g., Griffiths and Brooks 2022; Hart 2002)—and following Clarno, we scale downward to attend to the messiness of apartheid within the settler colonial matrix dynamics of Palestine/Israel.

We need to locate *urban* apartheid regime forms within a multifaceted and broader understanding of regulating power to facilitate the process of seizure and appropriation. Under these regulatory mechanisms, the urban political economy is based on the expansion of dominant interests, exploitation of marginalized groups, essentialization of identities, institutionalization of the "different and unequal," and hierarchical and coerced segregation (Yiftachel 2001).

In a similar fashion, Marik Shtern and Haim Yacobi (2019) suggest that any reading of Jerusalem demands attention to forces that do not necessarily correlate with neoliberal rationality in the context of state rescaling and globalization. This continues to flesh out the role that difference and its geographical expression play in smoothing and justifying neoliberal urban governance and begin to develop counter-geographies that link up the margins of the Global North and South. Today, however, planning and territorial appropriation in Jerusalem is transferred by the state to its agents, such as right-wing radical organizations like Ateret Cohanim, which claims to be "the leading urban land reclamation organization in Jerusalem, which has been working for over 40 years to restore Jewish life in the heart of ancient Jerusalem" (Jerusalem Chai 2021) or Elad, a right-wing nongovernmental organization (NGO) that is heavily involved in the Judaization of the Palestinian neighborhood and archaeological site in Silwan (Yacobi 2018). An additional example is provided by Michal Braier and Haim Yacobi (2017), who examine the production of dwelling configurations that have developed concurrently in Jerusalem over the last two decades against a background of the continued colonization of the city's spaces on the one hand and of the growing liberalization of planning processes on the other hand. Braier and Yacobi conclude that the privatization of space and spatial planning in Jerusalem is integrated into and complements the older patterns of organizing the ethno-national territory.

We agree, for example, that "creeping apartheid" is a useful analytical term. However, we are not sure whether apartheid itself, as a spatio-political category, has received sufficient critical examination. While apartheid operates as a system of divisions driving apart communities, its ability to endure as a regime depends on variegated modes of governance that foment integration—albeit extremely unequally—of the polity. Paradoxically, *apartheid exists in a system of governance (such as in Jerusalem) that operates through the production of constant divisions while seeking to spatially unite the city into a governable cohesive territory.* Thus, and similar to Hart (2008), we propose that the city is the main site where the multiplicity of neoliberalism needs to be understood as a political project that can transcend class projects, combine different forms of government rationalities, and articulate several ethno-racial narratives. Following this argument, we can perhaps better articulate how neoliberalism operates to bolster neo-apartheid. Our claim here is not that the state simply recedes, allowing market forces operating beyond its control to take hold; rather, the politics of (neo-)apartheid—facilitated by the settler colonial logic shaping the city as a node within the overall spatial matrix and in which the state remains a powerful actor—are being reorganized.

Consequently, we explore how Palestinians encounter apartheid not as a coherent form of control that operates to produce a divided polity but as a multiplicity of relational manifestations—that is, a neo-apartheid reality that is constituted by different power relations operating through interacting scales (neighborhood, city, state), logics (colonial, neoliberal, national), and physical structures (road networks, checkpoints, settlements). By carefully considering these multiple manifestations, we can also discuss the encounters that produce the complex realities that Palestinians and Israelis experience and reshape (Joronen 2019).

The Production of a Neo-Apartheid City

> What a glorious day—remember this moment! We are in
> Jerusalem, and we are here to stay, protected by the great
> soldiers of the IDF [Israel Defense Forces] who are protecting
> the borders of our state as we speak today. Jerusalem is and
> will always be the capital of the Jewish people, a city reunified
> so as never again to be divided. . . . Our people's unparalleled
> affinity to Jerusalem has spanned thousands of years, and is
> the basis of our national renaissance.
> —BENJAMIN NETANYAHU, May 14, 2018

Israeli prime minister Benjamin Netanyahu delivered these words as the Trump administration opened the new U.S. Embassy in Jerusalem amid fierce Palestinian protest in the Gaza Strip that resulted in multiple civilian casualties. Netanyahu's statement expresses the mainstream Israeli understanding of the city as "unified Jerusalem," a fixed territorial urban space and given subject of Israeli sovereignty and aspirations. In fact, the city is manufactured continuously by geopolitical practices including a military occupation and colonial planning that are mobilized to expand and fortify the Jewish population of and in the city at the expense of its Palestinian residents. We suggest reading these practices as territorial and scalar efforts to fashion a unified regime of separation between the different populations inhabiting the city.

Netanyahu's words should be read alongside current literatures (Abowd 2014; Dumper 2014; Jadallah 2014; Pullan et al. 2013) that analyze the urban dynamics in the city since its occupation in June 1967. Following the occupation, Israel began to reshape the city's urban territory, immediately annexing around seventy square kilometers of adjacent Palestinian villages to

Jerusalem and transforming them into urban neighborhoods, most usually referred to as East Jerusalem. In doing so, Jerusalem absorbed sixty-nine thousand Palestinians, who then became 26 percent of the city's population (today Palestinians compose 38 percent of Jerusalem's population). From 1967, and despite international objections, the Israeli government applied Israeli law to East Jerusalem and annexed 38 percent of Palestinian land to declare the city its unified capital. The sovereign annexation was enabled by applying the municipal regulation of Palestinian space—that is, by altering the status of Palestinians living in the city to "official residents" and giving them blue identity cards, which differ from the green ones issued in the West Bank and those held by Palestinian citizens of Israel (Tawil-Souri 2017, 60–61). The Palestinian residents of Jerusalem could participate in municipal elections but not vote for the Israeli parliament. Therefore, these territorial and scalar moves—that is, the annexation of land and the application of urban regulations to govern this land, respectively—produced the new city of a unified Jerusalem. It is within this "unified" Jerusalem that apartheid became a dominant form of political control.

In 1972 the Jerusalem municipality, backed by the Israeli Knesset, decided to maintain a demographic Jewish–Palestinian ratio of 73.5 percent to 26.5 percent, respectively, and expropriated twenty-six square kilometers in East Jerusalem for the purpose of building Jewish neighborhoods. In this regard, both state and city governments have persistently pursued the same general policy of the Judaization of Jerusalem—that is, the expansion of Jewish political, territorial, demographic, and economic control. From a planning perspective, this stage is characterized by the construction of settlements ("satellite neighborhoods") in East Jerusalem and by an extensive building of infrastructure (Nasrallah 2014; Nolte and Yacobi 2015; Pullan et al. 2007).

While development was an effective tool for Judaizing the city, de-development (Roy 1995) served as a complementary step; applied toward Palestinians, it took the form of a series of master plans that limited the growth of Palestinian neighborhoods (Jabareen 2015). By "de-development," we refer to the concentrated effort to maintain Palestinians' living space at a constant state of disadvantage in relation to Jerusalem's urban environment, which is mostly populated by Jewish residents. In other words, the "unification" of the city produces two distinct territories: one that is hyperdeveloped; the other, de-developed. This goal is achieved by what Braier and Yacobi (2017) has highlighted as the connection between the "hyper-planned" West Jerusalem built environment and the "unplanned" Palestinian neighborhoods of East Jerusalem. Though they seem antithetical to each other, both are outcomes of the privatization of space and spatial planning that are integrated into and complement the colonial patterns involved with organizing Jerusalem's space.

To give an illustrative example of this process, only 64 percent of East Jerusalem's Palestinian households are connected to the city's water system, and the area lacks approximately thirty kilometers of sewage pipes. The Israeli planning apparatus, backed by the Ministry of Internal Affairs and the municipality, also established five national parks and zoned at least 40 percent of East Jerusalem as open green spaces where Palestinian development is forbidden. Only 15 percent of East Jerusalem—and just 8.5 percent of the whole city—is allocated for Palestinian development. East Jerusalem's Palestinian neighborhoods—to repeat: where 38 percent of the city's population lives—are allocated just 1 *percent* of the municipality's sanitation budget. Furthermore, Palestinian neighborhoods are frequently targeted by Israeli security forces that raid houses, demolish buildings, and incarcerate residents (Nasrallah 2014; Shalhoub-Kerkovian and Busbridge 2014; Shlomo 2016). The state of de-development facilitates a political infrastructure of division that can be read as both territorial and scalar mechanisms of geopolitical separation. It separates Jerusalem's urban environment based on ethno-national identification and has severed the city from its immediate Palestinian surroundings to annex and unify it with the territory of the Israeli state (Abowd 2014; Jadallah 2014).

Within the context of Israel's overall policies, Jerusalem was to become a singular urban node with minimal access to Palestinian space beyond its metropolitan space. Israel splintered Palestinian space in the West Bank with the construction of the wall in 2002, effectively annexing another 160 square kilometers of the occupied territories in addition to the area annexed in the 1967 occupation of East Jerusalem. The barrier enforces Israel's de facto political border in Jerusalem, transforming it into the largest city in Israel, and is part of the spatial matrix that fragments Palestinian space, rendering Palestinian spaces precarious both inside Jerusalem and on its peripheries (Joronen 2019). Jerusalem emerges as a spatially segregated—or apartheid—city within a wider regime that overtly operates to facilitate spatial separation between different parts of Palestinian society. In reference to South African–apartheid urban planning (Maylam 1995), the route of the Israeli separation barrier restricts the movement of Palestinians between the walled city and the Palestinian hinterland.

Thus, at the territorial level, the wall disrupts the geographic continuum and functional integration of Palestinian neighborhoods, isolating them from their hinterland. It allows Israeli Jews to control the vast majority of territory and resources in the Jerusalem metropolitan area, while Palestinians are confined to disjointed enclaves without real sovereignty or control over their movement and natural resources.

At the scalar level, Israel deployed two different legal frameworks with two populations that share the same space. Palestinians living in Jerusalem are entitled to urban residency rights and can apply for citizenship, but as noncitizens, their residency can be revoked as they need to prove that Jerusalem is their "center of life" (see Jefferis 2012a, 2012b).[1] Palestinians who became Jerusalemites as their homes were incorporated into the city thus have been "foreignized" from their own surroundings and Palestinian neighborhoods. Furthermore, the wall reproduces the scalar relations upon which Palestinians' presence in the city is predicated. To remain part of the city, to maintain the limited privileges this urban citizenship awards, and, perhaps, to be able to claim full Israeli state citizenship, Palestinians must cling to their territorial location in and of the city. If, for instance, they choose to move to the West Bank, which is part of (the now completely splintered) Palestinian space, they will become foreigners to the city and join those without entitlement to any form of (Israeli) welfare privileges. The wall thus reaffirms both the territorial and the scalar elements of urban apartheid that produce Jerusalem as a unified city.

YACOBI AND RAM

Within the context of Israel's separation regime, Palestinians living in Jerusalem have become a category of their own, or a community that the state awards the special privilege of having a voice in municipal elections and recognizes as having a limited set of residency rights (Avni et al. 2022). In other words, *the apartheid state consists of the urban medium to differentiate between various Palestinian populations*—in this case, those who live in the city and those who live in the rest of the West Bank. East Jerusalem thus has become a differently occupied Palestinian territory. A discussion of Jerusalem's urban apartheid helps us to better understand the variegated and multiple meanings of apartheid in Palestine/Israel. It is a system that differs from one spatial formation to the other and shapes them in accordance to the particular context in which it is deployed. Nevertheless, the main binding logic—to ensure Jewish dominance over Palestinians—maintains throughout the area Israel controls.

Let us briefly reiterate our main argument: Israel's apartheid regime functions through spatial and scalar properties that organize the forms of governance the state deploys to control Jerusalem's urban space and Palestinian population. The city of Jerusalem awards Palestinians, who are identified by the state as urban residents, some form of legal protection. At the same time, the urban space is formed through the physical separation of the city from the rest of Palestinian territory. The reality of urban citizenship on the one hand and of territorial separation on the other reveals the messy existence of neo-apartheid and of Jerusalem as a neo-apartheid city.

In many ways, the urban processes specific to Jerusalem that we describe here resemble—though do not replicate—the South African apartheid system, where the state had a central and active role. In Jerusalem, too, a resident's rights and opportunities are determined, first and foremost, by their ethnicity, which is politically designated as a form of nationality ("Jewish" or "Arab"). Ethnicity in Palestine/Israel substitutes the role of race yet has the same function within the separation regime. The state makes a continuous, concerted effort to regulate one's mobility and to bring about a total separation between Israeli Jews and Palestinians in the spheres of housing, work, politics, and culture. However, while the apartheid state

4. "Do Not Sell Your House to Palestinians!" Courtesy of the author.

plays an active role in enforcing urban division and inequality (which shape Jerusalem's urban space through long-established forms of separation), in recent years novel practices—identified in the city's housing dynamics, among other areas—have set about rearranging the city's space, creating new forms of division. On the surface, they can be understood as "cracks" in the colonial project, as neutral development or infrastructure projects, or as familiar global-urban trends (Boano and Martén 2013). As we illustrate in the following section, these recent processes taking place in Jerusalem, in effect, reconstruct the city's colonial infrastructure as one facilitating a novel, and more radical, form of urban separation, one that we understand as indicative of the neo-apartheid city.

Banality and Urban Neo-Apartheid

Urban apartheid processes are advanced through seemingly "banal" acts, such as those involved in city planning, infrastructure provision,

YACOBI AND RAM

or housing construction. As already noted by Michael Billig (1995), territorialization is achieved through mundane actions that accentuate the ways by which everyday expressions construct geographical imagination, national boundaries, and jurisdictions. In the current discussion, the notion of banality relates to the question of personal relocation, with people moving around the city to look for better or more appropriate accommodations. In the apartheid city, such movements form a dynamic of colonial encounters between the different groups living in the city; these encounters expose the working mechanisms of Jerusalem's neo-apartheid regime. They can be clearly gathered from the activities of Jerusalem's housing sector, where the dual processes of house demolition and settlement development contribute to Israel's determination to gain and maintain demographic control in Jerusalem (Abowd 2014; Bimkom 2013; Braier and Yacobi 2017).

Yet, we would suggest that an additional phenomenon should also be considered—namely, the internal movement of Palestinians into "satellite Jewish neighborhoods." These areas are, arguably, the most "normalized" Jewish colonies (e.g., Talpiot-Mizrach, French Hill, Gilo, and Ramot, among others) in the sense that they are considered by their inhabitants, as well as in Israeli public discourse, as mainstream and apolitical. In recent years, these satellite neighborhoods have been undergoing a process of demographic transformation and have experienced an influx of Palestinians, both those with Israeli citizenship and those with Jerusalem residency certificates. Palestinians are moving to these areas because of the housing shortages created following the erection of the separation wall and the exclusionary planning against Palestinian housing construction (Yacobi and Pullan 2014; Shtern and Yacobi 2019). This phenomenon, according to Pullan and Yacobi (2017), highlights the paradox of the neo-apartheid city in an apartheid state. On the one hand, the Israeli settlements in East Jerusalem were planned, designed, and marketed as part of the attempt to Judaize the city; on the other hand, Palestinians who move to districts such as French Hill or Pisgat Zeev cross an invisible boundary that separates the colonized and the colonizers.[2]

5. A gated Israeli settlement in the Palestinian neighborhood/village of Jabel Mukaber in southern East Jerusalem. Courtesy of the author.

While Palestinians are moving into Jewish neighborhoods, right-wing NGOs have orchestrated the movement of Jewish settlers into the heart of Palestinian East Jerusalem neighborhoods. This process challenges in many ways the notion of clear-cut, separated urban spaces and reorganizes colonized space as a place shared—antagonistically, unevenly—by the two populations.

The "banal" colonization of East Jerusalem is usually understood as a static phenomenon, overlooking the microscale analysis of everyday life in the city and its effect on urban praxis. We would like to point out a more nuanced understanding of the urban dynamics at play by looking at a set of inversions, such as Palestinians moving to dwell in neighborhoods that were planned as Jewish colonies.

However, we cannot simply juxtapose Palestinian "movement" into Israeli settlements with that of Israelis into Palestinian neighborhoods. When

YACOBI AND RAM

Israelis (Jews) move into Palestinian neighborhoods of Jerusalem, they do so with the support and blessing of the state, and their entrance is enabled by a network of private companies, military and security operators, and legal protections that the state and the Jerusalem's municipality award. Such movement is an urban colonization that unfolds from the level of the individuals who seize Palestinian homes to that of NGOs to which the state delegates responsibility to ensure this colonization will be successful. Palestinians, however, move into Israeli settlements mostly as individuals, looking for better opportunities and possibly improved lifestyles. Like Israeli Jews who move to Palestinian neighborhoods, they maintain their political status, but unlike Israeli Jews, this status results in their precarious state of living. Thus, Israelis who move to Palestinian neighborhoods bring the state with them, while Palestinians who move to Israeli settlements do so at the risk of encountering that very state. This dynamic forms the inverted relationship between Palestinian movement to that of Israeli colonization as a paradoxical and messy phenomenon.

Palestinian residents of these neighborhoods relocate there for prosaic—or "apolitical"—reasons, for instance, to improve their living standards. Yet, at the same time, their movement is part of the territorial struggle for control over the city (Yacobi and Pullan 2014). Palestinians who move from East Jerusalem to the city's Jewish settlement neighborhoods are still urban denizens. The elements of the regime operating under the logic of the private market enable free movement, but they also coalesce with the juridical infrastructure that maintains the city's Palestinian population in a status quo of inherent inequality. The Jewish population in East Jerusalem organizes itself through a private network of contractors who support the transformation of the apartheid regime from one dominated by the state to one in which forces operate in the name of the state.

The attempt to politically and territorially annex East Jerusalem makes it harder to fully Judaize it. On the one hand are the territorial and scalar mechanisms that the apartheid state put in place to enforce division: the annexation of space, the splintering of existing communities from the rest of Palestinian territory, and the urban citizenship for Palestinians living in these segmented areas. On the other hand is the dynamic of the neo-apartheid city that enables movement and mobility, and is reformed by private market forces that shape new forms of political interfaces—that is, the movement of Palestinian urban denizens into the territorial nodes, or the Jewish urban neighborhoods, that were erected to ensure state control of the city.

Concluding Words

> The terror attack in Jerusalem on Wednesday night should
> not have surprised anyone. After all, two nations live in the
> Pretoria of the State of Israel. Unlike the other occupied
> areas, there is supposed to be a certain equality between the
> two peoples: blue ID cards available for everybody, freedom
> of movement, property tax payable to the municipality,
> national insurance—Israelis all. But Jerusalem is engulfed by
> lies. It has become the Israeli capital of apartheid.
> —LEVY 2017

Throughout this chapter, we have explored the emergence of the neo-apartheid urban regime in Jerusalem. We chose to focus on Jerusalem as a case that merits such an investigation as several important elements feeding the regime cohabit its urban environment. The contemporary version of this ancient and contested city is planned as a colonial locus, and a significant portion of its Palestinian population is excluded from the state that controls it; yet, these Palestinians are included within its fragmented urban fabric as residents. Hence, Jerusalem's history of domination based on racial categorization resonates and shapes the city to this day. We conclude by evaluating the effect of Israel's separation strategies (that are seldom explained as official policies) as the foundation of an apartheid state in the city. Israel's separation regime explicitly aims not to be straightforward and operates covertly rather than overtly.

As discussed throughout this chapter, the state's actions and policies (such as the erection of the separation wall for "security" reasons or the

YACOBI AND RAM

evolving neoliberal economy and its labor exploitation) create an urban regime that aims to maintain division and socioeconomic hierarchies. In parallel, the urban dynamics of living in the city and the separation tactics used to isolate Jerusalem from the West Bank, such as the construction of the wall, have paradoxically led to growing encounters between Palestinian and Israeli Jerusalemites. This paradox leads to the question: What is at stake in the dynamic we portray, especially against the seeming totality of the Israeli settler colonial project and its apparent success in bringing East Jerusalem under domination while separating it from the West Bank and, in the process, splintering the Palestinian lived environment?

Our aim is to think of the evolution of apartheid in the city as a dominant form of colonial governance upon which the settler colonial project is predicated. First, we delineated the materialization of apartheid, not necessarily as a clear-cut rule emanating from a centralized source but rather as a multisite and multi-scalar project of domination. Second, we noted the particular urban traits of the project to illustrate how the city is imbricated into the rationalities that guide apartheid regimes. Third, we delineated how a novel materialization of the apartheid regime, fueled by neo-liberal logic, produces spheres that become "open" for Palestinians while the very space for Palestinians in the city becomes enclosed, curtailed, and increasingly under siege.

To a certain extent, our discussion also draws from recent critical interventions in conceptualizing the postcolonial moment and the meaning of decolonization (Mbembe 2021). Jerusalem is a messy project that operates on various scales that both contrast and intersect. To think of encounters in the neo-apartheid city is to consider how the minute, everyday moments upon which the separation regime and the mechanisms of governance in the city are predicated can be ruptured and reaffirmed. What emancipatory powers can we identify in the neo-apartheid city? It is a complex question. To what degree does the movement of Palestinians into Jewish urban settlements in the city truly enable mobility and rupture the settler colonial reality on the ground? At the very least, it emphasizes the importance of evaluating the unintended consequences of the neoliberal ideology that dominates the urban transformation of the city and the scalar dimensions with which we evaluate the shape and form of apartheid today.

Here stand the very characteristics of the neo-apartheid city (rather than national or regional scales). The desires of the Israeli apartheid state to fully colonize the territories of East Jerusalem is in constant tension with the ongoing, increased presence of Palestinian inhabitants in everyday life within these territories. Such tension, stemming from the very nature of the city (such as density, shared infrastructure, involuntary encounters in public spaces), is expressed in individuals' aspirations to improve their housing conditions, secure employment, use urban services, or even to consume goods. Importantly, Palestinians with Israeli citizenship who can freely move within Israel are also migrating into other cities that were planned as Jewish strongholds as part of the colonial struggle over space. In such cases, these citizen Palestinians encounter various challenges from the urban authorities of these cities (Blatman-Thomas 2017). Therefore, the dynamic in Jerusalem should be placed within the larger context of reorganizing the urban and the territorial in Palestine/Israel.

This is, indeed, the paradox of colonial urbanism in Jerusalem. The forceful effect of the banalization of occupation was orchestrated by Israeli law, planning, and state regulations that privilege Jewish citizens (Shtern and Yacobi 2019). Importantly and in line with Yacobi and Pullan (2014), it would be misleading to idealize such a dynamic, which is based on asymmetric power relations and relies on the possibilities offered by what is considered a "free market," as a vehicle for Palestinians to achieve their right to the city. Apartheid in Jerusalem comes into full view via an analysis of movements between the level of the state to that of the city and emerges as a formation of relations between new apparatuses of territorial management and colonization.

Notes

1. From 1967 Israel revoked the status of at least 14,595 Palestinians from East Jerusalem. Authorities have justified most revocations based on a failure to prove a "center of life" in Jerusalem. The center-of-life policy pushes Palestinians to leave Jerusalem

in what are described as "forcible transfers." For more details, see Human Rights Watch 2017.

2. Official data indicates that in 2015, the number of inhabitants in the French Hill settlement neighborhood was 7,241, of which 78 percent were Jewish, 18 percent were Arabs (Muslim, Christians, and Druze), and 4 percent were non-Arab Christians and others (Israeli Central Bureau of Statistics 2017). For a detailed discussion, see Abowd 2007; and Shtern and Yacobi 2019.

References

Abowd, T. P. 2007. "National Boundaries, Colonized Spaces: The Gendered Politics of Residential Life in Contemporary Jerusalem." *Anthropological Quarterly* 80 (4): 997–1034.

———. 2014. *Colonial Jerusalem: The Spatial Construction of Identity and Difference in a City of Myth, 1948–2012*. Syracuse: Syracuse University Press.

Abu-Lughod, J. L. 1981. *Rabat: Urban Apartheid in Morocco*. Princeton: Princeton University Press.

Avni, N., N. Brenner, D. Miodownik, and G. Rosen. 2022. "Limited Urban Citizenship: The Case of Community Councils in East Jerusalem." *Urban Geography* 43 (4): 546–66.

Besteman, C. 2020. *Militarized Global Apartheid*. Durham NC: Duke University Press.

Billig, Michael. 1995. *Banal Nationalism*. London: Sage.

Bimkom. 2013. *Survey of Palestinian Neighborhoods in East Jerusalem: Planning Problems and Opportunities*. Jerusalem: Bimkom.

Blatman-Thomas, N. 2014. *Trapped by Planning: Israeli Policy, Planning and Development in the Palestinian Neighborhoods of East Jerusalem*. Jerusalem: Bimkom.

———. 2017. "Commuting for Rights: Circular Mobilities and Regional Identities of Palestinians in a Jewish-Israeli Town." *Geoforum* 78:22–32.

Boano, C. 2016. "Jerusalem as a Paradigm: Agamben's 'Whatever Urbanism' to Rescue Urban Exceptionalism." *City* 20 (3): 455–71.

Boano, C., and R. Martén. 2013. "Agamben's Urbanism of Exception: Jerusalem's Border Mechanics and Biopolitical Strongholds." *Cities* 34 (1): 6–17.

Bollens, S. A. 1998. "Urban Planning amidst Ethnic Conflict: Jerusalem and Johannesburg." *Urban Studies* 35:729–50.

Braier, Michal, and Haim Yacobi. 2017. "The Planned, the Unplanned and the Hyper-Planned: Dwelling in Contemporary Jerusalem." *Planning Theory and Practice* 18 (1): 109–24.

Brown, W. 2019. *In the Ruins of Neoliberalism: The Rise of Antidemocratic Politics in the West*. New York: Columbia University Press.

B'tselem. 2021. "A Regime of Jewish Supremacy from the Jordan River to the Mediterranean Sea: This Is Apartheid." January 12. https://www.btselem.org/publications/fulltext /202101_this_is_apartheid.

Cesari, C. 2019. *Heritage and the Cultural Struggle for Palestine*. Stanford: Stanford University Press.

Clarno, A. 2017. *Neoliberal Apartheid: Palestine/Israel and South Africa after 1994*. Chicago: University of Chicago Press.

Delaney, D. 1997. "The Political Construction of Scale." *Political Geography* 16 (2): 93–97.

Dubow, S. 2014. *Apartheid, 1948–1994*. Oxford: Oxford University Press.

Dumper, M. 2014. *Jerusalem Unbound: Geography, History, and the Future of the Holy City*. New York: Columbia University Press.

Economic and Social Commission for Western Asia (ESCWA). 2017. *Israeli Practices towards the Palestinian People and the Question of Apartheid*. Beirut: United Nations.

Ellis, D. 2019. "Apartheid." *Israel Studies* 24 (2): 63–72.

Erakat, N. 2019. *Justice for Some: Law and the Question of Palestine*. Stanford: Stanford University Press.

Gordon, N. 2009. *Israel's Occupation*. Berkeley: University California Press.

Graham, S. 2003. "Lessons in Urbicide." *New Left Review* 19:63–77.

Griffiths, M., and A. Brooks. 2022. "A Relational Comparison: The Gendered Effects of Cross-Border Work in Palestine within a Global Frame." *Annals of the American Association of Geographers* 112 (6): 1761–76. https://doi.org/10.1080/24694452.2021.2019572.

Haddad, T. 2018. *Palestine Ltd.: Neoliberalism and Nationalism in the Occupied Territory*. SOAS Palestine Studies. New York: Bloomsbury.

Hart, G. 2002. *Disabling Globalization: Places of Power in Post-Apartheid South Africa*. Berkeley: University of California Press.

———. 2008. "The Provocations of Neoliberalism: Contesting the Nation and Liberation after Apartheid." *Antipode* 40 (4): 678–705.

Human Rights Watch. 2017. "Israel: Jerusalem Palestinians Stripped of Status." August 8. https://www.hrw.org/news/2017/08/08/israel-jerusalem-palestinians-stripped-status.

Israeli Central Bureau of Statistics. 2017. *Jerusalem Population by Sub-Quarter and Religion, 2015*. Unpublished data (https://www.cbs.gov.il/en/Pages/default.aspx).

Jabareen, Y. 2010. "The Politics of State Planning in Achieving Geopolitical Ends: The Case of the Recent Master Plan for Jerusalem." *International Development Planning Review* 32 (1): 27–43.

———. 2017. "The Right to Space Production and the Right to Necessity: Insurgent versus Legal Rights of Palestinians in Jerusalem." *Planning Theory* 16 (1): 6–31.

Jadallah, D. 2014. "Colonialist Construction in the Urban Space of Jerusalem." *Middle East Journal* 68 (1): 77–98.

Jefferis, D. C. 2012a. "The 'Center of Life' Policy: Institutionalizing Statelessness in East Jerusalem." *Jerusalem Quarterly* 50:94–103.

———. 2012b. "Institutionalizing Statelessness: The Revocation of Residency Rights of Palestinians in East Jerusalem." *International Journal of Refugee Law* 24 (2): 202–30.

Jerusalem Chai. 2021. "Returning, Reclaiming, and Rebuilding a United Jerusalem." https://www.ateretcohanim.org.

Jonas, A. E. G. 2006. "Pro Scale: Further Reflections on the 'Scale Debate' in Human Geography." *Transactions of the Institute of British Geographers* 31 (3): 399–406.

Joronen, M. 2019. "Negotiating Colonial Violence: Spaces of Precarisation in Palestine." *Antipode* 51 (3): 838–57.

Kovel, J. 2007. *Overcoming Zionism: Creating a Single Democratic State in Palestine/Israel.* Ann Arbor: University of Michigan Press.

Levy, G. 2017. "Jerusalem, the Capital of Apartheid, Awaits the Uprising." *Haaretz*, October 23. https://www.haaretz.com/opinion/.premium-jerusalem-the-capital-of-apartheid -1.5318736.

Makdisi, S. 2018. "Apartheid / Apartheid / [ ]." *Critical Inquiry* 44 (2): 304–30.

Marshall, M. 1995. "Rethinking the Palestine Question: The Apartheid Paradigm." *Journal of Palestine Studies* 25 (1): 15–22.

Marston, S. A., J. P. Jones III, and K. Woodward. 2005. "Human Geography without Scale." *Transactions of the Institute of British Geographers* 30 (4): 416–32.

Massey, D., and N. A. Denton. 1993. *American Apartheid.* Cambridge MA: Harvard University Press.

Maylam, P. 1995. "Explaining the Apartheid City: 20 Years of South African Urban Historiography." *Journal of Southern African Studies* 21 (1): 19–38.

Mbembe, A. 2003. "Necropolitics." *Public Culture* 15 (1): 11–40.

——. 2021. *Out of the Dark Night.* New York: Columbia University Press.

McGahern, U. 2011. *Palestinian Christians in Israel: State Attitudes towards Non-Muslims in a Jewish State.* Oxon: Routledge.

Monterescu, D. 2017. *Jaffa Shared and Shattered Contrived Coexistence in Israel/Palestine.* Bloomington: Indiana University Press.

Nasrallah, R. 2014. "Planning the Divide: Israel's 2020 Master Plan and Its Impact on East Jerusalem." In *Decolonizing Palestinian Political Economy. Rethinking Peace and Conflict Studies*, edited by M. Turner and O. Shweiki, 158–75. London: Palgrave Macmillan.

Nogueira, A., and E. Davidson. 2012. *Roadmap to Apartheid.* Surrey: Journeyman Pictures.

Nolte, A., and H. Yacobi. 2015. "Politics, Infrastructure and Representation: The Case of Jerusalem's Light Rail." *Cities* 43:28–36.

Parnell, S., and A. Mabin. 1995. "Rethinking Urban South Africa." *Journal of Southern African Studies* 21 (1): 39–61.

Peteet, J. 2016. "The Work of Comparison: Palestine/Israel and Apartheid." *Anthropological Quarterly* 89 (1): 247–81.

Plonski, S. 2018. "Material Footprints: The Struggle for Borders by Bedouin-Palestinians in Israel." *Antipode* 50 (5): 1349–75.

Pogrund, B. 2015. "Israel Has Many Injustices. But It Is Not an Apartheid State." *The Guardian*, May 22. https://www.theguardian.com/commentisfree/2015/may/22/israel-injustices-not-apartheid-state.

Pullan, W., and H. Yacobi. 2017. "Jerusalem's Colonial Space as Paradox." In *Normalizing Occupation*, edited by M. Allegra, A. Handel, and E. Magor, 193–211. Bloomington: Indiana University Press.

Pullan, W., M. Sternberg, L. Kyriacou, C. Larkin, and M. Dumper. 2013. *The Struggle for Jerusalem's Holy Places: Radicalisation and Conflict*. London: Routledge.

Pullan, W., P. Misselwitz, R. Nasrallah, and H. Yacobi. 2007. "Jerusalem's Road 1: An Inner City Frontier?" *City* 11 (2): 176–98.

Rabie, K. 2021. *Palestine Is Throwing a Party and the Whole World Is Invited*. Durham NC: Duke University Press.

Richmond, A. 1994. *Global Apartheid: Refugees, Racism and the New World Order*. Oxford: Oxford University Press.

Roy, S. 1995. *The Gaza Strip: The Political Economy of De-development*. Washington DC: Institute for Palestine Studies.

Sabel, R. 2011. "The Campaign to Delegitimize Israel with the False Charge of Apartheid." *Jewish Political Studies Review* 23 (3/4): 18–31.

Schensul, D., and P. Heller. 2011. "Legacies, Change and Transformation in the Post-Apartheid City: Towards an Urban Sociological Cartography." *IJURR* 35 (1): 78–109.

Shalhoub-Kerkovian, N., and R. Busbridge. 2014. "(En)gendering De-development in East Jerusalem: Thinking through the 'Everyday.'" In *Decolonizing Palestinian Political Economy: Rethinking Peace and Conflict Studies*, edited by M. Turner and O. Shweiki, 77–94. London: Palgrave Macmillan.

Shlomo, O. 2016. "Between Discrimination and Stabilization: The Exceptional Governmentalities of East Jerusalem." *City* 20 (3): 428–40.

Shtern, Marik, and H Yacobi. 2019. "The Urban Geopolitics of Neighboring: Conflict, Encounter and Class in Jerusalem's Settlement/Neighborhood." *Urban Geography* 40 (4): 467–87.

Smith, D., ed. 1994. *The Apartheid City and Beyond: Urbanization and Social Change*. London: Routledge.

Soske, J., and S. Jacobs, eds. 2015. *Apartheid Israel: The Politics of an Analogy*. Chicago: Haymarket Books.

Stanley, B. 2017. "The City-Logic of Resistance: Subverting Urbicide in the Middle East City." *Journal of Peacebuilding & Development* 12 (3): 10–24.

Tatour, L. 2021. "Why Calling Israel an Apartheid State Is Not Enough." *Middle East Eye*. https://www.middleeasteye.net/opinion/why-calling-israel-apartheid-state-not-enough.

Tawil-Souri, H. 2017. "Surveillance Sublime: The Security State in Jerusalem." *Jerusalem Quarterly* 68:56–65.

Turner, M. 2019. "Fanning the Flames or a Troubling Truth? The Politics of Comparison in the Palestine/Israel Conflict." *Civil Wars* 21 (4): 489–513.

Turok, I. 2014. "South Africa's Tortured Urbanisation and the Complications of Reconstruction." In *Urban Growth in Emerging Economies*, edited by G. McGranahan and G. Martine, 143–90. London: Earthscan.

van Houtum, H. 2010. "Human Blacklisting: The Global Apartheid of the EU's External Border Regime." *Environment and Planning D: Society and Space* 28 (6): 957–76.

Weiss, Y. 2011. *A Confiscated Memory: Wadi Salib and Haifa's Lost Heritage*. New York: Columbia University Press.

Wilf, E. 2021. "How Not to Think about the Conflict." *SAPIR* 1:120–27.

Yacobi, H. 2009. *The Jewish-Arab City Spatio-politics in a Mixed Community*. London: Routledge.

———. 2015. "Review: Jerusalem: From a 'Divided' to a 'Contested' City—and Next to a Neo-Apartheid City?" *City* 19 (4): 579–84.

———. 2018. "'Silwan je t'aime': Vers une archéologie du présent." *Les Cahiers de l'Orient* 130:119–29. [In French.]

Yacobi, H., and S. Cohen, eds. 2007. *Separation: The Politics of Space in Israel*. Tel Aviv: Xargol.

Yacobi, H., and W. Pullan. 2014. "The Geopolitics of Neighbourhood: Jerusalem's Colonial Space Revisited." *Geopolitics* 19 (3): 514–39.

Yiftachel, O. 2001. "From 'Peace' to Creeping Apartheid: The Emerging Political Geography of Palestine/Israel." *Arena* 16 (3): 13–24.

———. 2006. *Ethnocracy: Land and Identity Politics in Palestine/Israel*. Philadelphia: University of Pennsylvania Press.

———. 2016. "The Aleph—Jerusalem as Critical Learning." *City* 20 (3): 483–94.

Yiftachel, O., and H. Yacobi. 2002. "Planning a Bi-National Capital: Should Jerusalem Remain United?" *Geoforum* 33 (1): 137–45.

———. 2005. "Walls, Fences and 'Creeping Apartheid' in Palestine/Israel." In *Against the Wall*, edited by M. Sorkin, 673–93. New York: New Press.

Zilbershats, Y. 2013. "Apartheid, International Law, and the Occupied Palestinian Territory: A Reply to John Dugard and John Reynolds." *European Journal of International Law* 24 (3): 915–28.

Zreik, R., and A. Dakwar. 2017. "On South Africa Then and Palestine/Israel: Apartheid and Its Conceptualisations." *Law, Society and Culture*: 185–220. [In Hebrew.]

7   Expectations to Fulfill

Anticipating the Familial Future in Palestinian Refugee Camps

Tiina Järvi

I met Rima in 2015, when she and her small daughter were visiting her parents. She had taken the short journey from a nearby Palestinian refugee camp located at the southern edge of the Lebanese coastal city of Tyre to a Palestinian gathering—or *tajamu'*, an unrecognized neighborhood outside of the official United Nations Relief and Works Agency for Palestine refugees (UNRWA) camp space (see Yassin, Stel, and Rassi 2016)—where she had grown up. I was there to visit her father, a political representative of the gathering, but I ended up chatting with Rima instead when she joined us in the salon of her parents' home. Rima had moved to the nearby camp after she married but visited her childhood home regularly. As in almost every longer encounter I had during my fieldwork, we ended up discussing the difficult conditions Palestinians faced in Lebanon and how emigration had become a prevalent way to imagine a better future. As we were talking, Rima stressed that "for us Arabs, family is very important." After a while she continued, "We would hope to stay close to our family," but she did so in an apologetic manner, with a quiet acknowledgment that many did, actually, end up leaving their families behind in Lebanon in search of better possibilities overseas.

In this chapter, I consider a specific form of encounter—that with the future. While the political futures of Palestinian refugees have been extensively explored in scholarship on Palestine (Farah 2006; Feldman 2016; Richter-Devroe 2013), here I instead concentrate on Palestinian refugees' futures in their more quotidian forms as they emerge via relations of kinship. My aim is to interrogate how familial relations, such as the closeness suggested in the discussion with Rima, emerge among Palestinian refugees in moments in which the prevalent conditions compromise the fulfilment of familial expectations. This, I claim, calls for a specific form of encounter with the future that involves anticipation. Thus, a second *cultural* sense of encounter is evoked here, whereby norms around family expectations—whether as *any* family or specifically as an often-evoked category of "Arab family" (see, e.g., Joseph 2018)—are impacted by, yet not fully confined by, the realities created by occupation, displacement, and exile. By taking such an approach, I direct attention to the familial practices of Palestinian refugees in their own right; even while refugee families are framed by Israel's colonial policies, they are not completely defined by them. Therefore, my intention is not to examine Palestinian lives as temporal encounters *within* Israeli colonialism (e.g., Griffiths and Joronen 2021) but to consider how cultural and societal expectations around family life, combined with the prolonged uncertainty and vulnerability of living in exile or under the settler colonial rule, push people toward anticipatory actions oriented to fulfill those expectations (see also Harker 2009).

On a conceptual level, this chapter contributes to the understanding of encounter in the sense of encountering temporality (Wilson 2017), as I consider *anticipation* as a form of encounter that aims to "tame" the unknowability of the future to make it correspond with the *expected*. These two "futural" modalities help articulate the ways that people—in this case, Palestinian refugees—attempt to fulfill obligations placed on them and, while doing so, face their precarious everyday conditions by predicting how things on the ground are likely to develop. This approach to the future allows us to consider how normative familial relations—*what is expected*—emerge in encounters with the future via *anticipatory* actions taken in the refugee camps where the lack of possibilities is endemic. While it would be possible to discuss familial futures also in relation to other futural modalities—for example, hope (Hage 2003; Kleist and Jansen 2016) and waiting (Hage 2009; Janeja and Bandak 2018; Peteet 2018)—it is in the entwinement between the normative and the precarities of the refugee condition that the notions of anticipation and expectation enrich our understandings. To act anticipatorily is to act with *preemption*—that is, on the basis of how situations *might* develop based on previous experiences and knowledge of the situation at hand—whereas in expecting we make an evaluation on *how things ought to be* and what *ought to happen* (see, e.g., Anderson 2010a; Bryant and Knight 2019). The focus on temporality here emerges from a base realization that so much of daily life is bound to the future, and while this notion has a certain generality, it also pertains specifically to the Palestinian refugees in Lebanon and the West Bank. Though markedly different in many respects, those contexts share a commonality with uncertainty, a feeling of lessening opportunities, and therefore a sense that undesirable outcomes might be mitigated via anticipatory actions. Hereon I suggest that among Palestinian refugee families, *that which is expected* creates a need for *anticipatory decisions and actions*.

Drawing on extensive ethnographic fieldwork with Palestinian refugees in Lebanon and the West Bank (see Järvi 2021), I address three interrelated issues: the culturally and socially enforced understandings and expectations around familial life, the conditions of refugee-ness as defined by Israeli colonialism and enduring rightlessness, and the lack of possibilities that create the need for anticipatory actions to fulfill familial expectations. As I show, for those I spent time with and spoke to during fieldwork, familial relations emerged in considerations, plans, and decisions as the future was encountered via anticipatory decisions and preparations that were seldom made individually but on the part of a family unit (see also Taraki 2006). The chapter is structured around vignettes in which my Palestinian interlocutors articulate the ways they encounter the future from the uncertainties of the present via anticipatory actions. The fieldwork, conducted between 2015 and 2019, forms the background for the themes discussed in this chapter, but I elaborate the more generally shared tropes of familial life mainly through three people, each of whom lives in a Palestinian refugee camp: Rima, Hassan, and Asma. At the time of my fieldwork, Rima was in her late twenties and lived with her husband and small daughter close to

Tyre, Lebanon; Hassan was in his forties and lived with his wife and five children at the outskirts of Dheisheh camp in the West Bank; and Asma was a nineteen-year-old, first-year university student who lived with her parents in another camp in Tyre, Lebanon. I begin the chapter by discussing expectations connected to familial relations, and how they are negotiated from the position that the refugees occupy, before then discussing how these expectations become part of the anticipatory actions taken by and within families. In this way, I aim to elaborate how the future was encountered in conditions framed by the vulnerabilities and precarities that are more broadly part of Palestinian refugees' lives in Lebanon and the West Bank.

Familial Expectations amid the Uncertainties of the Present

"We plan, but we don't know because the situation in this country is not guaranteed. You don't know what is happening tomorrow—because of the occupation. You have to plan for every day and every week and every year and every ten years, as people do but you don't know what will happen . . . the situation in this country is becoming more difficult and difficult."

In 2016 this was how Hassan from Dheisheh, a camp in the southern edge of Bethlehem, described the uncertainties that Israel's colonial practices create in the West Bank. We were sitting outside the home to which he had moved with his wife and five children less than a year before from a more confined apartment inside the camp. I had come to know Hassan through his younger brother, who had brought me to visit Hassan's family, and I ended up returning time and again during my fieldwork to chat, do laundry, and share iftar with them. On that particular occasion, Hassan described how the Israeli regime of control made it impossible to predict what the future might bring for him and his family but how they still had to prepare to their best capabilities. That was why he and his wife, Lama, for example, had taken three separate loans to buy land and build a house to provide a good environment for their children to grow up in. They wanted to ensure their children could continue to live in Palestine and have a good start in their lives even when Israeli occupation could easily render all such attempts futile. They were fully aware that life under occupation is difficult and reduces opportunities; therefore, they did their best to provide all the possibilities they could for their children to build their futures. Lama and Hassan felt strongly that it was their obligation to do so.

The discussion in this section emerges from an ethnography with Palestinian refugees in Lebanon and the West Bank conducted between 2015 and 2019, and I elaborate on the familial expectations at play in the lives of Palestinian refugees and the contexts in which they were acted upon. While different, both the West Bank and Lebanon can be considered as being in a state that Henrik Vigh (2011, 98) names "social hyper-vigilance": a "space of turmoil and uncertainty where society no longer is seen as moving toward a calm and coherent future but instead is viewed as being caught in a state of insecurity and uncertainty." By elaborating on familial expectations and the contexts in which Palestinian refugees try to reach them, I build an argument for considering anticipation as a form of encounter that aims to mitigate the unpredictability of the future and to secure the fulfillment of the expected.

Expectation connotes with how things *should* be, as "expectation is the ground on which the normative emerges" (Bryant and Knight 2019, 63–64). It simultaneously defines the "futurality of the future" by revealing its volatility: life might not, in the end, proceed as expected, and the future always retains its distance and is not entirely pulled into the present (Bryant and Knight 2019, 58; see also Koselleck 2004, 259). As the future-producing nature of expectation creates a sense of how things ought to be, it can reveal how familial relationalities are present in the ways that people prepare and plan. It does not, however, only reveal what *should* be but also what *could* be; expectation reveals wants and desires and thus functions as an expression of hope and hopefulness (Pijpers 2016; Weszkalnys 2008).

In a modality of *should*, the normative forms of familial life emerge inter alia in the obligations members of the family are expected to fulfill. While they should not be taken as essentialist, these obligations are nevertheless usually culturally specific in degree and quality, and in the context of my Palestinian interlocutors, they are also clearly gendered and tied to the generational position one occupies in the family. An example:

a friend and I were returning home from a walk when we passed by her father's workshop, exchanged greetings, and continued toward the family home. As we made our way, I asked my friend about her father's working situation, if he was doing well, and whether he had enough customers to earn a living for the family. I assumed that as the only breadwinner in a family with six children, he might find it challenging at times to bring in enough income for the household. To my surprise, my friend simply—and rather flatly—stated that her farther is obliged to work. I first found the answer a bit odd as it completely bypassed the limited control he has over his wage-earning situation. Yet, considered from the perspective of familial relatedness and the obligations it implies, my friend was merely (re)articulating the normative position her father occupied: as a husband and father, he was expected to provide for the entire family (see also Kelly 2008). In fact, one of the generally shared assumptions that Suad Joseph (2018) recognizes as associated with Arab families is a strong moral obligation between members of families. Joseph has elaborated the "care/control paradigm" specifically in the context of Lebanon, yet she maintains those same relationalities can be found also in other Arab countries. It defines what she calls "the kin contract," and it "raises expectations that kin care for each other, provide for each other, protect each other, love each other—above all others" (Joseph 2005, 156).

I repeatedly heard similar statements during the time I spent in Palestinian refugee camps: fathers are obliged to work, and parents should be able to provide a solid base for their children to build their futures. These sentiments emerged not only in the actions that parents took to fulfill their roles—helping to build an apartment, finding a way to emigrate, paying university tuition fees, or using connections to secure employment—but also in the gossiping and disapproval of others when someone failed to do so. This creates gendered horizons of expectations: men have the economic burden to provide and thus face, for example, the conditions of unemployment more acutely than women, whose role as a provider has more to do with nurturing and facilitating their children's opportunities and for whom the prevalent conditions usually seem more limiting when they hoped to achieve things in life other than marriage and motherhood (see also Allan 2021). Parents' obligations toward their children are, however, only one dimension of familial expectations, as children's obligations toward their parents and siblings also press on the ways that everyday lives are lived, futures are expected, and, inevitably, disapprovals are aired. The family, in fact, functions as a main locus of future making—first, as a progenitor of expectation and, second, as a collective forum of anticipatory action toward fulfilling that expectation.

The centrality of the family in future making was emphasized most pointedly by the father of my host family in Lebanon, Khalid. We were sitting on the balcony on a hot summer's evening when he explained what he considered the foundational aspects of his familial life. In his usual manner, he wanted to make me understand how *their* lifeworld differed from what he associated with *mine*—the Western, individualistic culture in which he placed me. We had been discussing his children's situation: his eldest son had recently emigrated to Germany, and his eldest daughter had graduated from university and was considering her next steps. He introduced the topic by stating that the family is "like a lock" and that he, his wife, and his children were tied together and hence functioned as a whole. When a decision concerning a member of the family needed to be made, such as a decision to emigrate or to get married, it was always discussed and made together. Khalid placed great emphasis on (and pride in) the fact that they talked over the issue from the perspective of the family rather than leaving the person most concerned to make the decision alone. Family, for Khalid, is conceived of as an inherent connection not only by birth but also *in being*, which is reflected in actions and decisions taken in everyday life.

That the family is the unit in which decisions are made suggests how kin is intrinsic to the self (Carsten 2004) and that it contributes in significant ways to how being in the world is perceived. Familial expectations should not therefore be considered as simply imposed on a person but rather as part of their relational being. Khalid's elaboration on family life reveals both the inherent character of kin and how it founds encounters with possible futures. While familial relations could also be a burden that produces (gendered) social control and discipline, more often, especially in the context of heightened uncertainty, family is viewed as a blessing that ensures one is not alone to face life's difficulties. Simultaneously, however, and as Rima also elaborated, the ideals of family life were hard to maintain in the present conditions of the limited possibilities Palestinian refugees have to build good lives. She sighed that their situation in Lebanon caused many social problems, which manifested in the refugee families. Her job as a teacher provided a window to the effects of poverty and the lack of possibilities that her students' families struggled with and that she saw as diminishing the children's ability to concentrate and learn in school.

To comprehend how family plays out in any given context, familial life can thus productively be considered in relation to the state (Joseph 2018) and, in the case of Palestinian—and a majority of other—refugees, to the lack of a state (Harker 2012). Since 1948 the culturally and societally enforced understandings on familial expectations have been framed by the conditions of exile and displacement in the statelessness in Lebanon and, since 1967, under the military occupation in the West Bank. In the West Bank, daily life and the kinship practices it entails "are deeply marked by the struggles between a colonial regime of control and dispossession and an unfulfilled national project of independence and sovereignty" (Johnson 2006, 53). Lives are lived amid Israel's settler colonial aspirations, and future making is framed by insecurities produced by Israeli visions of settlement growth that displace Palestinians, new laws that consolidate discrimination, violations and violence that continue to go unpunished, and everyday conditions that continue to deteriorate. Living in a refugee camp has its own specificities, such as a vulnerability to Israeli incursions (regardless of which area the camp is situated) and the compromised living conditions defined by inadequate housing and crowdedness in addition to the more general and severe restrictions faced by all Palestinians in the West Bank. Family life is foreshadowed not only by the threats of physical violence that constantly force Palestinians to stay alert but also by other manifestations of Israel's colonial policies that suffocate Palestinian communities socially, politically, and economically, creating an ever-present sense of heightened uncertainty (Allabadi and Hardan 2016; Giacaman and Johnson 2013; Griffiths and Repo 2020; Taraki 2006).

In Lebanon, familial life is more generally grounded in experiences of exclusion that have both economic and social dimensions (see, e.g., Hanafi, Chaaban, and Seyfert 2012). Of all Palestinian refugee communities, Palestinians in Lebanon are notably marginalized from the surrounding society, and while their continued refugee-ness is an outcome of Israel's denial to recognize their right to return, of more immediate consequence in the everyday is how they are placed within the state of refuge. The sectarian politics of Lebanon have positioned Palestinian refugees as a hostile presence that disturbs Lebanon's delicate—and often threatened—balance of power. Palestinians have been targeted by both Israeli and Lebanese militias, camp spaces have been violated, informal Palestinian gatherings are in a permanent state of uncertainty, and lacking employment rights has resulted in poverty, which has made the refugee community extremely dependent on the underfunded Palestinian refugee agency UNRWA both as a service provider and an employer (Allan 2013; Feldman 2017; Peteet 2005; Ramadan 2009; Stel 2016). From a position already defined by their marginalization and lack of possibilities, Palestinian refugee families in Lebanon thus face severe economic hardship amid diminishing resources in the country.

Obligations delineate normative forms of familial life and connect to the future(s) as families aim to secure a situation in which they would be able to fulfill the roles that familial relatedness place on them. To grasp how the future is encountered, it is thus important to acknowledge the culturally enforced understandings on expected achievements and obligations as they express ideas of how life *should* proceed and the forms it *should* take. For Palestinian refugees such as Rima, Hassan, Khalid, and others, however, not only culturally and socially produced expectations—which are usually doomed to fall short in any situation (Sahlins 2013; Stasch 2009)—press on decisions and choice but also the significant uncertainties of refugee-ness, statelessness, and rightlessness define the ways familial futures emerge in everyday life. These conditions inherently frame Palestinians' horizons of opportunities as the basis from which life is considered, and while the conditions of Palestinian refugees in the West Bank and Lebanon differ, in both places cultural expectations are negotiated amid a lack of possibilities. Placing obstacles in the way of reaching cultural expectations inherent in familial life creates a specific condition for negotiating expected forms of being. Therefore, Rima had to consider her family's situation and possibilities not only in light of normative ideals (e.g., around a gendered role as daughter, sister, mother) but also by taking into account those ideals in the context of the harsh realities Palestinian refugees face in Lebanon. Similarly in the West Bank, Hassan could not disregard the occupation, which is ever present and affects all dimensions of life from physical movement and housing to employment and a sense of (in)security. Palestinian refugees are thus forced to negotiate between the ideals and diminishing possibilities in Lebanon and the West Bank. These conditions make gestures toward different and sometimes foreboding futures that, in turn, invite anticipation—or anticipatory decisions to act *in the present* so as to change a situation to prevent it from worsening.

Anticipating the Future

The notion of encounter has been productively developed and deployed in geographical writing where difference is central to the object of analysis (Valentine 2008; Wilson 2017). Specifically, encounter refers to an engagement across difference (Faier and Rofel 2014) that brings attention to the relational coming together in moments in which "a lack of commonality is assumed" (Wilson 2017, 454). In what follows, I draw on the idea of encounter to address a specific engagement with the future—anticipation. In expecting, the future remains distant and is thus not yet encountered; in anticipating, an encounter, which consists of anticipatory decisions and actions, does take place. In fact, anticipations draw the future to the present and even overpowers it as decisions and actions are informed by what is presumed will happen in the future (Anderson 2010a, 2010b; Choi 2015; Griffiths and Joronen 2021). Anticipation aims to "tame" "the otherness, mystery or unknowability of things to come" (Anderson 2010b, 229) and is thus a way to encounter the inherent otherness of the future or an attempt to control its unpredictability.

Rebecca Bryant (2016, 27) has elaborated that "anticipation . . . is more than simply expecting something to happen; it is the act of looking forward that also pulls me in the direction of the future and prepares the groundwork for that future to occur." It is this active engagement with the future that makes encounter a useful concept in discussing anticipatory actions, as in these moments the future becomes the other that is encountered. In this section, I first briefly address anticipation as a futural modality that encounters the future to fulfill the expected in the contexts of Palestinian refugees; then I turn to ethnographic vignettes that demonstrate what this meant in practice for refugees living in the West Bank and Lebanon. The conditions described in the previous section often render it impossible for Palestinian refugees to trust that expectations can be met. Set in this context, reaching what is expected thus necessitates making anticipatory decisions that are greatly significant for one's life (e.g., regarding education, emigration, marriage, and so forth). Palestinian refugees I met took anticipatory actions against the assumed continuation of the present rather than, for instance, against unmaterialized threats that need to be governed to secure the perpetuation of the present, as anticipation is seen, for example, by Ben Anderson (2010a). Furthermore, as Palestinian refugees are constantly forced to anticipate the deterioration of their living conditions, for them "crisis" does not constitute an event that would render it impossible to anticipate the future (Bryant 2016) but rather has turned into a chronic condition (Vigh 2008) and is thus the basis from which anticipation emerges.

Consequently, the encounter with the future arises not only from the experienced present but also from the past, which significantly affects how the refugees see the yet to come. In light of the history of refugee-ness, anticipating adversities has become the most sensible response to the situation at hand. It has become Palestinian refugees' "horizon of expectation" (Koselleck 2004, 261–62). This was vocalized in the West Bank by Nada, a woman in her early twenties, when she tiredly acknowledged that Israel imposes new restrictions every day, narrowing the horizons of possibilities for Palestinians in multiple ways. In Lebanon, it was stressed that despite their decades-long presence in the country, Palestinian refugees still have nothing, no tools to build a decent life. The future was described as bringing the worsening of conditions. "Ma fi musta'bal houn" (There is no future here) was an often-repeated sentence. These conditions do not generate a sense of trust or hopefulness for the future; instead, they foment a feeling of existential immobility and "stuckedness" (Hage 2009). Therefore, while anticipation temporally draws the future to the present, it emerges from the conditions—the chronic crisis—at hand. This is reflected in the ways that Palestinian refugees encounter the future and consider the options and possibilities they have to build and support their families in the refugee camps. Encountering the future with anticipatory actions is how many of the people I met during fieldwork—not only Rima, Hassan, and Asma—aimed to escape the present, which is in many ways defined by a lack of possibilities. Anticipation thus seeks to counter the conditions that would continue to affect their lives if they took no actions to change them.

Importantly for Palestinian refugees, anticipation is a way to reach the *expected* forms of familial being. Expectation reveals the normative by delineating *how life should be*, but it is also—crucially—the modality that can initiate change; things could be different if steps are taken in a different direction. The holding of (and onto) expectations thus assumes horizons of possibilities, that a future could be achieved, and that somewhere achieving those normative forms of being would be possible. Thus, at a threshold of expectation and anticipation, futures are encountered.

Rima

Employment forms a basis for a smooth continuity of the everyday and is crucial for the fulfillment of many familial expectations. The most obvious economic obligation is related to the role of (male) breadwinner, but having a job also reflects possibilities to live a fulfilling life more broadly. A good job and a decent salary open doors even when life in general is defined by the occupation or statelessness. However, for refugees in both the West Bank and Lebanon, reaching economic security is not an easy task. In the West Bank, the Israeli occupation has crippled Palestinian economic life and created soaring numbers of unemployment and underemployment (UNCTAD 2018). In Lebanon, Palestinian refugees are barred from working in several fields altogether, and those jobs that are within reach necessitate a work permit, which is notoriously hard to obtain (ILO 2012; PHRO 2008, 2010). Hence, fulfilling the economic dimension of familial obligations has become increasingly hard, forcing families to consider different anticipatory options. These actions are informed and prompted by compromised conditions in the present and aimed at changing the situation so that meeting normative familial obligations could become possible.

Rima's brother was one of those who had been forced to "sit at home," making him, according to his sister, "extremely frustrated." As is the case for many Palestinian *shebaab* (young men) in Lebanon, he had difficulties finding employment, working seasonally as a house painter on construction sites and mainly staying home when that work slowed in the winter months. Therefore, as is common, he opted for emigration. Emigration is never an individual endeavor but involves the family as a whole, from making the decision to its practical implementation (Doraï 2008). In Rima's brother's case, the family borrowed from relatives and friends to cover his costs, and his aim was to reach Germany, where an uncle and other relatives were already living. The deciding consideration—one that looks forward into a specific expectation of how life should be—was, Rima explained, that "[while] the situation for him [is] still somewhat easy for now because he is still single [but] if he wants to have a family, to establish a house for his family, he can't make a living for them." In Lebanon, he would not have been able to fulfill the expected role of a male breadwinner; therefore, he decided to emigrate. His journey, however, halted in Ukraine when the borders became harder to cross in 2015. The situation then became a burden for the whole family, and their father was complaining that at every turn he needed more money, which they did not have to spare.

As elsewhere, in Lebanon emigration is an extremely common answer to an experience of being tied to a place and its constraining conditions, or what Ghassan Hage (2009) has termed "stuckedness." Emigration— and the *prospect* of emigration—is infused with hopes and driven by the social imagination of a globally defined field of almost limitless possibilities (Appadurai 1996, 31). While Rima saw that her brother could possibly bear the situation because he was still single, he had joined countless others on the extremely precarious journey to Europe. He had taken this anticipatory action to counter the precarities of the future, to find better chances to build his life and reach a situation in which it would become possible to fulfill the role of a breadwinner. Actually, Rima had a similar plan to emigrate from Lebanon. She had graduated with a degree in English literature and worked in UNRWA schools but was unable to secure a permanent position and worked sporadically, filling in for others on sick and maternity leave. However, her situation was different from that of her brother's, because as a woman she was not expected to be the main income source to the family. Also, unlike her brother, she was not ready to take the dangerous journey of an irregular migrant and had applied for a green card to travel to the United States with her husband. Her will to emigrate was defined by her role as a mother, as she wanted to provide better chances for her daughter. "I'm escaping for my children" was how Rima poignantly rationalized it.

The situation of Rima's family does not only exemplify the insecurities and limitations that Palestinians face in Lebanon and the common answer to them but is also indicative of how family and familial obligations emerge and are intensified as the future looms or as it is encountered. Rima's pondering on her brother's being single demonstrates the very taken-for-granted expectations placed on a man that her brother would not be able to fulfill had he continued to live in Lebanon. Their father's complaint of the burden of having to provide money for his son, in turn, demonstrates the obligation of parents to support their children, as does Rima's hope to emigrate to provide better possibilities for her daughter. Rima's negotiations for emigration also included an acknowledgment of children's obligations toward their parents: she stressed that it would have been better to stay close to her family but simultaneously lamented that the position of Palestinian refugees in Lebanon forced them to emigrate and thus live away from parents, siblings, and other relatives.

Hassan

Children are often considered a rather self-evident embodiment of the futurity (Jefferson and Segal 2019; Spyrou 2020; Whyte, Kyaddondo, and Meinert 2014), as it is in relation to them that futures are considered emergent. Therefore, almost as a matter of course, families take anticipatory actions to secure good lives for their children, as is exemplified by Rima and her husband's wish to obtain a U.S. green card. In so doing, they reiterated expectations placed on parents: they should look after their children and provide them the best possible chances. For Hassan and his family in Dheisheh in the West Bank, this theme was prominent, for instance, when his wife, Lama, recollected how Hassan's father was unable to provide support for him and how, with their five children, Hassan now was more determined that he would do so. Hassan acknowledged that the occupation and the uncertainties it created could render planning ahead difficult, futile even; nevertheless, he aimed to provide his children the support they needed via whatever means he was able to offer. As Hassan said, "Planning for the future . . . I don't know about my children and about the future. But I will do my best to protect this [their futures]. Give them advice, support them, and try to change their view about the future. When there is an obstacle, I can ease them, I do my best with my relationships. And hopefully I'll be successful in helping them. Here you have to support your child even when he is married, because the options here are very, very few."

Lama reiterated her husband's words when she stressed that in the difficult conditions created by the occupation, it was necessary to support their children and help them have the tools to build their lives. Therefore, she and her husband had enrolled their children in a private school instead of a UNRWA school, paid university tuition fees for their eldest daughters, and, when they built a new house outside the camp, added an apartment for their eldest son and his eventual family. Hassan often stressed that the bad economic situation and high unemployment created uncertainty in the West Bank. When his eldest son turned to him with his career plans, Hassan suggested, in an anticipatory fashion, that he apply to the Palestinian National Authority's police forces, which he considered to be the only institution that could provide at least some sort of economic security for the future.

The changing conditions of refugee-ness have forced families to reconfigure ways to anticipate their children's futures. While education has provided ladders for social mobility—and Palestinian refugees have embraced the path of education with the expectation that it can enhance living conditions for the whole family (Rosenfeld 2004)—it has, for people such as Lama and Hassan, become perceived as a less reliable course toward realizing familial expectations. Hassan saw the value of education had declined from the times he was at school because it could not provide a secured path to an economically stable future. This was true also in Lebanon, where limited working rights make it seem futile to spend time studying. While education as an anticipatory action has not disappeared, its centrality as such has been diminished. Therefore, rather than supporting his son's wish to study business administration at a university and seek employment in the commercial sector, Hassan suggested they would use their "good name" to help him get into the security forces. He wanted his son to be able to "start his life normally" and "in time" instead of being stuck in endless waiting before he could start a family of his own.

Furthermore, Hassan was certain that the difficulties faced in everyday life made many consider emigration, and he supported his children precisely to allow them to continue living in the West Bank. He said he did not want his children "to think of leaving this country for another country. Because when you have problems in living, problems in housing, problems in finding a job, you start to think *why not leave and live outside*." Hassan stressed that he wanted them to stay in Palestine because "being here is a matter of resistance. . . . Israel needs this land empty." Staying on the land is, in fact, a form of *sumud* (Schiocchet 2011), or steadfastly withstanding the occupation and refugee-ness. While staying in Palestine or in the refugee camps is linked to the broader political futures of Palestinian refugees, it also has a familial dimension, as Hassan's insistence on supporting his children to make them stay demonstrated. It was the family who hoped, or at times even insisted, to keep their children close by. The possibilities to build a decent life in the West Bank were, nevertheless, generally recognized as limited. A common exchange—with vendors, taxi drivers, friends—focuses on the lack of opportunities for people in the West Bank. I especially recall a man whose children were each living in different parts of the world and who acknowledged that no matter how much he wanted his children to remain in Palestine, "there's nothing for them here."

Asma

The direction that anticipatory actions took was not always self-evident or straightforward. Multiple expectations—familial, political, and others—are at play in people's lives, and the prioritized position affects the way in which the future is encountered. Even within a familial frame, there are discrepant expectations, as becomes evident with Rima: as a daughter she wished to stay close to her parents, but as a parent she hoped to provide better chances for her own daughter. She prioritized the latter role when she applied for a U.S. green card. In Lebanon, Asma struggled precisely because she faced multiple expectations that could not be realized simultaneously. In her late teens as a first-year university student, she was at a point where she had to make decisions for her adult life, and as with a majority of people in Lebanon, emigration was an open question. But for her, the lack of possibilities in Lebanon was not the only way the future presented itself; Asma was the only child still living at home. Her brother was working in the Gulf, one of her sisters had emigrated to Germany, and another was living in Beirut with her husband. Asma felt that leaving would not be a good idea for her nor did she want to, mainly because her aging parents would then be left alone with none of their children living nearby. While families usually supported the sons' wish to emigrate—due to gendered understandings on what is "appropriate" and what familial expectations are placed on sons and daughters—in Asma's case her parents, especially her mother, insisted she should prioritize her own future and leave Lebanon. She had hoped to continue her studies after completing a bachelor's degree, and as master's programs were extremely expensive in Lebanon, her only option was to apply for a scholarship for a European university. Though her relatives had already emigrated to Europe, she did not have a desire to follow them. She spoke frankly that she had no passion for European countries and that she did not wish to live the life people lived there. For her the only reason to even visit Europe was to see her sister, whom she had not seen for a long time and missed terribly.

For Asma, anticipating the aging of her parents created expectations she could not meet were she to think only from an individual perspective. She had several examples of relatives facing difficult situations that emigration could cause, such as that of her cousin who left Lebanon "irregularly" (i.e., without travel documents) and whose risk and precarity had thus been exacerbated. If Asma ended up paperless like her cousin, then she would not be able return to Lebanon to visit her parents before gaining a regularized status in Europe, a process that can take years. As emigration has become the prevalent way to imagine a better future among the Palestinian refugees in Lebanon, many have turned to irregular routes to other countries or, once there, have overstayed their visas. They were thus unable to travel back and forth to visit their families. Contact was kept via WhatsApp and Messenger, but such forms of contact could not, naturally, replace the closeness people were used to. In this way, both those who remain and those who leave experience separation. While emigration could provide much sought-after privacy and independence with the physical distance from the often-prying family and community, it also meant those who had emigrated had to manage on their own. Emigration does often follow a preset path taken by relatives, but it also involves loneliness in the separation from immediate kin. It was, in fact, stressed that the significant relations were in Lebanon and that the familial connections and obligations they implicated would have been reasons to stay, but they were not usually enough. While the lack of possibilities was inherently linked to their position as Palestinian refugees, it was also a quality of living in Lebanon itself. Hence, many thought they had little option but to emigrate.

The ideal of closeness often conflicted with other familial obligations, and while many refugees—both men and women—stressed a desire to stay near family, the present conditions did not provide such a choice. Rather, emigration was how the anticipated precarities of the future were encountered. Families supported their children's emigration, often extensively, even when they knew that it meant extended periods apart. The desire to provide their children better opportunities outweighed the wish to keep them close. Because they knew that life both in the occupied West Bank and in Lebanon had little to offer, emigration became *an* anticipatory action for them to reach for a decent life. The parents' desire to see their children prosper, earn prestigious degrees, or just possibly find work and start a family of their own was what drove parents to support, and even encourage, their children to leave them behind.

Conclusion

At the beginning of this chapter, I proposed analyzing anticipation as a way of encountering the future when reaching the expected is compromised by the precarious conditions defined by the lack of rights and possibilities. More specifically, I brought attention to the quotidian practices of Palestinian refugees' kinship and family life, and how they and the obligations related to them emerge temporally as futural modalities of anticipation and expectation. Hence, my aim has been to interrogate how the family functions as a central component of the future, both for which and through which futures are considered. Palestinian refugees, as I have shown, often hope to build a future in which they can provide for their families, and it was their families who made plans and supported each other in reaching those futures. Such decisions and support, however, take place in a context defined by decades-long refugee-ness, statelessness, and Israel's colonial practices, as well as a deteriorating economic situation. The future was thus encountered in the discrepancy of the ideal forms of familial relatedness and the compromised everyday conditions that required actions to better the situation. In this way, anticipatory actions emerge as a way to encounter the future to reach culturally and societally expected forms of being.

It is fair to say that for Palestinian refugees in Lebanon and the West Bank, the capacities to affect the future—whether in the long term or even tomorrow—are extremely limited; thus, expectations become a complicated matter. Often the obligations of family life are referred to apologetically, as an acknowledgment of how things should be but that are simultaneously understood as hard to reach. Economic difficulties compromise opportunities to provide hoped-for standards of living, and familial proximity is sacrificed to pursue other culturally set expectations. In this sense, the particular mode of encounter with the future tells us much of the haves and have-nots of choice and future making; many Palestinians whose testimonies are included here can only dream of a situation in which they would be "able to await the future rather than having always to anticipate it" (Bryant and Knight 2019, 70). While it is entirely possible that anticipatory actions do not produce the expected outcomes—that education may not secure employment or social mobility, that building a house does not prove sufficient for starting a family, that emigration might not bring greater opportunity—families nevertheless encounter the future with the presumption that they could.

While Israel's colonial policies in themselves have not been at the forefront in this chapter—on the contrary, they have been wittingly set aside to situate Palestinian refugees' lives beyond them—they are an undeniable part of the everyday condition as practices of displacement and exclusion that shape both short- and long-term choices and opportunities. The general unknowability of the future is heightened by conditions of refugee-ness and occupation, and the rightlessness that ensues from them; thus, they not only frame but also in some ways define the culturally and societally enforced expectations that Palestinian refugees try to reach. In this complex and wider encounter between culturally shaped prospects and those curtailed and denied by Israel's colonial project, Palestinians face their own temporal encounter with the future, one that prompts a range of anticipatory decisions and actions angled toward a promise of fulfilling familial expectations.

References

Allabadi, Fadwa, and Tareq Hardan. 2016. "Marriage, Split Residency, and the Separation Wall in Jerusalem." *Jerusalem Quarterly* 65:69–85.

Allan, Diana. 2013. *Refugees of the Revolution: Experiences of Palestinian Exile*. Stanford: Stanford University Press.

———. 2021. "Mothers Gather: The Fractured Temporalities of Palestinian Motherhood." *Geografiska Annaler: Series B, Human Geography* 103 (1): 367–79.

Anderson, Ben. 2010a. "Preemption, Precaution, Preparedness: Anticipatory Action and Future Geographies." *Progress in Human Geography* 34 (6): 777–98.

———. 2010b. "Security and the Future: Anticipating the Event of Terror." *Geoforum* 41 (2): 227–35.

Appadurai, Arjun. 1996. *Modernity at Large: Cultural Dimensions of Globalization*. Minneapolis: University of Minnesota Press.

Bryant, Rebecca. 2016. "On Critical Times: Return, Repetition, and the Uncanny Present." *History and Anthropology* 27 (1): 19–31.

Bryant, Rebecca, and Daniel M. Knight. 2019. *The Anthropology of the Future*. Cambridge: Cambridge University Press.

Carsten, Janet. 2004. *After Kinship*. Cambridge: Cambridge University Press.

Choi, Vivian Y. 2015. "Anticipatory States: Tsunami, War, and Insecurity in Sri Lanka." *Cultural Anthropology* 30 (2): 286–309.

Doraï, Mohamed Kamel. 2008. "Itineraries of Palestinian Refugees: Kinship as Resource in Emigration." In *Crossing Borders, Shifting Boundaries: Palestinian Dilemmas*, edited by Sari Hanafi, 85–104. Cairo: American University in Cairo Press.

ESCWA (Economic and Social Commission for Western Asia). 2020. *Poverty in Lebanon: Solidarity Is Vital to Address the Impact of Multiple Overlapping Shocks*. Policy Brief 15. Beirut: United Nations. http://www.unescwa.org/sites/default/files/pubs/pdf/covid-19-beirut-explosion-rising-poverty-en.pdf.

Faier, Lieba, and Lisa Rofel. 2014. "Ethnographies of Encounter." *Annual Review of Anthropology* 43:363–77.

Farah, Randa. 2006. "Palestinian Refugees: Dethroning the Nation at the Crowning of the 'Statelet'?" *Interventions: International Journal of Postcolonial Studies* 8 (2): 228–52.

Feldman, Ilana. 2016. "Reaction, Experimentation, and Refusal: Palestinian Refugees Confront the Future." *History and Anthropology* 27 (4): 411–29.

———. 2017. "Humanitarian Care and the Ends of Life: The Politics of Aging and Dying in a Palestinian Refugee Camp." *Cultural Anthropology* 32 (1): 42–67.

Giacaman, Rita, and Penny Johnson. 2013. "'Our Life Is Prison': The Triple Captivity of Wives and Mothers of Palestinian Political Prisoners." *Journal of Middle East Women's Studies* 9 (3): 54–80.

Griffiths, Mark, and Jemima Repo. 2020. "Women's Lives beyond the Checkpoint in Palestine." *Antipode* 52 (4): 1104–21.

Griffiths, Mark, and Mikko Joronen. 2021. "Governmentalizing Palestinian Futures: Uncertainty, Anticipation, Possibility." *Geografiska Annaler: Series B, Human Geography* 103 (4): 352–66. https://doi.org/10.1080/04353684.2020.1871299.

Hage, Ghassan. 2009. "Waiting Out the Crisis: On Stuckedness and Governmentality." In *Waiting*, edited by Ghassan Hage, 97–106. Melbourne: Melbourne University Press.

Hanafi, Sari, Jad Chaaban, and Karin Seyfert. 2012. "Social Exclusion of Palestinian Refugees in Lebanon: Reflections on the Mechanisms that Cement Their Persistent Poverty." *Refugee Survey Quarterly* 31 (1): 34–53.

Harker, Christopher. 2009. "Spacing Palestine through the Home." *Transactions of the Institute of British Geographers* 34 (3): 320–32.

———. 2012. "Precariousness, Precarity and Family: Notes from Palestine." *Environment and Planning A* 44 (4): 849–65.

ILO (International Labour Organization). 2012. *Palestinian Employment in Lebanon—Facts and Challenges: Labour Force Survey among Palestinian Refugees Living in Camps and Gatherings in Lebanon*. Geneva: ILO. https://www.ilo.org/beirut/publications/WCMS _236502/lang--en/index.htm.

Janeja, Manpreet K., and Andreas Bandak, eds. 2018. *Ethnographies of Waiting: Doubt, Hope and Uncertainty*. London: Bloomsbury.

Järvi, Tiina. 2021. "Negotiating Futures in Palestinian Refugee Camps: Spatiotemporal Trajectories of a Refugee Nation." PhD diss., Tampere University.

Jefferson, Andrew M., and Lotte Buch Segal. 2019. "The Confines of Time—on the Ebbing Away of Futures in Sierra Leone and Palestine." *Ethnos* 84 (1): 96–112.

Johnson, Penny. 2006. "Living Together in a Nation in Fragments: Dynamics of Kin, Place, and Nation." In *Living Palestine: Dynamics of Place, Survival and Resistance*, edited by Lisa Taraki, 51–102. Syracuse: Syracuse University Press.

Joseph, Suad. 2005. "The Kin Contract and Citizenship in the Middle East." In *Women and Citizenship*, edited by Marilyn Friedman, 149–69. Oxford: Oxford University Press.

———. 2018. "Introduction: Family in the Arab Region: State of Scholarship." In *Arab Family Studies: Critical Reviews*, edited by Suad Joseph, 1–14. Syracuse: Syracuse University Press.

Kelly, Tobias. 2008. "The Attractions of Accountancy: Living an Ordinary Life during the Second Palestinian Intifada." *Ethnography* 9 (3): 351–76.

Kleist, Nauja, and Stef Jansen. 2016. "Introduction: Hope over Time—Crisis, Immobility and Future-Making." *History and Anthropology* 27 (4): 373–92.

Koselleck, Reinhart. 2004. *Futures Past: On the Semantics of Historical Time*. New York: Columbia University Press.

Peteet, Julie. 2005. *Landscape of Hope and Despair: Palestinian Refugee Camps*. Philadelphia: University of Pennsylvania Press.

———. 2018. "Closure's Temporality: The Cultural Politics of Time and Waiting." *South Atlantic Quarterly* 117 (1): 43–64.

PHRO (Palestinian Human Rights Organization). 2008. *Lebanese Labor Laws . . . Palestinian Refugees Recent Situations: The Palestinians' Contributions to Lebanon's Economy*. 2nd ed. Beirut: PHRO. http://www.palhumanrights.org/rtw%20campaign/Right-to-work/Labor%20Study-English.pdf.

———. 2010. "Law Adopted by Lebanese Parliament on 17 August 2010 Regarding Palestinian Refugees' Right to Work and Social Security." Position Paper. Beirut: PHRO. http://www.palhumanrights.org/var/Position%20Paper%20-RTW%20and%20Social%20Security%20Amended%20Laws.pdf.

Pijpers, Robert J. 2016. "Mining, Expectations and Turbulent Times: Locating Accelerated Change in Rural Sierra Leone." *History and Anthropology* 27 (5): 504–20.

Ramadan, Adam. 2009. "Destroying Nahr el-Bared: Sovereignty and Urbicide in the Space of Exception." *Political Geography* 28 (3): 153–63.

Richter-Devroe, Sophie. 2013. "'Like Something Sacred': Palestinian Refugees' Narratives on the Right of Return." *Refugee Survey Quarterly* 32 (2): 92–115.

Rosenfeld, Maya. 2004. *Confronting the Occupation: Work, Education, and Political Activism of Palestinian Families in a Refugee Camp*. Stanford: Stanford University Press.

Sahlins, Marshall. 2013. *What Kinship Is—and What It Is Not*. Chicago: University of Chicago Press.

Schiocchet, Leonardo. 2011. "Palestinian Sumud: Steadfastness, Ritual and Time among Palestinian Refugees." Working Papers 2011/51. Birzeit: Birzeit University. https://ssrn.com/abstract=2130405.

Spyrou, Spyros. 2020. "Children as Future-Makers." *Childhood* 27 (1): 3–7.

Stasch, Rupert. 2009. *Society of Others: Kinship and Mourning in a West Papuan Place*. Berkeley: University of California Press.

Stel, Nora. 2016. "The Agnotology of Eviction in South Lebanon's Palestinian Gatherings: How Institutional Ambiguity and Deliberate Ignorance Shape Sensitive Spaces." *Antipode* 48 (5): 1400–1419.

Taraki, Lisa. 2006. "Introduction." In *Living Palestine: Dynamics of Place, Survival and Resistance*, edited by Lisa Taraki, xi–xxx. Syracuse: Syracuse University Press.

UNCTAD (United Nations Conference on Trade and Development). 2018. *The Economic Costs of the Israeli Occupation for the Palestinian People and Their Human Right to Development: Legal Dimensions*. Geneva: UNCTAD. https://unctad.org/webflyer/economic-costs-israeli-occupation-palestinian-people-and-their-human-right-development.

Valentine, Gill. 2008. "Living with Difference: Reflections on Geographies of Encounter." *Progress in Human Geography* 32 (3): 323–37.

Vigh, Henrik. 2008. "Crisis and Chronicity: Anthropological Perspectives on Continuous Conflict and Decline." *Ethnos* 73 (1): 5–24.

———. 2011. "Vigilance: On Conflict, Social Invisibility, and Negative Potentiality." *Social Analysis* 55 (3): 93–114.

Weszkalnys, Gisa. 2008. "Hope & Oil: Expectations in São Tomé e Príncipe." *Review of African Political Economy* 35 (117): 473–82.

Whyte, Susan Reynolds, David Kyaddondo, and Lotte Meinert. 2014. "Chapter Six: Children." In *Second Changes: Surviving AIDS in Uganda*, edited by Susan Reynold Whyte, 152–66. Durham NC: Duke University Press.

Wilson, Helen F. 2017. "On Geography and Encounter: Bodies, Borders, and Difference." *Progress in Human Geography* 41 (4): 451–71.

Yassin, Nasser, Nora Stel, and Rima Rassi. 2016. "Organized Chaos: Informal Institution Building among Palestinian Refugees in the Maashouk Gathering in South Lebanon." *Journal of Refugee Studies* 29 (3): 341–62.

8 Surreal Resistance in Elia Suleiman's *Divine Intervention*

Arun Saldanha

The question of how to resist the occupation by the Israeli military is entwined with an exploration of what "Palestine" is and could be, despite Israel's doing its utmost to deny even the fact of Palestinian existence. Resistance is a process of survival and militant opposition, but this depends on an affirmative process of invention that envisages a future beyond mere opposition, beyond imagining a community. Within Palestinian media and international discourses on the conflict, this question of self-creating resistance has usually been posed in terms of social realism or melodrama. What kind of quotidian humiliations do Palestinians suffer? What brings someone to suicide bombing? How does the colonized relate to the colonizer? What is their *situation*? How are fleeting moments of love and poetry nevertheless possible?

Elia Suleiman's films take for granted there is such a depressingly familiar reality of settler colonialism and legal apartheid as reported for decades in left-leaning news sources, with Edward Said (1979) among the first to theorize the racist biases, both archaic and fully modern, in how the region is apprehended by the West. But instead of either facts or redemptive stories, instead of a frontal critique of Zionist violence, Suleiman's cinema probes into the occupation's more ridiculous dimensions. Responding to the Israeli state becomes for him a haphazard exercise in imagination before or adjacent to the ceaseless labor of securing a home from bulldozers and bomb campaigns, something more than strategizing within an atmosphere of despair. Palestinian futurity thereby departs partially from inherited models of anticolonial nationhood and internationalist solidarity—of which Frantz Fanon (1963) is the thinker par excellence—and invites the impossible, or what seems impossible, by engaging the otherworldly and the speculative, even to the extent that a veritable ethos emerges of not taking one's own national identity seriously at all.

Suleiman's cinema can be seen to expand on the rich archives of the avant-garde of Paris and to an extent New York (metropolises he lived in), from Baudelaire's poetics of urban estrangement to the humor in Jacques Tati and Jean-Luc Godard to underground electronic music. *Divine Intervention: A Chronicle of Love and Pain* won the Jury and International Critics Prize at the 2002 Cannes Film Festival, but in an ironic instantiation of the lack of a people that Suleiman's films explore, it couldn't be nominated for an Oscar as there is no country of Palestine that would officially select his film. Through a series of sometimes-correlated vignettes, *Divine Intervention* follows the lives of a number of ordinary middle- and working-class Palestinians in and around Nazareth, an Arab-majority city in Israel, and a Palestinian man from Jerusalem called ES played by Suleiman himself. The two easily discernible storylines involve ES's efforts to meet with his unnamed young woman lover from Nazareth, a process that necessitates negotiating the infamous Al-Ram checkpoint between Jerusalem and Ramallah, and how he deals with his father's stroke and hospitalization.

The movie has little dialogue and music. Its emphasis on corporeal action enhances the deadpan humor emerging from the situations similar to that in silent cinema (apart from Tati, Buster Keaton is one of Suleiman's influences). In an interview with the *Journal of Palestine Studies*, Suleiman (2003, 68) says, "I think silence is very political—what it conveys depends on how you use it. Silence is a place where the poetic can reign. If there's anything the authorities hate, it is poets, because of poetry's potential for liberation. And silence is a real magnifier of poetic space." Without dialogue, scenes can become a lot more bizarre and polysemous so that, emphatically against mainstream Hollywood, the audience is unsure of what is "really" going on or how the parts are supposed to hang together, let alone what Suleiman's moral takeaway might be. Why does the movie open with a

Santa Claus stabbed and hunted by young Palestinian boys? What's with the wearied limousine Mercedes turned yellow taxi? This is the post-Freudian power of surrealism: the juxtaposition of items both banal and strongly perverse furnishes a necessarily idiosyncratic approach to the violences inherent in the everyday.

The construction of a "poetic space" therefore renders undecidable the boundary between reality and imagination, and exhibits what is potential in the here and now. We cannot know which scenes might be conjured in a character's mind. "I didn't want to do what a lot of filmmakers do, which is segregate the fantasy from the reality by putting the dream in blurry images or showing that it's a flashback in some other technical way, signaling that what we are about to look at is nonreality. What I wanted to do in this film was to bring the imagined to potential reality and vice versa" (Suleiman 2003, 69). To cinematically inhabit the fractured geographies of Israel/Palestine with a surrealist approach is "political" in a different way. Instead of presenting more shameful facts about Israel/Palestine, or putting a personalized, "human" face on the blatant injustices and monotonies, *Divine Intervention* enjoins us to consider fundamental questions around how various populations relate phantasmally to this colonial reality.

The film stages encounters between conflicting desires and knowledges. What do Palestinians want, and what do "we" as viewers want of and for Palestinians? There is surely no invitation to identify with the characters, as none are particularly likable or interesting. The film does not aim to generate empathy for an Arab Other whom the West has otherwise demonized for a thousand years. While ES's love object is certainly beautiful, and three times she uses her sexuality to insurgent effect against Israeli state violence, she remains distant like a mirage, even to ES, so we are left uncertain whether love triumphs. Neither ES nor the other many characters seem to be interested in political militancy even as structural violence is an omnipresent backdrop. As Suleiman (2003, 64–65) notes, "*Divine Intervention* is the very early stages of a volcanic eruption, before it actually spews the lava, but where you can see the sparks and all the warning signs that you have to evacuate immediately." Refreshingly, how this rumbling of antagonism is channeled into everyday affects among neighbors, within families, between lovers, between locals and tourists, and relating to occupying forces can clearly be very funny.

In one hilarious encounter, a young French woman outside Jerusalem's Old City approaches a police van to ask for directions to the Church of the Holy Sepulchre. The cop wants to be helpful but, after looking at her map, quickly gives up and fetches a Palestinian locked up in the back. Handcuffed and blindfolded, the arrestee gives the tourist precise directions, but the cop is impatient and leads him back into the van even as he is still talking. The tourist waits until the cop is back next to her, thanks him, and continues her walk. This whole scene is congenial. The three speak perfect English, each in his or her accent. The sun shines. The woman is entirely oblivious to both the Palestinian's captivity and the irony that a local policeman, charged with regulating mobilities in the world's most fraught urban labyrinth, does not know the location of Christianity's holiest site—the church, consecrated in 335 CE, having been built on the spot where Jesus was crucified and buried. The policeman presumes, correctly, that a Palestinian in his custody does know (whether the latter is in fact Christian does not matter much).

There is serious commentary here: in thanking the policeman and not the Palestinian, the woman normalizes settler colonialism. The colonizer can, as a matter of course, usurp the colonized's geographic knowledge, which then automatically becomes the colonizer's own in the eyes of the visitor. Furthermore, a tourist in Jerusalem for a week has a right of movement that is denied to a population who has lived there for centuries. But there are more ironic and idiotic twists to settler colonialism. The cops and soldiers are all stupid in this movie, clueless about what they're doing, waiting all day and night for instructions over the radio, at times crazy from boredom or their own firepower. And the willful ignorance among most pilgrims about the slow ethnic cleansing taking place in the Holy Land is a symptom of the structural hypocrisy and Islamophobic resentment of Christianity worldwide. As Michel de Beistegui (2022) argues, inspired by Gilles Deleuze, stupidity has become a key feature of hegemonic discourses.

It cannot be combated with reason, facts, or morality alone. Perhaps one requires a sense of irony to see how it works.

Later in the film, the tourist returns, and the policeman greets her heartily as if an acquaintance. She is apologetic for being lost again. "Again!" they both say. Now she needs directions to the Haram esh-Sharif and the iconic gold-plated Dome of the Rock, Islam's third holiest site; built in the seventh century and rebuilt in the eleventh, it is where Muhammad ascended into heaven and the Last Judgment will play out. This makes the cop instantly anxious. He mutters, "Just, just a minute," as he again goes to the back of the van for help. Whatever he sees there makes him panic, and without a word, he runs and jumps into the driver's seat, switches the siren on, and skids off around the woman, who is left puzzled and without directions. Was he ashamed that without the help of a Palestinian this time he couldn't help the European visitor? Or was it the fact that Israel's presence is ineradicably built on the burying of the Islamic past that shamed him? Did he discover that his arrestee had escaped? Or maybe the vehicle wasn't empty, and the Palestinian lay unconscious or dead on the floor? Whatever the case may be, that the vignette ends in polysemous panic brings home the acute absurdities of Israel's repressive apparatus and the extreme convolution of sacred spaces it is meant to control and rationalize.

Surrealism traffics in surprise. In one scene, ES eats an apricot while driving and throws the pit nonchalantly out of his window. The pit instantly detonates, blowing up an Israeli tank on the roadside in a spectacular explosion filmed in slow motion. Parodying 1980s action movies, there is an unabashed eroticization of physical destruction. The random presence of a tank along the highway (albeit not so uncommon in the region) and the fortuity that a piece of thrown-away plant waste would blow it up make for a perfect allegory of the extreme asymmetry between Israel's bloated military-industrial complex and a puny Palestinian intellectual lost in thought and on his way to his lover. Presumably this is one place wherein Suleiman seeks to turn what a character is daydreaming (imagine if I had a magic anticolonial apricot!) into what he called "potential reality." While it is conceivable that a fruit pit could annihilate a piece of massive military gear in a cathartic blast, it would take quite a bit of planning. Or, indeed, divine intervention. Realism in politics, as much as in epistemology, depends on linear stories and being able to assess what is likely and what is not. Surrealism does not ask us to ponder plausibility, however, only to feel abrupt incongruence to, perhaps, make us think again. What we can say for sure is that some kind of violence happens. Inserting this explosion out of nowhere without narrative preparation or ramification jolts the viewer into participating in a momentary fantasy of dismantling occupation. And how significant is this outrageous aside? If it is but a daydream, then might it only exacerbate the angry incapacitation felt by Palestinians facing the military machine?

The film's most-discussed scene is when ES shows an ingenious tactic for distracting checkpoint soldiers so that he and his lover can drive past them. He lets loose a red balloon with a cartoon face of Yasser Arafat that gently floats toward the checkpoint, tricks the soldiers, and comes to adorn Jerusalem itself. This scene probably references Albert Lamorisse's famous 1956 fantasy short *The Red Balloon* about a mute boy's friendship with a red balloon accompanying him across Paris. Suleiman's soundtrack, however, parodies Ennio Morricone's compositions to create the preposterous tensions we associate with Westerns, although instead of the lethal standoff in cowboy duels, our heroic lover is solving militarized tensions with a toy. An icon of third world resistance, Arafat's face was a favorite for cartoonists, many gleefully accentuating racial elements and giving him thick lips, a big nose, small eyes, a scruffy beard, and a keffiyeh, which became known, indeed, as the Arafat scarf. The troops are mesmerized by this cartoon face. Surely it announces the balloon is somehow in service of the enemy? Could this be a new method of terrorist attack? When a trigger-happy soldier wants to fire, the rest stop him to check with their superiors over the radio whether to retaliate against this object "trying to get through." The soldiers are ordered to let it be and remain dumbstruck after encountering something so extraordinary—the ludic within a warzone. The balloon steers itself face forward across the Jerusalem cityscape, like a floating tourist, making sure to fly past the Church of the Holy Sepulchre before circling a few times around the crescent atop the Dome of the Rock, and ending its supernatural journey right there.

How are we to interpret this chimerical gliding object? When Gilles Deleuze and Félix Guattari ([1980] 1987) invented the term "faciality" (*visagéïté*) to sharply critique the ways image-saturated colonial capitalism boxes subjects into self-generative grids of identities and differences by virtue of their corporeal characteristics, they needed to leave room for elements that, somewhat enigmatically, escape this facializing machine. They called them *têtes chercheuses*, which is translated as "probeheads" (literally search heads, or guided missiles; also a slang term for penis). Faciality is about instant recognition, knowing your place, and a quasi-sacred halo emanating from the most important faces. Waging war on faciality for Deleuze and Guattari implies devising infrapersonal bits and pieces that the machine cannot figure out and that will thereby jam it. Thus, the projectile ES devises puts an over-publicized face to use to momentarily escape the panoptic eye that makes certain bodies, like his own, criminal. There is a victory of sorts, with a hero's face serving to defacialize ordinary individuals under occupation, not through actual combat or peace negotiations but by the mere surprise of its appearing in this form.

And what about this form? Why a balloon? Moreover, why does the climax of the balloon's journey take place at the tip of the monumental mosque visible from all around? Arafat's own secularism and ES's (and Suleiman's) Christianity would suggest that this balloon of liberation is not, finally, about celebrating the perseverance of Islam or about a love (for which the balloon's magic was instrumentalized) that only occurs on the way to and under the sign of religion (the magic hinted at of ending the ritualized geopoliticking since 1948). Definitely, the movie's title seems to suggest that in this scene, as in others, there is an intervention from a transcendent realm, whether it is a protagonist's dream or it is "really happening." But if there is a structure of feeling that surrealism and Dadaism poke fun at first and foremost, it is religion, so something far more ironic must be going on with this balloon. Whether deliberately or not, perhaps Suleiman is making use of some very basic affects exuding from this particular object—soft and hard at the same time, inflatable, searching the skies but fragile.

Sigmund Freud ([1917] 1973, 188) said in his 1916 lecture on dream symbolism:

> The remarkable characteristic of the male organ which enables it to rise up in defiance of the laws of gravity, one of the phenomena of erection, leads to its being represented symbolically by *balloons, flying-machines* and most recently by *Zeppelin airships*. But dreams can symbolize erection in yet another, far more expressive manner. They can treat the sexual organ as the essence of the dreamer's whole person and make him himself *fly*. Do not take it to heart if dreams of flying, so familiar and often so delightful, have to be interpreted as dreams of general excitement, as erection-dreams.

The phallic nature of rockets has been often commented upon, but if we take these brief examples of Freud's seriously, we can push further and ask what the apparent frivolousness of balloons might mean for masculine fantasies about power. ES's (fantasy of the) soft weaponization of a balloon bearing the face of the foremost male political leader of his people to get through a deadly bottleneck toward his lover can be said to index the clashes among fundamental authoritative subject positions—of planning, projectiles, surveillance, the "international community"—subject positions most traditionally found in bodies with penises. But what is essential in the psychoanalytical concept of "manhood" and symbolic masculinity, especially in Jacques Lacan's ([1958] 2006) formalized notion of the phallus as no longer tethered to concrete things such as umbrellas and pistols, is that it is always already threatened by castration. Flaccidity is around the corner for every erection. As with few other symbol-objects, a balloon stands in for the seeming airborne-ness of masculine authority whose aggressive self-inflation is nothing but the masking of a primordial weakness. True, ES's balloon was victorious over the soldiers, but that was through its strangeness, not through force. And it was, by definition, a fleeting moment. At any moment, a bird or the crescent on the Dome of the Rock could prick it. The higher and farther it flies, the likelier its end is nigh.

For all his earnest dedication to science, Freud's thesis that phantasmic objects ultimately refer to sex organs has for decades been heartily ridiculed. From his side, Suleiman's professed absurdism could well lean Dada more than Freudian, and he may explain his choice of objects such as the balloon, the apricot pit, or the ubiquitous cigarette as more or less arbitrary. But can any series of signs really be composed randomly? This would deny there is an unconscious tout court. Perhaps the audacity and seeming ridiculousness of psychoanalytic interpretation are to be further deepened instead of feared and thrashed, at least in some especially evocative instances. Perhaps Freud's own claims to scientific reason are made more complex by a certain surrealist and comical artistry or mythologizing proper to early psychoanalysis itself. If it is posited, for example, that the Arafat balloon = an intellectual's erection dream = Palestinian castration complex, the question is not whether this can be "proven" through whatever psychotherapeutic and public health records; instead, it is to be creative, as an interpreter, in delineating what makes an Arafat balloon above Jerusalem beguiling. By following a strange coupling presented in the film, we see how fantasies around masculinity, impotence, and authority are intermeshed with the realities of occupation.

If the balloon scene is in fact an "erection dream" of the male protagonist working through his immobilization by the regime, then its launching a geopolitical iconicity would seem to invite some commentary on how authority under heteropatriarchy operates at the level of states (and would-be states). Nothing in the movie would lead us to think ES believes in official Palestinian politics, tied up as he is with the difficult encounters with his girlfriend and father. To the contrary, the balloon clearly signals ambiguity around Arafat's authority. It did not take long for Arafat's legitimacy among the general Palestinian population to start its steady decline when it became clear the Oslo Accords he had worked on were not only leaky by design but would be actively ignored by settlers. Suleiman is probably not poking fun at Arafat the person but at the failures of the Palestine Liberation Organization (PLO) and the Palestinian National Authority by the time of the Second Intifada to provide workable responses to Israel's ethno-nationalist expansionism. In rendering Arafat's face a probehead to wage a personal war against the facializing authorities, the face's auratic function is used in a direction opposite from propaganda—as a comic instrument to consume love. The sometimes-romanticized notion of an anti-imperialist hero in Arab and progressive Western discourses of the 1970s and 1980s—one that had affected Deleuze, too—was precisely what fooled the soldiers. Transported by a sexually equivocal object, the Arafat face was just authoritative enough to hold their attention. When Deleuze (1998) wrote of Arafat's "grandeur," he was defending the PLO against attacks coming both from the West and from Islamist radicals, and could not have been thinking of quite such a paradoxical approach to magnificence. In Suleiman's hands, the anticolonial struggle pushes weirdness over its edge to deal with the absurdities that accumulate in a legacy of oppression.

As a style of thought, surrealism and Dadaism smudge the boundaries between eroticism and politics, between fun and war. This makes them supremely irreverent and possibly irksome to anyone trying to forge dependable political subjectivation. The strength of surreal resistance lies not merely in its illegibility to power and its demonstration of power's stupidity but also in its ridiculing of one's own (always gendered) claim to counterauthority. As for the gendering of resistance, the balloon tactic of ES is rather infantile in comparison to his girlfriend's approach: she bravely strides through hostile situations, using her dashing femininity to full effect. While ES never dares leave his car while engaging in (dreaming) subversive acts, his girlfriend's superhero status comes into its own at the end of the film, as she turns ninja-militant and, in a brilliant kung fu–, *The Matrix*–, and folk dance–inspired fight, overcomes five Zionist vigilante gunmen and an Apache military helicopter. She uses Islam darts, a slingshot (of intifada and David-and-Goliath fame), and her own veil as magic weapons. As with the Arafat face, the fight scene is an over-the-top reference to the Palestinian effort at nation-building. The soundtrack and dust again recall those of Westerns. But however outlandish, somehow it seems more difficult to call this scene ridiculous or to consider it as a feminine counterpart to ES's erection dream, the articulation of a wish for solid personhood under conditions of sociospatial and erotic frustration that, as suggested above, is interpretable as self-deprecation and an ironizing of anticolonial struggle. Maybe this is because we see militarism defeated by his girlfriend's courage and bodily determination instead of the randomness of an apricot pit, a balloon, or a mere mention of the Dome of the Rock. Or maybe if the phantasmatic power of combat is presented in and through a feminine figure instead of the usual male one, then the belief in the possibility of justice in the anticolonial viewer (of whichever gender) is less open to ironical twists. Within the cauldron of surrealism, a strange, nonempirical kind of realism about revolution's murkier regions arises.

Divine Intervention is the second in Suleiman's trilogy of semi-autobiographical films, which started with *Chronicle of a Disappearance* in 1996 and ends with *The Time That Remains: Chronicle of a Present Absentee* of 2009. The latter, whose title probably repeats that of Giorgio Agamben's ([2000] 2005) study of messianic futurity in Saint Paul and Marxism, follows a Palestinian family from the Nakba to the present. Even on this longer timescale, instead of presenting a linear arc of growing political awareness, Suleiman stresses the fragmentation and rut of Palestinian survival against the backdrop of the insidious but as a rule unimaginative process of Israelization. Though less funny as a movie, the tragedies of displacement and pillaging again double as absurdities of state power. While Suleiman's art has no takeaway message about what "Palestinian" might mean, and does not articulate any hope for a "solution to the conflict," at the very least it has a sense that the reality of colonialism is never about fully formed identities confronting each other. The Palestinian experience since 1948 cannot be captured just by the notion of "nation."

In a fascinating twist, Suleiman says that the singularity of diasporic cosmopolitanism so hated by anti-Semites has now been forced upon Palestinians: "What may be most Palestinian about me is that anti-nationalistic sense." Zionism has from the beginning threatened to strangle the vibrancy and open-endedness that had characterized Jewish intellectual and artistic life over so many centuries. Palestinians have, in fact, become more "Jewish" than Israelis. "Israel came and handed us their Jewishness and off we went.

The Israelis became racist tribalists, and we became the diasporic people. And now we are the ones who are feeding on non-centered cultures, on resisting power structures" (Suleiman 2003, 73; compare Alain Badiou's [(1982) 2006] controversial thoughts on this topic, as well as Judith Butler's [2012]). Suleiman qualifies his statement that it is privileged exiles like himself who manage to turn being deterritorialized into creative projects. And of course, Jewishness includes a unique legacy of exile and genocide that cannot be adopted. What matters is the idea of identities being at play, interpenetrating, and excessive of their nationalist territorializations. While Suleiman's poetic space and ironic twists cannot take the place of the militant struggle for self-governance in the present, a decolonization through the exploration of the colonizer's suppressed history of forced self-reinvention could be one entry point for a Palestinian futurism.

References

Agamben, Giorgio. (2000) 2005. *The Time That Remains: A Commentary on the Letter to the Romans*. Translated by Patricia Dailey. Stanford: Stanford University Press.

Badiou, Alain. (1982) 2006. "Israel: The Country in the World Where There Are the Fewest Jews?" In *Polemics*, 167–71. Translated by Steve Corcoran. London: Verso.

Butler, Judith. 2012. *Parting Ways: Jewishness and the Critique of Zionism*. New York: Columbia University Press.

de Beistegui, Miguel. 2022. *Thought under Threat: On Superstition, Spite, and Stupidity*. Chicago: Chicago University Press.

Deleuze, Gilles. 1998. "The Grandeur of Yasser Arafat." Translated by Timothy S. Murphy. *Discourse* 20 (3): 30–33.

Deleuze, Gilles, and Félix Guattari. (1980) 1987. *A Thousand Plateaus: Capitalism and Schizophrenia*. Translated by Brian Massumi. Minneapolis: University of Minnesota Press.

Fanon, Frantz. 1963. *The Wretched of the Earth*. Translated by Constance Farrington. New York: Grove.

Freud, Sigmund. (1917) 1973. *Introductory Lectures on Psychoanalysis*. Translated by James Strachey. Harmondsworth: Penguin.

Lacan, Jacques. (1958) 2006. "The Signification of the Phallus." In *Écrits*, 575–84. Translated by Bruce Fink, in collaboration with Héloïse Fink and Russell Grigg. New York: W. W. Norton.

Said, Edward W. 1979. *The Question of Palestine*. New York: Vintage.

Suleiman, Elia. 2003. "The Occupation (and Life) through an Absurdist Lens." Interview by Linda Butler. *Journal of Palestine Studies* 32 (2): 63–73.

9 Queering Esthesis
Unsettling the Zionist Sensual Regime

Walaa Alqaisiya

The violence of Zionist settler colonial conquest in Palestine—and the ongoing Nakba—is central to the policies that Israel has promulgated around liberal sexual values for the past twenty or so years. Framing such policies as "pinkwashing,"[1] Palestinian queer activists have documented, analyzed, and resisted the dangers of colonial violence masked as liberalism, providing crucial understandings of "how Israel divides, oppresses, and erases Palestinians on the basis of gender and sexuality" (alQaws 2020). Scholarly analyses of pinkwashing have similarly provided analytical critiques of Zionist sexuality politics, drawing on wider postcolonial and de-colonial queer discourses that enable a clear articulation of the relations between sexuality and colonial violence (e.g., Alqaisiya 2018; Britt 2015; Elia 2012; Morgensen 2012a, 2012b; Puar 2011). In this chapter, I build on this work by engaging with pinkwashing as a site of legitimizing a sensual regime of violence that expands Zionist power in Palestine. I examine racialized, sexualized, and gendered configurations of settler colonial domination to outline the value of de-colonial queering esthesis that Palestinian artistic productions generate. In doing so, the chapter takes Palestine as a site for expanding the political and theoretical significance of de-colonial geographies (Daigle and Ramírez 2019; Naylor et al. 2018), tracing the generative spatial and epistemic value that emerges from across settler colonial, decolonizing, native feminist, and queer studies.

The chapter begins by identifying the functionality of pinkwashing as a settler sensual regime. I focus on theorizing the relationship between sex

(sex/gender systems) and sense (sensory structures including emotive and affective dimensions of politics) that supports a Zionist structure of native elimination. Drawing on Israel's (inter)national promotion of its pluralistic (gendered and sexed) self in the context of Netta Barzilai's victory at the 2018 Eurovision Song Contest (Europe's most widely viewed annual television event), I show how the sovereign parameters of a settler colonial consensus mediate the sensorial and liberatory effect of global queerness. In section 2 I analyze the production of the Palestinian "gay victim" in Israeli pinkwashing discourses that helps to ground processes of settler indigenization via an explication of Zionist sensual encroachment onto the pain of a native Other. Against this backdrop, section 3 proceeds to unpack the value of queering esthesis, articulating a form of native resistance that challenges the violence of the Zionist sensual regime. I focus on three Palestinian queer artistic productions: the cinematic lens of Nadia Awad, the activist/artist musical tracks of alQaws, and the story of the late dancer Ayman Safiah. In conclusion I substantiate the argument that the politics of queer esthesis functions on multiple levels. On one level, it challenges the Zionist configuration of sex and sense, where the projections of sexual pluralism and the moral superiority of Israeli humanist values coalesce. On a second level, queer esthesis articulates the native's bodily ways of doing, being, and enunciating epistemologies for revival, life, and return to home, grounding the willingness to challenge the native's own political imaginary as it succumbs to the imperatives of a settler sensual regime bent on instilling the native's *ghorba* (exile) from her land, histories, and desires.

Pinkwashing: Settler Grammars of Sex and Sense

Netta Barzilai's victory at the 2018 Eurovision Song Contest provided another moment to hail Israel as a country of "difference and acceptance." In her celebratory speech, Barzilai beamed: "Thank you so much for accepting differences between us. Thank you for celebrating diversity. Next year in Jerusalem!" Barzilai's achievement came twenty years after her fellow Israeli Dana International won the 1998 contest with a performance "considered one of the all-time Eurovision greats—with its classic Eurodance

Queering Esthesis   213 rhythms and typically Israeli melody, it is irresistibly camp" (Barlow 2018). Dana was the first transgender winner in the history of the contest, and her victory helped establish Eurovision as a space for celebrating lesbian, gay, bisexual, transgender, and queer (LGBTQ) identity. Barzilai's 2018 entry, "Toy"—which includes the line "I am not your toy, you stupid boy"—is similarly celebrated for addressing women's empowerment via what the singer describes as "the awakening of female power and social justice, wrapped in a colourful, happy vibe" (Barzilai cited in Adams 2018). For some European and Israeli media commentators, the song is (hyperbolically) labeled "the voice of the #MeToo movement" (Cabral and Matthieussent 2018), while Barzilai herself embodies a woman who, uninhibited by her plus-size looks, gender, or sexual orientation, dares to encourage others to think outside of the box, to break societal constraints, and to be happy about themselves.

Crucially, Barzilai frames her success and sexually progressive politics in a specific way: they show how "amazing Israel is," showcasing its "good values" and challenging the "bad PR that we have in the world."[2] Predictably, Benjamin Netanyahu and other prominent politicians such as Nir Barakat, the mayor of Jerusalem, welcomed her statements with joy, making Barzilai something of a cultural ambassador for Israel (Kreshner 2018)—especially since her victory and Jerusalem statement coincided with "Jerusalem Day" (Yom Yerushalayum), the state's official commemoration of the "reunification" (i.e., the violent conquest) of East Jerusalem in 1967.[3] Barzilai's win thus encapsulates the dynamics of Israel's pinkwashing policies, where queer and trans rights are readily used to "distract from and normalize Israel's occupation, settler colonialism and apartheid" (PACBI 2019). Recognizing this, Palestinian queer activists called on international solidarity groups to boycott Eurovision and the 2019 Tel Aviv Pride event. Palestinian queer groups' actions and analysis expose the role of pinkwashing within the Zionist political regime: pinkwashing articulates Zionist settler colonialism as a gendered and sexually progressive self while denying and regulating a Palestinian native Other.

The framing of Barzilai's victory signifies another moment that reinforces Israel's status within a liberal democratic order that is also an extension of

Europe itself. Israel participates in and wins the continent-wide contest under the rubric of an esthetic/political regime that makes visible the celebratory narratives of feminism and LGBTQ progress. My understanding of esthetics in relation to politics draws on the work of Jacques Rancière, arguing that the esthetic regime entails the distribution of sense, which is inherently connected to the ways in which the "police" regime organizes the hierarchical orderings of "sense" (Rancière 1999, 2004). Camp esthetics and liberatory "vibes" structure and animate the sense of pride and happiness folded into the spectacle of multicultural internationalism. In this way, Barzilai's victory functions as an affective form of geopolitical (re)mapping where Israel's place in the model of Euro-Western queer citizenship is affirmed. Eurovision is a space that "allow[s] performers and fans alike to be part of an international order that is said to simultaneously claim and disavow regional, national, and continental identities," enabling them to "to maintain a sense of cultural identity while critiquing essentialism" (Tobin 2007, 28). The claim to non-essentialism and internationalism that this space maintains, however, obscures the very exclusivist either/or logic upon which "non-essentialising" scripts of queer geopolitical relations stand (Weber 2014). The non-essentialism of a global queer citizenship is mediated through the sovereign parameters of a Euro-Western consensus, whose constituent grids on development, immigration, and nation-state formations underpin hierarchizing processes of racial and sexual imbrications. In the case of the settler colonial project, one can go further to situate the establishment of a settler-sovereign nation-state within the structures of elimination—in both negative (genocidal) and positive (regulatory) forms (Wolfe 2006)—entrenching the continuity of the settler presence on native land.

Barzilai's victory thus situates Israel's gendered and sexual values within "a narrative of progression in terms of sexual citizenship linked to European liberalization" (Cook and Evans 2014, 9). At the same time, and importantly, it also reveals the historical continuity of a settler colonial project, whose sex-gender system coheres with a racializing constitutive (native/settler) context that always already aligns with Euro-Western notions of space and time (Alqaisiya 2020). The process of Israel's constitution as a settler sovereignty is born of Euro-Western imaginaries of conquest as a modernizing schema, which renders the native's disappearance as a necessity for the civilizing enterprise. The contemporary colonization of Palestine, as is well documented, began in earnest with the British Mandate for Palestine, whose sanctioned vision of governance aligned with European parameters of state sovereignty (Erakat 2019). The proclamation of state sovereignty, the defining principle of which is "Jewish and democratic," is both predicated on and productive of the "legal fiction of Palestinian non-existence" (Erakat 2019, 54). This disappearing logic of the natives renders them necessarily conquerable. Settler colonial policies and laws—inherited from an "internationally" backed mandate regime[4]—stipulated the necessity of transforming a people and a land whose physical replacement enabled it to bestow Jewishness on "a place in the modern family of nations," as Israel's first president Chaim Weizmann so proudly put it (quoted in Said 1979, 13). Modernity is a defining factor of the Zionist imaginative sovereign self, which simultaneously undergirds a process of settler indigenization or the settler's own effort at indigenizing or naturalizing their settlement (see Morgensen 2011; Veracini 2010).

The recognition of Israel and "proud" Israelis, such as Barzilai, as a place and the subjects of sexual pluralism and modernity stands as another marker of settler sovereignty, reproducing the Nakba for Palestine. Barzilai's call for "next year in Jerusalem!" corresponds to the de facto conquest of the city and the legitimacy conferred upon it by the Euro-American powers whose economic and cultural support has enabled settler indigenization in Palestine for more than a hundred years. In the assertiveness of an indigenized settler self that naturally extends an invitation to her own hometown and thanks the Eurovision judges (i.e., the tens of millions of voting public)—"you chose diversity, and for accepting difference amongst us"—Barzilai thus demonstrates "a civilised nature marked by race, gender, or sexuality that defines their own national character or universality" (Morgensen 2012b, 9). The Zionist state and settler subjects heavily invest in the globalized promulgation and consumption of the spectacles that market

Israel as an international and progressive space on gender and LGBTQ issues. Numerous Israeli state institutions, such as the Ministry of Foreign Affairs, Ministry of Tourism, and the Tel Aviv Municipality, as well as Aguda, Israel's LGBTQ Task Force, have participated in the promotion of the city of Tel Aviv as an LGBTQ haven (see Alqaisiya, Hilal, and Maikey 2016).

The eventual decision to host Eurovision in Tel Aviv rather than in the "controversial" and "ultra-orthodox" Jerusalem was taken precisely because of the city's "pink" image; as Tel Aviv mayor Ron Huldai claimed, "Eurovision is a perfect fit for our city, which has been internationally acclaimed for its vibrant energy, creative spirit, its lively cultural scene and its celebration of freedom" (cited in Holmes 2018). The municipality's official promotional videos exalt Tel Aviv's internationalist and vibrant progressive image, where the display of a Middle Eastern LGBTQ utopia accompanies songs celebrating an obsession with the color pink.[5] "The hot men of Tel Aviv" also welcome tourists into the Pride parade, night life, and tastes of its "orientalist-culinary" arts.[6] Similarly, the Eurovision 2018 promotional video featured the return of Dana International—who flamboyantly emerges from rainbow ribbons[7]—to emphasize the city's (and by extension Israel's) friendly and progressive pink image. Euro-American media narratives further promoted this message: Madonna's appearance beside Dana and the 2014 Austrian winner, the drag artist Conchita Wurst, also contributed to Euro-American narratives promoting the message that the Tel Aviv event would be "the queerest" yet (Alled 2019).

These events show the global reach of the settler sensual regime, or what Magid Shihade (2015) calls "Global Israel." The creation of the Israeli settler state activated a structure of domineering global settler mobility exemplified by "violence and repression, arms trade, and technologies of surveillance, and militarisation that shape Israeli [settler] mobility locally, regionally, and globally" (Shihade 2015, 15). Bringing attention to the very mobility, expansion, and intersection of Israel's power in military, economic, and cultural terms is part and parcel of what the global boycott, divestment, and sanctions (BDS) call strives for. Palestinian queer work in particular, and boycott campaigning more generally, highlights the sensual aspect of this mobility and normalizing of Israel's violence. While expanding globally, this sensual regime is constructed in relation to gender and sexual modernity to reify its structure of native elimination. It makes visible, sayable, and audible a modern and pluralistic gendered and sexed self by rendering invisible and inaudible a Palestinian native Other—one who is marked for erasure and the theft of their pain. It is to this theft that I now turn.

The Theft of Native Pain

The political and esthetic manifestation of Tel Aviv as a space of sexual democracy rests upon the projection of the Middle East and especially adjacent Palestinian spaces and subjects as homophobic, terroristic, and sexually pathological. Palestinian queer subjects are only conceivable within the framework of victimhood in a culture of honor or terror. Israeli production of movies such as *The Bubble* (2007, directed by Eytan Fox) or *The Invisible Men* (2021, directed by Yariv Mozer) disseminates this "reality" of Palestinian suppressed LGBTQ people whose only way to find shelter from their homophobic families is by seeking refuge in the gay haven city of Tel Aviv.[8] This channeling of a victimhood image (Alqaisiya, Hilal, and Maikey 2016) enables the activation of a colonial-savior sense, whose underlining racial and sexual imbrications constitute a structure of feeling (Anderson, 2014) that is part of the "forming and formative processes" of ongoing native dispossession (Rifkin 2011, 32). At the same time, and as a complement, settler subjects are at pains to demonstrate a solidarity with native queer suffering. For instance, in the follow-up to recent incidents of violence toward Palestinian LGBTQ groups and individuals, Israeli institutionalized support was noticeably heightened, and a number of "solidarity marches" began to take place. The discourses reproduced in such solidaristic acts, where Jewish Israeli analyses and institutional support dominate, cement the colonial self-generated fantasy of the Zionist state as a refuge space for Palestinian queers, a fantasy in which Palestinian queers are constituted as inherently denied the freedom that their colonizer can offer (Maikey 2019). Spaces of multicultural Israeli-ness and expressions of solidarity with Palestinian suffering thus exemplify a facile settler sense of empathy with the pain of the native Other, or what I call, following Sherene Razack's (2007) "Stealing the Pain of Others," the settler theft of native pain.

As Razack (2007, 378) argues, an element of pleasure instructs the master's sense of "embracing the pain" of the slave. This relates to the former's position of observer and consumer that has historically cemented the master's role in relation to a voyeuristic enjoyment of the slave's suffering. The examples discussed so far—spanning Barzilai's Eurovision victory to state institutional support of pinkwashing—alongside complementing narratives of saving and protecting LGBTQ Palestinians, indicate this same relational dynamic. It reifies a Zionist humanist sense that remains morally superior and thus more worthy of legitimacy than a native sovereign constituency. The settler colonial theft of native pain reaffirms legitimacy and naturalizes settler conquest. It takes place within an "international" ceremonial hailing of settler subjects, such as Barzilai, who are construed as belonging to a pluralistic state that chooses diversity. At the same time, and crucially, it obscures the role of the state, its settler subjects, and the "international spectator/realm of the global" by effecting a "will-full ignorance" (Vimalassery, Pegues, and Goldstein 2016) of, on the one hand, Palestinian queer voices and political appeals for boycott and, on the other, the state's existential dependence on native dispossession.[9]

That Barzilai invites spectators to Jerusalem is illustrative of the day-to-day encroachment of the settler regime onto its native Other. Palestinian feminists draw our attention to Zionist occupation of the senses for Palestinians in the city, where the structure of settler colonial dispossession is performed by the "sensory technologies that manage bodies, language, sight, time and space in the colony" (Shalhoub-Kevorkian 2016, 1279). The violability of the native's most intimate and bodily terrain explains the encroachment of the settler sensual regime across orthodox and liberal ideologies and reveals the continuum of the structural reality of the Nakba. A pointed and tragic example of this sensual regime is the burning and killing of the Palestinian boy from Jerusalem, Muhammed Abu Khdeir, by Orthodox Jews in 2014 and its misrepresentation by the Israeli liberal camp's discourse as an "honour crime" conducted by the boy's "homophobic" family. The circulation of an image of Abu Khdeir on social media with the tag in Hebrew that "Arabs had killed him because he was gay" demonstrates the affective parameters of a settler rescue empathy that is not to be disavowed from the very genocidal structure it serves and perpetuates. This rescue-empathy logic also interlinks with the production of a native sense of guilt, which intermeshes with a settler sense of innocence.

This sense of innocence, held strongly, abrogates settlers from their responsibility in native dispossession by virtue of endowing conquest with humanist value, encapsulating the human/man notion of the settler colonial trap (Mignolo 2006). Yet, the former locks the native within the psycho-political imperatives that toy "with [the] colonised psyche" (Shalhoub-Kevorkian 2016, 1296) and "destroys [natives'] sense of being a people" (Smith 2005, 3). The native's sense of guilt inscribes the compulsion to reenact, on subjective and objective scales, the inevitability of the native's failure to govern or imagine a sovereign (sensual) self. This failure, as I have argued elsewhere (Alqaisiya 2020), is a fundamental element of hetero conquest; it captures how Palestinian political imaginaries remain subsumed by the inevitability of settler presence, thus obstructing a native's self-recognition and willful initiation beyond the colonizer's gaze and regime of sensual configurations. Thus, the Palestinian/Arab subjective reproduction of the taxonomies of freedom within pinkwashing narratives—that is, *Palestine as homophobic/Israel as gay haven*—tallies with the imaginaries of liberation that Palestine has undergone, from the First Intifada to the rise of the Palestinian National Authority (PNA) in the aftermath of the Oslo Accords.[10] Both scales accept and normalize the logics of Zionist presence and—by extension therefore—hetero and sensual dominance.

Queering Esthesis: Video Art, Songs, and Dance

In this final part of the discussion, I reflect on how Palestinian queer artistic expressions refuse to normalize the Zionist sensual regime that does not allow the colonized to see beyond the stricture of its subjugation. By enacting a politics of refusal (Simpson 2014) via what I call de-colonial queering esthesis, the artworks I discuss here usher forms of resistance and native resurgence that attempt to delink (Mignolo and Nanibush 2018) from and challenge the violence of the esthetic sensual regime fixing the native in and out of place. These artistic works resonate with what Walter Mignolo identifies, drawing on Frantz Fanon, as the geared sensibility of the colonized to undo settler encroachment on and wounding of the native's subjecthood and sensual sovereignty (Mignolo 2014).

In 2009, after a shooting at a Tel Aviv gay bar, thousands of people attended a vigil. The short film *A Demonstration* (2014) focuses on the event and reflects on the gathering with these words from its director, the Palestinian visual artist Nadia Awad: "I expected a small candlelit vigil with fifty activists. To my surprise, 10,000 people had gathered in Rabin Square. The vigil was, in fact, a benefit concert where Israeli government officials gave speeches equating the youth bar shooting to the Holocaust and suggesting that [David] Ben-Gurion's Zionist vision included LGBT communities."[11] In her film, Awad's camera wanders among the crowds in Rabin Square in central Tel Aviv as they gather to hear a speech that is also projected onto a giant screen. The camera catches glimpses of the screen, and the emotionally loaded speech runs throughout the film's audio. As the camera zooms in on the speaker (see figure 6), his dramatic expressions come into view, as do streams of tears on his face. His speech begins by lamenting how "bad this week" has been "for all of you good people who are here today in Rabin Square," before reflecting on how the Jewish "refuge," in direct reference to the Israeli state, has become "a slaughterhouse for a despicable murder." Through his tears, the speaker alludes to the strong "never again" discourse in Israel as he refers to a Holocaust poet who "found it impossible to recount what happened there" and praises the work of Aguda.[12] He rallies: "Your presence here . . . proves something. We are a nation that really does oppose violence and wants peace. Violence destroys the foundations of Israeli democracy, it must be denounced, expelled, shunned for the sake of the state of Israel." Finally, the speaker, whose name is never given, draws our attention to the "nice little place called Bar Noar . . . the only place that serves orange juice and salad with mini rainbow flags on one side and Israeli flag on another."

The cinematography of *A Demonstration* imposes a certain sense of distance from the events depicted, preventing the viewer from developing an affinity with or empathy toward those in the crowd. While the lens looks on at the event, we are kept at a distance, hovering hesitantly around the crowds, as the other cameras (presumably) attempt a more proximate depiction. The speaker is only (partially) captured on a big screen, giving the viewer the impression of observing a movie set. Through Awad's lens, the speech and the speaker are imbued with a sense of theatricality; focusing on the speaker makes the viewer aware of such theatrical elements. In other words, while the viewer watches what could be described as "a representation of a representation," the video reveals the performative character of the esthetic performance at play (Butler 1999, 173). Awad's distant and detached lens work accentuates the distance between her viewers and what is portrayed on the screen, further inhibiting the emergence of empathetic feelings. In what follows, I argue that Awad's visual production of *A Demonstration* is rooted in her native exilic positionality vis-à-vis the esthetic sensual regime that constitutes a de-colonial queering lens.

Awad's *A Demonstration* presents a form of de-colonial queering esthesis that seeks to enunciate a native sense that queers and interrupts the esthetic-political field of the settler encroachment on the native's existence. It emanates from what she describes as "outside-of-time subjecthood" that links to her growing up as a 1948 displaced Palestinian in a U.S.-Christian evangelical context (in Florida). Awad explains how her "questioned subjecthood" and the persistent negation she faces "when claiming any entitlement or even relationship to Palestine" are fundamental to understanding her work.[13] Such negation is compounded with Christian evangelicals' commonly enthusiastic support for the state of Israel that Awad saw openly demonstrated when church collections would fund guns to be shipped to Israel for waging its "holy war." In these biographical details, Awad's questioned subjecthood becomes a way both to experience the globalized mobility of a settler structuring of sense and self (as described above) and to challenge it from a queer native lens.

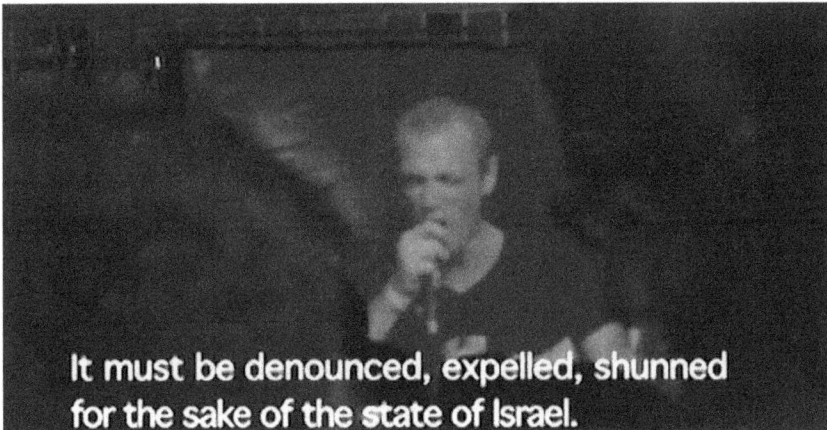

It must be denounced, expelled, shunned for the sake of the state of Israel.

6. Still from *A Demonstration*. Nadia Awad, 2014.

In *A Demonstration*, Awad synthesizes fragments of different films to "rip apart" their meaning and unsettle their esthetics. She "watch[es] them over and over and over" to remake them anew, using contemporary visual and audio techniques whose purpose is to undermine the visual and rhetorical logic of the films and to "draw attention to the ways in which they construct truth claims and potentially sympathetic viewing positions" (Awad and Jankovic 2012, 139). Awad's artistic techniques convey a de-colonial esthesis that reconfigures dominant settler sensual structures.[14] She reflects on how, while at the vigil in Rabin Square, she had to make sure "not to slip as a Palestinian"; she felt revealing herself as Palestinian would have been a risk given the "highly nationalistic Jewish Zionist sentiment at the event."[15]

A Demonstration, therefore, relays a native sense of haunting (Gordon 1997) that emerges from an "outside-of-time" subject position, one excluded from and potentially threatened by the nonviolence of liberal Jewish democratic values. Awad's queer lens therefore reveals and undermines the Zionist configuration of sex and sense, where the projections of the sexual pluralism and moral superiority of Israeli humanist values collide. It demonstrates how pinkwashing emerges from the "histories that cannot rest" (Coddington 2011, 748), thus exposing and dramatizing the esthetic elements of the "reality" on screen. In doing so, Awad's cinematic lens bespeaks a native "seething presence" that "meddles" (Gordon 1997) with the spectacles that celebrate and equate Israeli-ness to sexual modernity and the negation of violence.

A second example of queering esthesis that I wish to discuss is found in "Ghanni A'an Taa'rif" (Singing Sexuality), a musical project led and produced by one of Palestine's prominent queer organizing groups, alQaws for Sexual and Gender Diversity in Palestinian Society. Its spaces foster creative energy to imagine a different Palestine. "Ghanni A'an Taa'rif" was launched by alQaws in 2013 to bring together volunteers—activists, artists, and singers—from across Palestine to share with their wider society the *hikayat* (stories) that are often not told within communities.[16] The latest production of "Ghanni A'an Taa'rif," titled *Minkom O Feekom* (We are from you and continue to live among you), is a medley of four music tracks based on the traditional folk music of Palestine and the wider Shami region (greater Syria). According to alQaws (2020), *Minkom O Feekom* is "a colloquial way for us to say we are an integral part of society, a statement against social denial and colonial narratives isolating Palestinian queers from Palestinian society, and an invitation for our society to engage in a discussion around sexual and gender diversity in Palestine." In the following, I draw on two tracks—"Ala Dal'oona" (which has many meanings, among them the name of a Canaanite lover and to ask someone for help) and "Ya Zarif Al-Toul" (Tall handsome man)—to build an account of a queering esthesis that works for the enunciation of a liberatory native sensuality.

Palestinian folk music emanates from the wider region of Greater Syria (*bilad al sham*)—comprising Syria, Lebanon, Jordan, and Palestine—and its indigenous folkloric *turath* (heritage). In the last century, Zionist settler colonialism and the Palestinian Nakba have contributed to the carving out a distinct form of Palestinian folkloric artifacts such as dance, music, and embroidery. Concurrently, and driven by a sense of fascination and reclamation of indigenous Palestinian-*ness*, the logic of replacement and conquest has also operated at the level of cultural production; since the 1930s, settlers have appropriated indigenous cultural productions, such as the *debkeh* dance (see Kaschl 2003). Jewish Israeli performances of debkeh—it has, for instance, become a mainstay of the Arabized version of the Israeli national anthem "Hatikvah"[17]—in place of Palestinian natives serve to reaffirm the settlers' presence and natives' disappearance. It thus comes as no surprise that the Palestinian reclamation and revival of a folkloric turath has become an integral part of the struggle for freedom and liberation. This process of revival became prominent following the establishment of the PLO and during the launch of the Palestinian *thawra* (revolt) in the late 1960s, and a Palestinian folklorist dedication to historicize and document the lyrics of liberation songs reached its zenith with the First Intifada (Al-Bargouthi 1994). Folk genres of *ataaba* and *aal'ouna*, and the song "Ya Zarif Al-Toul," are poetic forms of orally transmitted melodies usually set around repeated maqam phrases and have gained particular prominence as distinct forms of Palestinian musical turath (see Al-Bargouthi 1980). Characteristic of these musical forms is their malleability in accommodating lyrical alterations within the tradition of oral poetic singing known as *zajal*.[18]

The nationalization process of Palestinian turath music takes place within and reveals the relations between ideas of nation and gender. Masculinity comes through as integral to the Palestinian national project in the role of protector, thereby designating a protectee role to women (see, e.g., Kanaaneh 2002; Massad 1995). Weddings, for instance, became a prominent site for nation-building and singing, with protest songs being sung as often as wedding songs were sung at protests, if such a distinction could even be made (McDonald 2013, 4). David McDonald's (2010) ethnomusicology relates the poetics of masculinity within wedding celebrations as an effect of a nationalist operationalization of indigenous wedding songs and dances, turning them into acts of engendering resistance and sacrifice for the nation. Here, one can understand how the PNA's recent use of violence against alQaws's activities in the West Bank relates to the masculinist and heteronormative vision of a free Palestine, which is inscribed in the colonized failure to see beyond the regime of a settler sensual configuration (Alqaisiya 2020). In contrast to the existential and political conditions of the PNA, alQaws's Palestinian turath music opens the way toward a native sovereign sensuality, allowing an escape from the grip of the colonizer. Here is an extract from "Ala Dal'oona":

منكم وفيكم بنضلنا هونا
منضلنا هونا بلادك وبلادي
حنّوا علينا الوطن حنونا

منكم وفيكم، وبعدو الشارع
مش عارف إحنا فعل مضارع
ما زهق فينا، فينا يصارع
بدل ما يحارب اللي احتلونا

منكم وفيكم، يما ويا يابا
حرام نتشرد ونروح غرابا
حرام يروحوا من الأرض صحابا
في دفا دياركم والله خلونا

منكم وفيكم: إسأل المراية
طلطل ع روحك واسمع الحكاية
فيكم ما زلنا من البداية
كبرنا بوطننا مثل الزيتونا

Ala Dal'oona, Ala Dal'oona
We are from you and we continue to live among you
We remain here, this is my country and your country
Let's be compassionate to one another, our homeland is the land of compassion
We came from you and we continue to live among you
Yet somehow you doubt our presence
Have you not tired from fighting us, instead of fighting our colonizer
Oh mother and father, we are from you and deserve to remain with you,
    so not to disperse and
Become estranged from one another
How sorrowful would be for our land to lose its people
In the warmth of our home, let us remain
We are from you and we continue to live among you: look in the mirror
Reunite your soul, and listen to the tale
Since the beginning, we have been here
Like the olive trees we have continued to grow in the homeland

"Ala Dal'oona" is one of the most popular folkloric songs in Palestine and is sung at almost every Palestinian wedding celebration. Of its four hemistich stanzas, the first three have similar endings, and the fourth usually ends with the long sound "nā," which is the sound used in performing the debkeh. The group alQaws appropriates "Ala Dal'oona" to tell the queer hikaya, one that is long silenced within nationalist esthetic productions, leading to societal "doubtful[ness] [of] our presence." The singers repeatedly and affirmatively declare the phrase *minkom o feekom* (we are from you and we continue to live among you) and that "like the olive trees we have continued to grow in the homeland." The adoption of "Ala Dal'oona" emanates from the song's significance in proliferating the value of the Palestinian political model of *sumud* (steadfastness) and in offering a liberatory vision of "fighting our colonizer." Thus, it animates a native grounded knowledge of queering, a healing from the sorrows of dispossession, captured in the native exile from home. It is a call for a queering of the homeland, striving to make heard and felt the urgency for "the warmth of our home" and a reunion of the soul.

The queering tale from alQaws turns away from the colonizers' sensual regime-casting of the native self away from home by looking inward to recognize oneself: "Look [at yourself] in the mirror." Here, the song offers a reconfiguration of home that is woven into the embodied experiences and modalities of indigenous sensual ways of knowing and feeling in and of a place: "We have been here like the olive trees" that "since the beginning . . . have continued to grow." The narrative of "Ala Dal'oona" (re)maps (see Goeman 2013) the sensual and spatial grammars governing native life and obstructing the native's connection to her roots. It reinvigorates native spatial and bodily topographies, unsettling settler colonial sensual violence that imposes an outside-of-time subject position. alQaws's work and esthetic productions enact a politics of reorientation in a native liberatory project away from the hetero-conquest mode that subjugates in the first place (Arvin, Tuck, and Morrill 2013). The queering of "Ala Dal'oona" proposes an alternative conjuring of a native past, going beyond the gendered and sexed schemas of "authenticity" and "purity" that underpin nationalist rhetoric. This articulation exemplifies the openings and the yet-to-come futural directions (spatio-erotic) that the queering esthetic reimagining of a native past enables. This emerges further in "Ya Zarif Al-Toul":

يا ظريف الطول وقف تاقولّك
رايح عالغربة وبلادك أحسنلك
خايف يا ظريف تروح وتتملّك
وتعاشر الغير وتنساني أنا

يا ظريف الطول، أسمر ولطيف
غنولك كتير وغنوا عن التعريف
بس ما حد عرفك زيي يا ظريف
بستنّاك أنا مية ألف سنة

يا ظريف الطول يا سن الضحوك
إيدك بمسكها قدام امك وابوك
لو تقول أهلك عني ابعدوك
بنهرب بالليل ونعلن سرنا

O, zarif al-Toul,
Stop so I can tell you
You are going abroad but your country is better for you
I am afraid you will get established there
And find someone else and forget me

O, zarif al-Toul, with a nice dark skin
They sang for you and sang about who you are (sexuality)
But none of them knows you like I do
I shall wait for you a hundred years

O, zarif al-Toul, with a wide grin
I shall hold your hand in front of your mother and father
If you say that your family has torn us apart
We shall run away at night, and announce our secret

The song recounts the story of a Palestinian forced into exile, or ghorba, and is traditionally sung from a first-person perspective of he who has stayed behind, lamenting the condition of exile that has separated the man from his homeland. In the second and third stanzas, queer sexuality emerges subtly yet directly as the male narrator flirts with the beauty of his tall handsome lover's "nice dark skin" and "wide grin," evoking an amorous relation or connection: "None of them knows you like I do." The singer also daringly says that "I shall hold your hand in front of your mother and father" and hints at "run[ning] away at night" to "announce our secret."

This is yet another example of a queering turath that tackles indigenous conditions of ghorba while articulating a yearning, or desperate waiting for the beloved: "I am afraid you will get established there and find someone else and forget me." alQaws's production thus (re)orients the native's past to accommodate the rhythms of a queer sensuality in a specific way that draws on the Palestinian indigenous zajal tradition. As noted, zajal refers to a traditional form of oral poetry that is semi-improvised and adapted to the context; it is usually sung between *zajjalyin* (poets) in the local dialect. In its productions, alQaws's use of zajal is situated within the very recitational queer modality of native turath, conferring the changeability of each song's lyrical content according to the local context or situation and the speakers involved. It unveils the malleability of indigenous oral turath as per the long-existing diversities of genders and sexuality within Palestine. This perfectly coheres with what zajal does as "a thunderous form of music opposed to aristocratic and serious poetry of classical Arabic, containing subversive laughter of the lower classes as well as metaphors of the lower bodily strata" (Zuhur 2001, 135). The *zajjal* (singer) in alQaws's production aligns with the very premise of queer playfulness and subversion that is already at the heart of native esthetic and sensual configurations (esthesis). The readaptations of "Ala Dal'oona" and "Ya Zarif Al-Toul" animate the value of a de-colonial queering esthesis that maps the native return or that encompasses desires and relationships that are generative of the life denied to them within the structures of the settler sensual regime. Such a return simultaneously challenges the native's own political imaginary, as it succumbs to the imperatives of a settler sensual regime bent on instilling the native's ghorba from her land, histories, and desires.

Before sketching out concluding comments, I want to finally and briefly turn to one more example of queering esthesis—the case of the late Palestinian dancer Ayman Safiah. In a video production called *In Your Absence* (2014), Safiah performs a whirling dervish dance within the ruins of the Palestinian depopulated village of Kufr Biraim. His dancing evokes a phantom figure that seems to continually appear and disappear as we (the viewer) and another dancer in the film search desperately for the phantom-like dervish. Ayman's movement among the ruins of Kufr Biraim alludes to Palestinian refugees—the video closes with the words "I will be complete, the land says, when the refugees come back"[19]—and the sense of ghostly haunting they trigger against taken-for-granted realities within the settler state (Gordon 1997). In May 2020 Ayman's body washed ashore close to Atalit, a Palestinian depopulated town south of Haifa (Akil 2018), where he had been swimming with friends before a violent wave swept him away. His friends and family searched for him desperately for days, organizing volunteer search teams with hundreds of people and criticizing the lack of help from Israeli emergency services. On reporting the incident to Israeli police, its first response was, as is so often the case, "Jewish or Arab?" Upon his disappearance, a media campaign was waged in the search for Ayman. Videos and articles were shared not only about his work but also about his determined spirit as someone who never shied away from expressing himself, including a transgressive sexuality and a love of performing modern forms of dance that might be frowned upon or discouraged. Despite the challenges Ayman faced, he expressed in one emotional video a defining moment in his life where his father asked, "Ayman, won't you come home?" Ayman replies, in that moment, "I realized that my father understood all along." Ayman then continues tearfully, "If I am lucky with one thing in my life, it is the presence of my parents and family" (Makan 2020).

Reflections on losing Safiah to the violent sea that marked a Palestinian disintegration from home and Nakba compound the analysis of his figure as one of determination and persistence. Ayman dies, but his dancing never stops; it continues as his body moves along Haifa's coast off two depopulated villages in the south (Kfr Lam and Tantura) (see Fusha 2020) until

7. Still from *In Your Absence*. Khalil, 2012.

finally reaching the shore of yet another depopulated Palestinian town, Atalit. As Safiah whirls, everyone is on the lookout for the phantom figure. By acknowledging and recognizing Palestinian refugees' right of return, Ayman's previous whirling dance showed native persistence in the face of settler denial; later, the very utterance of "Jew or Arab?" breathes life into death. Such a life was further brought to celebration during the funeral of the whirling figure; the joyous ceremony marked and recognized the life and unity his dance ushered into the world around him as thousands came together from across different communities to honor him, to sing, and to join in the dance. His funeral was exceptional in that his body was laid to rest in the Islamic cemetery while the local church opened its doors for people paying their condolences to the family (Khatib 2020). This unifying moment stands against the structuring of a native sense of failure, which is bent on reproducing native misrecognition through the creation of stratified identities and intercommunal native conflict (see Alqaisiya 2020).

Conclusion: Queering Esthesis and Native Life Encounters

In this chapter, by unraveling the entwinement of sex and sense to the continuity of Nakba, I have aimed to show how at the heart of the Zionist settler regime in Palestine lies an esthetic and political regime. Netta Bar-zilai's winning of the 2018 Eurovision song competition is an example of what Palestinian queer activists call the pinkwashing policies of Israel; they serve as a crucial site for understanding the mechanisms of native disap-pearance and regulation within both the local and global spheres of settler colonial mobility. It reveals how a settler sensual regime—mediated by the esthetic configuration of Israel as a place of gender and sexual pluralism—encroaches on its native Other via the spectacles that fix the native in and out of place. A Zionist sensual regime confers modes of in/visibility, in/audibility, and un/sayablity about Palestinian queerness. That is, queerness via-à-vis Palestine is either nonexistent or only conceived via colonizers' humanist rescue-empathy frame, thereby locking the native within the psycho-political imperatives of ghorba, or exile, and misrecognition.

The examples of queering esthesis that this chapter engages via Awad's cinematic lens, alQaws's singing voices, and Safiah's dancing body capture the labor of refusing and unsettling settler modalities of sex and sense that are bent on colonizing the native land and being. Such unsettling does not simply articulate the value of undoing esthetic modalities of sexual violence that govern native life but also enables the activation of conceptual, politico-historical, and subjective unseen forces (Simpson 2014). The queering music of alQaws complements the political work that the group proliferates in Palestine and internationally, channeling de-colonial queering against the forces maintaining "out-of-time subject positions." The group's appropri-ation of turath songs to narrate the queer hikaya long silenced within this same regime further elucidates the significance of inhabiting a world of de-colonial queer erotics. This world celebrates the revival of communities and bodily mappings, carving the way for indigenous homecoming. Ayman Safiah's whirling dance also animates a Palestinian homecoming within a queer futurity that dares, in the processes of "opening a life" (Ahmed 2010, 20), toward a reconstructed sense of self and nation and to imagine how to be truly free.

Overall, the artistic productions explored in this chapter exemplify native methodologies for life that capture a geography of encounter where an indigene's forms of "life persist, and, at times, transcend mechanisms of political oppression" (see Griffiths and Joronen's introduction to this volume). Indigenous feminist and queer political theories have a crucial role to play in advancing a geographical encounter of Palestine that remains attuned to the irreducibility of the native's cultural and political life forms. Queering esthesis challenges the approaches of political geography that tend to reproduce the amnesia of settler colonialism by lacking a serious engagement with the openings that a de-colonial knowledge of queer esthetics generates. Such openings pertain to the possibilities that the work of de-colonial queering activates through initiating forms of native sovereign sensuality and home-return praxes, especially one that "gives voice, spreads love and maintains continuities" while also being "a critical space of becoming" (Shalhoub-Kevorkian and Ihmoud 2014, 377). Queering esthesis, therefore, invokes Palestinian epistemologies of en-*countering* the set of conceptual and geopolitical scripts disabling the native's sensual will to de-colonially exist.

Notes

1. See Pinkwatching Israel (@pinkwatcher), Twitter, accessed August 2020, https://www.twitter.com/pinkwatcher?lang=en.
2. Associated Press, "Netta on Israel: 'We Get Such Bad PR in the World,'" YouTube, July 26, 2018, https://www.youtube.com/watch?v=Uq2M0GKEEvU.
3. Prime Minister of Israel (@IsraeilPM), Twitter, accessed August 20, 2020, https://twitter.com/IsraeliPM/status/995620627003465728; and Archive: Mayor Nir Barakat, Twitter, May 13, 2018, https://twitter.com/ArchiveNir/status/995585653495816192/photo/1.
4. The term "internationally" refers to the League of Nations, which was another tool for legitimizing the mandate regime and thus the continuity of colonialism under the guise of self-determination. For further explication, see Erakat 2019, 35.
5. Shefita, "Pink (Moran Kariv Remix) [Aerosmith cover] TLV pride 2016," YouTube, accessed August 20, 2020, https://www.youtube.com/watch?v=ZRHKrH2UHyc.
6. Arisa, "Tel Aviv Pride 2013—Arisa feat. Omer Adam," YouTube, accessed August 20, 2020, https://www.youtube.com/watch?v=srOFki9PGM0. In his welcoming speech to Eurovision, the mayor of Tel Aviv talks about special culinary arts of the city. The Tel Aviv Municipality's website provides promotional videos of local culinarians that include hummus and falafel, which are appropriated from Palestinian cuisine.

See Tel Aviv Municipality, "Amazing Tel Aviv," YouTube, accessed August 20, 2020, https://www.youtube.com/user/telaviv.

7. See Dana International, "Dana International Is Preparing the City for Eurovision," YouTube, accessed August 20, 2020, https://www.youtube.com/watch?v=3zdwvtIGcA4.

8. StrandReleasing1 (2007), "The Bubble—US Trailer," directed by Eytan Fox, YouTube, accessed August 20, 2020, https://www.youtube.com/watch?v=Ou4UFIiY1wk; and Journeyman Pictures (2016), "The Invisible Men Trailer," directed by Yariv Mozer, YouTube, accessed August 20, 2020, https://www.youtube.com/watch?v=P3JmudV1wIo.

9. Israeli subjects such as Barzilai are mandated to serve in the Israeli army, which kills and dehumanizes Palestinians daily.

10. For a full explication of that process, see Alqaisiya 2020.

11. Video at Vimeo, accessed August 20, 2017, https://vimeo.com/99671737.

12. See the website for Aguda: The Israeli National LGBTQ Task Force, https://www.nif.org/tag/the-aguda-israels-lgbt-task-force/.

13. See Tag Archives: The Aguda—the Association for LGBTQ Equality in Israel, New Israel fund, https://www.nif.org/tag/the-aguda-israels-lgbt-task-force/; and conversation with Nadia Awad, 2015.

14. Mignolo and Vazquez (2013, 8) explain: "The first is a concept that now belongs to the sphere of philosophy; the second to language in general, in any language. Thus, if aestheTics is indeed modern/colonial aestheTics and a normativity that colonized the senses, decolonial aestheSis has become the critique and artistic practices that aim to decolonize the senses, that is, to liberate them from the regulations of modern, postmodern, and altermodern aestheTics."

15. Conversation with Awad, 2015.

16. See "About the Project," accessed August 20, 2020, http://www.ghanni.net/#about.

17. See Daniel Saadon, "Hatikvah—Al-Amal," YouTube, April 17, 2018, https://www.youtube.com/watch?v=ywq1wXU_HZs.

18. The etymology of "zajal" is related to play and musical entertainment in Zuhur 2001.

19. See Muhamad Saleh Khalil, *In Your Absence*, YouTube, accessed August 20, 2020, https://www.youtube.com/watch?v=pJhPZ-dAYQk.

References

Adams, William. 2018. "'We Are All Equal'—Netta and Dana International Speak Up for Israel's LGBT Community amid Surrogacy Bill Protests." *WiwiBlog*, July 20. https://wiwibloggs.com/2018/07/20/netta-and-dana-international-speak-up-for-israels-lgbt-community-amid-surrogacy-bill-protests/224831/.

Ahmed, S. 2010. *The Promise of Happiness*. Durham NC: Duke University Press.

Akil, Muhammad. 2018. "Atalit: Land and Memory Arab 1948." *Arab 48*, April 16. https://www.arab48.com/%D9%85%D8%AD%D9%84%D9%8A%D8%A7%D8%AA/%D8%AF%D8%B1%D8%A7%D8%B3%D8%A7%D8%AA-%D9%88%D8%AA%D9%82%D8%A7%D8%B1%D9%8A%D8%B1/2018/04/16/%D8%B9%D8%AA%D9%84%D9%8A%D8%AA-%D8%A7%D9%84%D8%A3%D8%B1%D8%B6-%D9%88%D8%A7%D9%84%D8%B0%D8%A7%D9%83%D8%B1%D8%A9-. [In Arabic.]
Al-Bargouthi, Abdellatif. 1980. "Palestinian Folk Literature: Ya Zareef al-Tool." *Al-Turath wa al-Mujtama* 13 (7): 20.
———. 1994. "The Role of Arab Popular Songs in the Palestinian Intifada." Amman: Markez Ahaya al-Turath al-'Arabi.
Alled, Dan. 2019. "Eurovision 2019: The Queerest—and Most Controversial—Yet?" NBC News, May 18. https://www.nbcnews.com/feature/nbc-out/eurovision-2019-queerest-most-controversial-yet-n1007201.
Alqaisiya, Walaa. 2018. "Decolonial Queering: The Politics of Being Queer in Palestine." *Journal of Palestine Studies* 47 (3): 29–44.
———. 2020. "Palestine and the Will to Theorise Decolonial Queering." *Middle East Critique* 29 (1): 87–113.
Alqaisiya, Walaa, Ghaith Hilal, and Haneen Maikey. 2016. "Dismantling the Image of the Palestinian Homosexual: Exploring the Role of alQaws." In *Decolonizing Sexualities: Transnational Perspectives, Critical Interventions*, edited by Sandeep Bakshi, Suraiya Jivraj, and Silvia Posocco. London: Counterpress.
alQaws. 2020. "New from Singing Sexuality: Minkom O Feekom." alQaws News, March 2. http://www.alqaws.org/news/New-from-Singing-Sexuality-Minkom-O-Feekom?category_id=0.
Anderson, B. 2014. *Encountering Affect: Capacities, Apparatuses, Conditions*. Farnham: Ashgate.
Arvin, M., E. Tuck, and A. Morrill. 2013. "Decolonizing Feminism: Challenging Connections between Settler Colonialism and Heteropatriarchy." *Feminist Formations* 25 (1): 8–34.
Awad, Nadia, and Collen Jankovic. 2012. "Queer/Palestinian Cinema: A Critical Conversation on Palestinian Queer and Women's Filmmaking." *Camera Obscura* 27 (2): 135–43.
Barlow, Eve. 2018. "Viva la Diva: How Eurovision Dana International Made Trans Identity Mainstream." *The Guardian*, May 10. https://www.theguardian.com/music/2018/may/10/viva-la-diva-how-eurovisions-dana-international-made-trans-identity-mainstream.
Britt, Brett Remkus. 2015. "Pinkwashed: Gay Rights, Colonial Cartographies and Racial Categories in the Pornographic Film Men of Israel." *International Feminist Journal of Politics* 17 (3): 398–415.
Butler, J. 1999. *Gender Trouble: Feminism and the Subversion of Identity*. London: Routledge.

Cabral, Thomas, and Delphine Matthieussent. 2018. "Netta Barzilai Is the Voice of #MeToo at Eurovision." *Times of Israel*, May 10. https://www.timesofisrael.com/netta-barzilai -is-the-voice-of-metoo-at-eurovision/.

Coddington, Kate Shipley. 2011. "Spectral Geographies: Haunting and Everyday State Practices in Colonial and Present-Day Alaska." *Social & Cultural Geography* 12 (7): 743–56.

Cook, Matt, and Jennifer Evans. 2014. "Introduction." In *Queer Cities, Queer Cultures: Europe since 1945*, edited by Matt Cook and Jennifer Evans, 1–12. London: Bloomsbury.

Daigle, Michelle, and Margret Marietta Ramírez. 2019. "Decolonial Geographies." In *Keywords in Radical Geography: Antipode at 50*, edited by the Antipode Editorial Collective, 78–84. Hoboken: Wiley Blackwell.

Dirbas, Nahid. 2019. "Ayman Safiah: Life Is Dance." *Al Arabi al Jadeed*, July 18. https:// www.alaraby.co.uk/%D8%A3%D9%8A%D9%85%D9%86-%D8%B5%D9%81%D9 %8A%D8%A9-%D8%A7%D9%84%D8%B1%D9%82%D8%B5-%D9%87%D9%88- %D8%A7%D9%84%D8%AD%D9%8A%D8%A7%D8%A9-0?fbclid=IwAR0kTKXG5J -YJg4spqsztVsXGp36eNTJY5ZAeQKIpLXW8kEXeYiEHOe5N9o. [In Arabic.]

Elia, Nada. 2012. "Gay Rights with a Side of Apartheid." *Settler Colonial Studies* 2 (2): 49–68.

Erakat, Noura, 2019. *Justice for Some: Law and the Question of Palestine*. Stanford: Stanford University Press.

Fusha. 2020. "Ayman Safiah Swam in the Air like a Feather." *Arab 48*, May 27. https:// www.arab48.com/فسح ة /جسد لر قص /2020/05/27/أيمن -صفي ة -سبح -في -الهواء -لخفته [In Arabic.]

Goeman, Mishuana. 2013. *Mark My Words: Native Women Mapping Our Nation*. Minneapolis: University of Minnesota Press.

Gordon, Avery. 1997. *Ghostly Matters: Haunting and the Sociological Imagination*. Minneapolis: University of Minnesota Press.

Holmes, Oliver. 2018. "Eurovision 2019 to Be Held in Tel Aviv instead of Jerusalem." *The Guardian*, September 13. https://www.theguardian.com/tv-and-radio/2018/sep /13/eurovision-song-contest-2019-tel-aviv-confirmed.

Kanaaneh, Rhoda Ann. 2002. *Birthing the Nation: Strategies of Palestinian Women in Israel*. Oakland: University of California Press.

Kaschl, Elke. 2003. *Dance and Authenticity in Israel and Palestine: Performing the Nation*. Leiden: Brill.

Kershner, Isabel. 2018. "'Next Year in Jerusalem!': In Israel, Eurovision Win Is Seen as a Diplomatic Victory, Too." *New York Times*, May 13. https://www.nytimes.com/2018 /05/13/world/middleeast/israel-eurovision-jerusalem.html.

Khatib, Isac. 2020. "Kufr Yasif: Thousands Participate in Funeral of Ayman Safiah." *Makan*, May 28. https://www.makan.org.il/Item/?itemId=60228. [In Arabic.]

Maikey, Haneen. 2019. "Tel Aviv Protecting Queers?" *MITRAS*, November 9. https:// metras.co/%D8%AA%D9%84-%D8%A3%D8%A8%D9%8A%D8%A8-%D8%AA %D8%AD%D9%85%D9%8A-%D8%A7%D9%84%D9%85%D8%AB%D9%84%D9

%8A%D9%8A%D9%86%D8%9F-%D8%A3%D8%B3%D8%B7%D9%88%D8%B1
%D8%A9-%D8%A5%D8%B3%D8%B1%D8%A7%D8%A6%D9%8A%D9%84/.
[In Arabic.]

Makan. 2020. "Ayman Won't You Come Home?" Facebook video, May 27. https://www
.facebook.com/Makan.Digital/videos/646190472602685.

Massad, Joseph. 1995. "Conceiving the Masculine: Gender and Palestinian Nationalism."
Middle East Journal 49 (3): 467–83.

McDonald, David A. 2010. "Geographies of the Body: Music, Violence and Manhood
in Palestine." *Ethnomusicology Forum* 19 (2): 191–214.

———. 2013. *My Voice Is My Weapon: Music, Nationalism, and the Poetics of Palestinian
Resistance*. Durham NC: Duke University Press.

Mignolo, Walter. 2006. "Citizenship, Knowledge, and the Limits of Humanity." *American
Literary History* 18 (2): 312–31.

———. 2014. *A Demonstration*. Vimeo. https://vimeo.com/99671737.

Mignolo, Walter, and Nanibush, W. 2018. "Thinking and Engaging with the Decolonial: A
Conversation between Walter D. Mignolo and Wanda Nanibush." *Afterall: A Journal of
Art, Context and Enquiry*, March 26. www.afterall.org/article/thinking-and-engaging
-with-the-decolonial-a-conversation-between-walterd-mignolo-and-wanda-nanibush.

Mignolo, Walter, and Ronald Vazquez. 2013. "Decolonial AestheSis: Colonial Wounds/
Decolonial Healings." *Social Text-Periscope*, July 15. http://socialtextjournal.org
/periscope_article/decolonial-aesthesis-colonial-woundsdecolonial-healings/.

Morgensen, Scott Lauria. 2011. *Spaces between Us: Queer Settler Colonialism and Indigenous Decolonization*. Minneapolis: University of Minnesota Press.

———. 2012a. "Queer Settler Colonialism in Canada and Israel: Articulating Two-Spirit
and Palestinian Queer Critiques." *Settler Colonial Studies* 2 (2): 167–90.

———. 2012b. "Theorising Gender, Sexuality and Settler Colonialism: An Introduction."
Settler Colonial Studies 2 (2): 2–22.

Naylor, Lindsay, Michelle Daigle, Sofia Zaragocin, Margaret Marietta Ramírez, and Mary
Gilmartin. 2018. "Interventions: Bringing the Decolonial to Political Geography."
Political Geography 66:199–209.

PACBI (Palestinian Campaign for the Academic and Cultural Boycott of Israel). 2019.
"No to Eurovision Pinkwashing: More Than 100 LGBTQ+ Groups Call for Boycott of
Song Contest in Israel." BDS movement, January 29. https://bdsmovement.net/news/no
-eurovision-pinkwashing-more-100-lgbtq-groups-call-for-boycott-song-contest-israel.

Puar, Jasbir. 2011. "Citation and Censorship: The Politics of Talking about the Sexual
Politics of Israel." *Feminist Legal Studies* 21 (1): 133–42.

Rancière, Jacques. 1999. *Disagreement: Politics and Philosophy*. Translated by J. Rose.
Minneapolis: University of Minnesota Press.

———. 2004. *The Politics of Aesthetics: The Distribution of the Sensible*. Translated by G.
Rockhill. Bloomsbury: London.

Razack, Sherene. 2007. "Stealing the Pain of Others: Reflections on Canadian Humanitarian Responses." *Review of Education, Pedagogy and Cultural Studies* 29:375–94.

Rifkin, Mark. 2011. "The Erotics of Sovereignty." In *Queer Indigenous Studies: Critical Interventions in Theory, Politics, and Literature,* edited by Qwo-Li Driskill, Chris Finley, Brian Joseph Gilley, and Scott Lauria Morgensen. Tucson: University of Arizona Press.

Said, Edward. 1979. *The Question of Palestine.* New York: Quadrangle.

Shalhoub-Kevorkian, Nadera. 2016. "The Occupation of the Senses: The Prosthetic and Aesthetic of State Terror." *British Journal of Criminology* 57 (6): 1279–300.

Shalhoub-Kevorkian, Nadera, and Sarah Ihmoud. 2014. "Exiled at Home: Writing Return and the Palestinian Home." *Biography* (University of Hawaii Press) 37 (2): 377–97.

Shihade, Magid. 2015. "Global Israel: Settler Colonialism, Mobility, and Rupture." *Borderlands* 14 (1): 1–16.

Simpson, A. 2014. *Mohawk Interruptus: Political Life across the Borders of Settler States.* Durham NC: Duke University Press.

Smith, Andrea. 2005. *Conquest: Sexual Violence and American Indian Genocide.* New York: South End Press.

Tobin, Robert Deam. 2007. "Eurovision at 50: Post-Wall and Post-Stonewall." In *A Song for Europe: Popular Music and Politics in the Eurovision Song Contest,* edited by I. Raykoff and R. D. Tobin, 25–36. Aldershot: Ashgate.

Tourist Israel. 2020. "Why Tel Aviv Is the Ultimate LGBTQ Travel Destination." https://www.touristisrael.com/why-tel-aviv-is-the-ultimate-lgbtq-travel-destination/26062/.

Veracini, Lorenzo. 2010. *Settler Colonialism: A Theoretical Overview.* Houndsmills: Palgrave Macmillan.

Vimalassery, M., J. H. Pegues, and A. Goldstein. 2016. "Introduction: On Colonial Unknowing." *Theory & Event* 19 (4).

Weber, Cynthia. 2014. "Queer International Relations: From Queer to Queer IR." *International Studies Review* 16 (4): 596–601.

Wolfe, Patrick. 2006. "Settler Colonialism and the Elimination of the Native." *Journal of Genocide* 8 (4): 387–409.

Zuhur, Sherifa, ed. 2001. *Colors of Enchantment: Theater, Dance, Music, and the Visual Arts of the Middle East.* Cairo: American University in Cairo Press.

10 Life of the Wounded

Rethinking Settler Colonial Power in Palestine

Mikko Joronen

> If it is true that so many power relationships have been
> developed, so many systems of control, so many forms
> of surveillance, it is precisely because *power was always
> impotent* [emphasis added].
> —MICHEL FOUCAULT (1989, 258)

As Ann Laura Stoler (2016) suggests in *Duress: Imperial Durabilities in Our
Times*, tracing the contours of colonial power requires not necessarily a
more thorough explication of forms and types of colonialism—imperial,
settler colonial, "hybrid," and so on—but a sharper focus on where such
power fails and becomes newly (re)formed and undone, and so associates
with the debris and waste it produces (see also Velednitsky, Hughes, and
Machold 2020). During the last two decades, a particular type of eliminatory colonial power—settler colonialism—has become sedimented as
one of the prominent critical frameworks in thinking of the structural
features of over a hundred years of violence, colonization, occupation, and
war in and of Palestine (e.g., Barakat 2018; Englert 2020; Khalidi 2020a;
Shalhoub-Kevorkian 2015; Yiftachel 2002). To be sure, the framework of
settler colonialism itself is hardly novel; despite the way many contemporary
authors anchor the debate, its roots go beyond the often-cited works of
the anthropologist Patrick Wolfe (e.g., Wolfe 2006). At the turn of 1970s,
for instance, several authors writing in the aftermath of the 1967 Israeli
occupation of the Palestinian territories (oPt) debated the overlapping

and coexisting phases of "internal" and "foreign," as well as the "imperial," "military," and "settler"-based, forms of colonial history and power (e.g., Abu-Lughod 1971; Abu-Lughod and Abu-Laban 1974; Jiryis 1976; Rodinson 1973; Said 1970a, 1979; Sayegh 1965 [2012]; Zureik 1979). In the years since, the debate has expanded enormously as Israeli uses of power and forms of violence have been shown to include numerous, often coexisting modalities ranging from forms of necro- and thanato-power to biopower and sovereign exception, with each spreading differently across the territorial fragments of the occupied Palestinian territories (e.g., Amir 2013; Gordon 2008; Griffiths 2022; Mbembe 2019; Lentin 2016; Parsons and Salter 2008; Puar 2016; Shenhav and Berda 2009; Weizman 2009).

In this chapter, my aim is to critically (re)think the way that power is conceptualized in political geographies of colonization, violence, and governing in Palestine. By approaching power on two fronts—one, by rethinking the *functions* of power, conceptually and empirically, from the perspective of the woundedness of life; and two, by asking what such woundedness can tell us of the *nature* of power itself—I wish to tackle what I see as the key problems related to different ways of ontologizing structural features of power in research on Palestine. Such an endeavor naturally contains a certain sense of grandiosity that goes beyond the question of Palestine: it is not only about offering an innovative frame for thinking how Israeli apparatuses function, for instance, to harm, wound, and maim Palestinian bodies (Puar 2016), nor of comprehending how these apparatuses operate by installing vulnerable and hyper-precarious conditions in which Palestinians dwell and cope (Hammami 2016; Joronen 2017b), but also about a tentative experiment to find ways for approaching the functions and conditions of power through a fundamental field that accounts for power's *indebtedness* to what I refer to as "wounded life" (see also Joronen and Rose 2020).

Considering the breadth of the task, in this chapter I limit my focus to two crucial points. First, I show how the indebtedness of power to woundedness changes the way of approaching functions and relations of power, as well as those tangible forms power has taken in Palestine. Such a change of approach, however, should not be taken to offer yet another novel "ontology of power" that undoes, for instance, the work on eliminatory forms of settler colonialism; rather, attending to woundedness asks us to clarify our take on both power *and* ontology. My second aim is precisely to think of power and woundedness without succumbing to install the meta-ontological (or "metaphysical," "onto-theological") scaffoldings that authors such as Martin Heidegger and Jacques Derrida questioned throughout their oeuvres (e.g., Derrida 1992; Heidegger 1998, 2002). It is the woundedness of living, I rather argue, that makes power both possible *and* impotent; I further show, by drawing on some of my existing work on ontology (e.g., Joronen 2016b; Joronen and Häkli 2017), that woundedness forces us to approach the question of ontology in ways that cannot strive to ontologize peculiar ways of becoming (and being) related. My aim to rethink power as indebted to woundedness should be thus understood, not as a novel ontological framework but as an attempt to approach ontology without ontologizing power as a primary frame in understanding the colonization of, and the colonial violence in, Palestine. This is not to deny the devastating effects of Israeli mobilizations of power or the ways of governing and the historical forms of violence they constitute. It is rather to explore the vast consequences of recognizing all forms of power, not only as *indebted* to woundedness but also as bound up to *encounter* with what makes power possible in the first place—that is, the exposure of the wounded life. "Encounter" in this reading is not a reaction of Palestinian life to forms of power cast upon them but rather the opposite: it names the *originary* situation, where the *always already impotent claims of power become imposed upon the always already wounded life*. Encounter, in short, denotes a life that is dealing with the relations of influence to which it is exposed.

To reach these aims, I open the chapter with a discussion of existing works in Palestine on power. In doing so, I shift the focus from the types and rationalities of power and the subtle arts of governing the "conduct of conduct" (Foucault 2000) to the originary event of encounter—that is, to the life of those forced to deal with the consequences of governing. While this can be further connected to ethical questions on Palestinian agency (see Griffiths 2017; Kotef and Amir 2011) and the victimization of those targeted by power (Joronen 2017a; Marshall 2014), to limit the reading to these facets alone would miss the depth of the argument. Woundedness, I contend, compels us to inquire, through the lives of those living with the wounds, what makes power "powerful" in the first place. The second section shows how woundedness forces us to think of power not as ontologically capable, affective, or powerful (e.g., Pile 2009; Ruddick 2017) but as epiphenomenal to woundedness itself (e.g., Joronen and Rose 2020; see also Dekeyser and Jellis 2020). Power, I suggest here, not only is enabled by the exposure of life to power (the woundedness *to* power) but also names a form of relating that is inherently vulnerable, limp, incapable, fragile, and so prone to failure (the woundedness *of* power). Indebted to woundedness, power is never more than a wounded power, one incapable of subsuming those it targets and is always seeking another form, technique, or way of relating in the face of its own impotence. Ultimately, the discussion in the second section shows that, in important ways, *power cannot be defined as a mere type or a form but through its own impotentiality*. The final section then explores some of the dynamics that the *woundedness of and to power* takes in the fieldwork materials I have collected over recent years in the West Bank and East Jerusalem. I show, first, how *woundedness to* power is used as an instrument not only where physical wounds can turn into long-lasting social, emotional, and political vulnerabilities but also where a constant maintaining of vulnerable sociopolitical conditions wounds Palestinian daily life and the family sphere in profound ways. When it comes to the *woundedness of* power, I show how it opens up various avenues for Palestinians to encounter and play with the woundedness of power, further expanding the cracks in all constellations of power. Through these discussions, my aim is to show how the "of/to" relationship between power and woundedness gives a renewed understanding of (colonial) power in Palestine as impotent, wounded, and indebted to a life that might be exposed but was always already there. The empirical discussion thus offers a way of thinking of power as an ever incomplete and inherently fragile process—that is, as indebted to its own impotentiality, or its incapacity to be no more than a wounded claim upon wounded life.

Settler Colonialism, Governing, and Ethics of Agency

Despite various authors, such as Edward Said, Elia Zureik, Sabri Jiryis, Maxime Rodinson, Fayez Sayegh, and Ibrahim Abu-Lughod, raising awareness of settler colonial and imperial traits in Palestine already during the years after Israel occupied the Palestinian territories in 1967, for a long time mainstream public and academic discussion on such traits of Israeli rule were more or less, at least in the West, conspicuous by their absence. Such silence was not merely due to various (geo)political reasons, which were reflected in the comments of key intellectuals of that time, including figures such as Michel Foucault, Jean-Paul Sartre, and Simone de Beauvoir (Said 2000; see also Medien 2019); this silence was also prevalent in core academic fields, such as postcolonial studies, whose main critical tools were, quite paradoxically, founded on the work of Palestinian scholar Edward Said. According to Stoler (2016), this echoed partly the failure to read Said's two key works—*Orientalism* (1978) and *The Question of Palestine* (1979)—as a singular effort; both were influenced by the grave gap Said saw, as Rashid Khalidi (2020b) explains, between post-1967 events in Palestine and the Western perception of them (see also Bayoumi and Rubin 2019; Said [1970b] 2019). Without a doubt, the decades following these early works on colonialism in Palestine have brought a significant change to this state of affairs, particularly after authors such as Oren Yiftachel (2002), Lorenzo Veracini (2006), Nadera Shalhoub-Kevorkian (2015), Zureik (2016), Wolfe (2006), Khalidi (2020a), and many more have consistently brought up the colonial legacies and nature of the present situation in Palestine (see also Abu Hatoum 2020; Barakat 2018; Jabary-Salamanca 2016; Velednitsky, Hughes, and Machold 2020). This is not to say that the academic debate on colonialism and the colonial present in Palestine would have disappeared since the publication of the early works (see, e.g., Gregory 2004; Ram 1999; Shafir 1999; Yiftachel 1996); rather, it is only during the last twenty years that the focus on settler colonialism has become paradigmatic for critical scholarship on power in Palestine.

Evidently the debate on settler colonialism has opened fruitful avenues for unfolding the nature of Israeli occupation, not as a "temporary" solution (as the word "occupation" indicates) but as part of the longer legacy of eliminatory practices inseparably entwined to the use and settlement of colonized territories. As Zureik (2016) has argued, it is also the case that settler colonial elimination—operating not only through the negative means of expulsion, genocide, and ethnic cleansing but also by "positive" means of assimilating the native to social and legal reorganization (e.g., Wolfe 2006)—has been, and still is, elementally entwined around other colonial and imperial means, ranging from the political economies of exploiting cheap labor to the extraction of material resources (such as ground water) (see, e.g., Braverman 2019; Shenhav and Berda 2009; Tawil-Souri 2009). While Zureik's (2016) suggestion to think of Palestine as a grand example of "hybrid colonialism" pays proper attention to the simultaneity of even opposing forms of colonial and imperial governing, it also demonstrates some of the focal problems of thinking of Palestine through a *type* or a *form* of power or governing. Here, Palestine becomes framed through the traits of a type, or at best through a mixture of originally separate types (as hybrid), as if these formations of power, or the Palestinian lives and spaces they shape, could be reduced to a blending of originally "pure" categories. Even in cases where these forms are seen more as "ideal types" that are always messy when actualized, the approach raises the issue of framing the field of power with types whose structural features are not only idealized and categorical but also identifiable beforehand. In this way, Palestine becomes framed as, and so reduced to, a place of a particular form of eliminatory drive. In a sense, such framings are understandable against the need to recognize structural forms of exploitation, violence, and oppression in Palestine (Shalhoub-Kevorkian 2015); yet, they are less apprehensible, as I show below, when considered against the theoretical challenges of approaching power in general and its nuances in Palestine in particular.

First of all, it is crucial to notice that these problems are not unique to the debate on settler colonialism alone; they also characterize more recent literatures focusing on the diverse modalities and tactics of power that Israel has mobilized in different territorial enclaves of the oPt (and within Palestine of 1948). In these works, the focus is perhaps less on recognizing the types and mechanisms of colonial domination and elimination in

Palestine and more on thinking of those manifold forms of power that Israel's rule in the oPt has taken over the decades. Whether elaborating on the biopolitical ways of regulation (Winter 2016), the traits of sovereign power and its logics of exception (Lentin 2016), or the thanato- and necro-politics of killing, maiming, and threatening (Ghanim 2008; Joronen 2016a; Leshem 2015; Mbembe 2019; Puar 2016; Weizman 2009), these discussions have nevertheless focused keenly on articulating the inner logics of Israeli control—namely, their onto-historical forms of operation. It is, to follow Chris Harker (2009), as if Palestine is seen first and foremost through the spaces of occupation—as if *Palestinian* spaces and lives were only epiphenomenal and nonexistent prior to the rationalities, forms, and techniques of power that the Israeli regime of power mobilizes (see Weizman 2007). In his book *Israel's Occupation*, Neve Gordon (2008), for instance, traces the genealogies of Israeli power precisely to show how the historical evolution of Israeli ways of governing the oPt makes understandable the symmetric forms Palestinian resistance have taken against them.

Perhaps a more subtle approach to governing, at least in a sense of being able to step outside structuralist readings and narrow "domination-reaction" symmetries, can be located in works on governmentality (e.g., Amir 2013; Azoulay and Ohpir 2009; Griffiths and Joronen 2021; Parsons and Salter 2008; Plasse-Couture 2013; Shlomo 2017; Zureik, Lyon, and Abu-Laban 2011). In such works, governing is approached through ways of governmentalizing power as a *structure of actions* ultimately based on the decisions and the behavior of those targeted by power. Often following Foucault's later thinking, the focus in these works is more on the art of governing, not as it comes forth as a process of domination but as a way of positioning people to behave in a certain (desired) manner. These works focus on the manifold ways of regulating the "conduct of conduct"—the field of possibilities where acting takes place—and the "art of governing," which refers to those "governmentalities" through which Palestinians internalize power. Such a process of "subjectification" can of course contain many historically formed techniques and forms of governing, but the crux here is that they are seen as actualized through the management of those conditions that encourage certain actions, not merely by forcing them but also by positioning them as desirable, favorable, rational, or less threatening ones to choose—that is, by "managing the possibilities" that actualize in action (i.e., as self-governing) (Foucault 2000, 341; see also Griffiths and Joronen 2021). Certainly, some of the works mentioned above—those focusing, for instance, on the thanato-politics of threat, particularly on how threats function by creating anticipation, self-regulation, and self-governing—have also pointed out the need to look at the ways in which power, as a relation of governing, always traverse subjectivities and so ultimately lean on how the governed act and regulate their own conduct. In fact, at times it might be hard to draw a clear line between the accounts focused on the modes and rationalities of domination and the ones centered on the governmentalization and the "art of governing" the field of possibilities. What ultimately unites both of these strains, however, is their ultimate aim to trace the ways through which *power works to govern, regulate, dominate, and control.* While in the former case, these functions are traced by looking at the structures, apparatuses, and rationalities of governing, in the latter the focus is more on the ways in which Palestinians internalize the logics of governing through their own conduct.

As several authors have acknowledged, these approaches raise several ethical and ontological dilemmas. In the worst-case scenario, they frame Palestinians as passive victims of power and trauma (Marshall 2014), thus robbing them of an ethical capacity to act politically. While in literatures on governmentality the internalization of governing is naturally seen to demand certain conduct or active forms of self-regulation, such works also raise questions related to the proper acknowledgment of Palestinian voice(s) and politics beyond internalized regulation and, ultimately, of the (ir)reducibility of Palestinian life to Israeli claims and rationalities of governing (see Leshem 2015; Harker 2009). As Hagar Kotef and Merav Amir (2011, 75) sum up, such approaches are in danger of reducing Palestinians to passive "objects" of Israeli apparatuses, so erasing Palestinian "agency, experience, voice and, most importantly, strategies of resistance." This is particularly problematic as Palestinians themselves refuse to be caught within forms of victimization and often find ways of acting that remain utterly irreducible—and in asymmetric relationship—to the aims of governing (Joronen 2017a).

The final approach that serves as an example on governing is the still relatively small body of literature, at least if compared to broader lines in current geographical thought, that focuses on *affects* of governing in Palestine (e.g., Curti 2008; Griffiths 2017; Joronen and Griffiths 2019; Kouri-Towe 2015). Perhaps not so tightly related to self-regulation as to the pre-subjective conditions from which affective states manifest (as bodily sensations), affect is elaborated as a *capacity* to make bodies act via certain states (of fear, threats, anxiety, waiting, hope, and so on) that are engendered by uses and forms of power and violence (e.g., also Anderson 2014). In other words, while capable of affecting, bodies are positioned by and affected through certain "atmospheric configurations" (Hitchen 2019) and "affective maneuvers" (Woodward and Bruzzone 2015) that hamper, diminish, or encourage particular states of acting and affecting. Here, the capacity to act thus follows from pre-subjective components and relational connections that already position, condition, and affect acting and feeling bodies (see also Plasse-Couture 2013; Laurie and Shaw 2018).

While the works on affect and the ethical concerns related to Palestinian agency both afford important additions that help in directing attention to how bodies are positioned and affected, as well as to how and under what conditions Palestinians can act on the prevalent state of affairs, they remain tightly entwined around a certain ontological take. Power, whether dominating, encouraging, insinuating, regulating, or emancipating, is ontologically defined in terms of its *ability*—that is, its capacity to influence, be affective and effective, and remain powerful. What I wish to argue next is that ultimately the approaches discussed thus far frame the forms of governing, and the counter-politics they might engender, in terms of their *capacity* to act and affect—that is, in terms of their ability to be powerful. While the voices here are manifold, the problem is, I argue in the next section, not only that of ontologizing power as capacious but also of approaching ontology as a way of framing how the process of worlding takes place. What I instead argue—first theoretically and then empirically—is that power should be considered neither a *type* nor as *capacious* but as a claim inherently indebted to *woundedness*. Woundedness, I show, does not merely move the focus from the aims of governing to the bodies, spaces, and lives of those who remain wounded but also engenders an approach to power as inherently wounded—that is, as a wounded power emerging through the sites of its indebtedness. Through this insight on how power operates as indebted to and by encountering the woundedness of life, I show the question of colonial power in Palestine can be opened to a radically renewed understanding.

Ontological Woundedness, Impotent Powers

The first step here is to recognize that woundedness, instead of being reducible to the wounds inflicted on those who live under colonial violence (e.g., Puar 2016), indicates life as *originally* exposed and fragile (for more, see Butler, Gambetti, and Sabsay 2016; Joronen and Rose 2020; Rose 2014). Palestinian everyday life and the Palestinian spaces of dwelling thus remain inherently *irreducible* to the spaces of occupation, not merely because Palestinians are capable of resisting and counter-(re)acting or because there is an ethical demand to look at the views and decolonizing counter-actions of the oppressed but also because of the original *woundedness of/ to power*. In other words, life cannot be reduced to a power, whose claims are ultimately impotent in nature, and these impotent claims of power are always posed upon a life that already existed, prone to influence. It is to this twofold sense of woundedness—of *life* as originally exposed and *power* as inherently impotent—that I anchor my discussion of power here.

Woundedness, as understood in this sense, operates on two closely related planes. First, it becomes impossible to think of ontology as a realm where the fundamental constitution of things, relations, and their ways of coming to being (i.e., worlding) are grounded in nominators such as power, force, or capacity. Certainly, the various takes on power (and governing) discussed so far deal with the questions of ontology and ontological framing in very different ways. Foucault (1997), for instance, talked about power in relation to historical ontologies, hence approaching prevalent forms of power as temporally grounded and closely related to multiple everyday operations. Yet, there remains a question of why such operations and temporal forms should be first and foremost considered as questions of *power*. Given the diversity of current debates on ontology (e.g., Ash 2020; Blaser 2014; Jan 2019; Joronen and Häkli 2017; Joronen and Rose 2020; Sundberg 2014), what I wish to underline here is specifically the need to think of ontology beyond setting a predefined framework of inquiry. My aim is to ask what happens to power if we start by thinking of ontology as a wounded "event," or as a site of spatial relatedness that preserves its ontological conditions, not through predefined frameworks of inquiry but through those events that remain utterly wounded. In other words, what if we think of power through those events of gathering and coming-to-being that woundedness allows to take place, not only as fragile compositions but for their finite time as well. Such ontologies are, in other words, *ontogenetic*—not in a sense of offering preset ontological axioms that are formed and finalized in their emergence (Massumi 2002) but in a sense of generating their incomplete formations through those *limited durations that woundedness allows to abide*. Woundedness therefore calls us to examine ontology through those formations that the world comes to being, at the same time showing the inherent *finiteness* and *fragility* of the "ontological"—that is, its limitedness and incapacity to offer lasting grounds for capturing the world (see also Malpas 2006). Woundedness, in this important sense, renders all aims to ontologize power incapable from the beginning.

This leads to the second plane—namely, one where woundedness ensures that power cannot be framed as an inherent capacity of things, or as something that defines things as capacious and altogether capable in their doings. Woundedness rather names all that power remains fundamentally indebted, or "beholden," to; it makes power possible by simultaneously rendering it impotent, resulting in a limited and a fractured *claim to power* (Joronen and Rose 2020). In this regard, woundedness cannot be considered something that merely undoes, unarms, and unpowers the capacities of power; it also constantly exposes life to various influences and relations of power that simultaneously render it as wounded and incapable of fulfilling power's claims. Woundedness, in other words, operates as power's innermost limit. It is this limit—present in those ways in which power remains cracked, fragile, impotent, and incapable—that characterizes power's indebtedness to woundedness to the extent that power cannot overcome or resolve what ultimately sets a limit to its own powerfulness. In this regard, woundedness comes to the fore as an impotentiality of power: it is manifested through power's constant fragility, incapacity, and proneness to fail in the task of upholding those capacities it claims for itself. *Power*, to conclude, *is not approached here as a type or a form* but through *its own impotentiality*.

Encounters: Woundedness of and to Power in Palestine

As the discussion so far has shown, power should not be defined through its types or forms, nor through its capacities, effects, and "doings," but through its elemental indebtedness to woundedness. Such indebtedness, I have further shown, contains an inherent *duality*: woundedness grants power its capacities, while at the same time it ungrounds those abilities that power comes to claim for itself. This realization has radical consequences for thinking of power and woundedness in Palestine: it moves the focus away from types of power to a wounded life, one exposed to the (impotent) claims of power. In spite of being impotent, power is hence never merely powerless, or completely incapable of having any effect whatsoever on how life within Palestinian spaces becomes organized. Rather, woundedness defines power in action through two peculiar routes that importantly make life *irreducible* and *exposed* to power: through the woundedness *of* and the woundedness *to* power.

I start my empirical discussion here from the latter notion, the *woundedness* (of life) *to* power. Here, it is crucial to acknowledge, my aim is not simply to move the focus on those forms and rationalities of governing that power takes to wound; rather, I look at wounding(s) through the originary site of encounter—that is, through the *life of those who become exposed* to power. This brings to the fore encounters that life, in the sites of exposure, has with (themselves wounded) forms of power. With the second notion—the woundedness *of* power—the aim is to further show how Palestinian lives, in their ways of becoming wounded, remain irreducible to the uses of power. It is due to such *woundedness of* power that life can always play with the cracks, fractures, and incapacities—the impotency—of power.

Certainly, lives can become wounded via numerous routes: via physical and bodily wounds, via structural vulnerabilities or prospective insecurities, and via ways that are slow and unspectacular (e.g., Hammami 2016; Joronen 2017b). Wounding is never merely about the bullets of Israeli soldiers, even when our focus might be on the bodily wounds (e.g., Puar 2016). Consider an example from my fieldwork on the contrasting realities of two groups of Palestinian women living only a few kilometers apart in the West Bank.[1] In a workshop in one of the refugee camps in the Bethlehem Governorate, the women discussed situations where Israeli soldiers had wounded and maimed their children with bullets, even to the extent that one child had his leg amputated. All the mothers (sixteen in this particular workshop group) described the shock of these events often taking place when the children were playing football in the only available site located near the separation wall or when Israeli soldiers entered to raid the camp. In the beginning, all the workshop participants recalled, the strong social ties of the camp were helpful in offering support and care to the families with children wounded by Israeli military violence. In the long run, however, the prevalence of the events revealed the profound significance of being maimed. The mothers talked heartbreakingly of their kids, many of whom "loved playing football," not only "losing their dreams" but also reacting in various ways: becoming less sociable, "spending too many hours on social media and with video games," or "go[ing] to the playground . . . to watch, only to watch others play." Some refused to go to back to school, not only because one often needed to be in a "different class than his friends" but also, as several mothers sadly recalled watching their children "lose their happiness," because of the depression, stress, and fears the children have experienced. The violent events and permanent disabilities thus became something the whole family was exposed to and obliged to live through. One mother summed up her own feelings: "I'm always stressed that Israeli soldiers will come to take him [her son] back and cannot sleep when I know that soldiers are around." This is particularly the case, as she later recalled, since "the general of the soldiers who invade the camp continually threatens to make our children handicapped."

As these cases exemplify, physical wounds alone can expose life to long-lasting affectual, social, and political vulnerability, ranging from stress, depression, and a sense of insecurity to a constant "worry about the future." Further, the prevalent sociopolitical vulnerabilities can also wound Palestinian lives in profound ways. This was revealed in a second workshop organized in one of the villages surrounded by the Israeli settlements of Gush Etzion (a settlement block). The inhabitants of these strangulated spaces are not only subjected to the arbitrariness of settler and military violence but also prevented from farming their former agricultural lands, which now are mostly allocated to the expanding settlements (see also Joronen 2017a). This has resulted in a worsening economic situation and forced families to seek job opportunities outside the village, mostly as laborers in Israel or East Jerusalem (Farsakh 2005; see also Englert 2020; Tawil-Souri 2009). As documented by many (e.g., Griffiths and Repo 2020; Tawil-Souri 2017), due to detours, settler-only roads, and slow passage through the checkpoints, workdays become, almost without exception, considerably long. "My husband works inside Israel," a woman in her late forties said in one of the group meetings. "I swear some days he didn't see his children at all. He comes back from work either late or tired and cannot engage anyone." The cycle starts again the next morning as the men need to leave early to pass through the checkpoint—a process that alone can take several hours—and reach work on time. As an outcome, all the women with husbands working long days in Israel or East Jerusalem lamented the need to "carry all the responsibility," from "taking care of children" and "being their mum and dad" to "paying bills" and "taking care of all house needs." While acknowledging the role of the occupation in creating these vulnerable conditions—the social and economic problems, the stress, the constant presence of aggression, the sense of everyday insecurity, and the need to work outside their home villages in the first place—the men's absence added another layer of insecurity to their lives. As one woman concluded, at times she felt her husband had become "almost a stranger," yet she still wanted him to come sleep at home as she was "afraid the soldiers might break into the house."

The vulnerabilities of everyday life, as described by the fourteen women in this second workshop group, are closely related to ranging conditions, such as economic insecurities or the everyday familial matters of organizing life in hostile political environments. However, these vulnerabilities become comprehensible and often visible only by looking at the *intersections* of wounds *within* everyday Palestinian life. The focus on woundedness, in other words, requires an equal focus on the everyday *encounters* and various layers of resulting mundane harm. As the examples on the aftereffects of maiming Palestinian children and the need to seek job opportunities outside the strangulated communities both highlight, these ways of wounding often emerge slowly as part of everyday life—as spaces of "ordinary sufferings" (Povinelli 2011)—thus creating less visible and less spectacular ways of becoming wounded (see also Hammami 2015; Joronen 2021). These mundane woundings can be connected quite readily to spectacular events (for instance, to the physical maiming of Palestinian children, as discussed above) that over time turn into chronic wounds, while in other instances it is impossible to detect the events that first wounded as they are not instantly visible. In both cases, we are witnesses to the slow intrusions of mundane wounding, intrusions that ultimately use the woundedness of life as their asset (see Joronen 2017b; Rose 2014).

However, even here we are faced with a power that might be able to wound life—to mobilize the woundedness of living as its asset—but that nevertheless itself remains utterly wounded as maimed children were able to adapt to new realities, communities showed care and support to families with maimed children, women and families supported one another in strangulated communities, and so on. To further highlight the incapacity of power to reduce life under its forms of domination—the woundedness *of* power—I want to draw attention to discriminatory administrative processes that Palestinians living in the above-mentioned parts of Area C need to cope and deal with as part of their daily lives. Take, for instance, the infrastructural shortages, such as the lack of building permits, electricity, and running water, that are inseparable from the strict permission policies of the Israeli Civil Administration, a military body dealing with civilian matters in the oPt. Lacking proper access to water, some Palestinian communities secretly take water from the pipes running from aquifers located on Palestinian lands that serve the settlements. At other sites, when building permits are not allowed for Palestinians, they construct buildings slowly or covertly, or they might do so quickly during the Jewish holidays as a legal process for demolishing a finished house is significantly more complex than issuing of "stop construction" order. Similarly, Palestinian communities and farmers have mobilized renewable energy solutions in parts of the West Bank, where infrastructural shortages are chronic and continuing. Finally, when there has been a lack of running water, rainwater filtering systems have been built and alternative, self-sustainable farming methods imposed (for more on these options, see Joronen and Griffiths 2019; Joronen 2017a; Meneley 2020).

What is at stake here is not merely a constitutive form of (legal-administrative) power that mobilizes the woundedness of living to the extent of using the profound exposure of life (to power) as its asset. It is also the case that no power can ever be more than a wounded power—a power that not only is fractured and cracked open to all sorts of manners of canceling, ignoring, in-operationalizing, and countering its effects but even more importantly is incapable of forcing Palestinian lives and spaces into its claims and forms of governing. Woundedness is thus never merely a condition for acts of wounding; it also allows ways of *encountering and playing with* the woundedness of power. Such a de-colonial mining of the cracks of power naturally takes numerous other forms that are often unspectacular and mundane in nature. What the examples above help to underline is the way that the woundedness *of* power not only opens up various avenues for Palestinians to play with power's own impotencies but also reveals the incapacity of power to bring life within its capture. Encounter, in this regard, is never simply a Palestinian reaction to presumably prior and constitutive techniques of power. It rather names the originary situation, where the impotent operations of power become imposed upon the already wounded, yet irreducible life—that is, where Palestinian life deals with the relations of influence to which it is so exposed but is always inexhaustible. Such power can only ever be a claim of power upon what remains utterly irreducible to it.

Conclusion: Being Wounded

In this chapter, I have suggested approaching power in general and settler colonial forms of power in particular as inherently indebted to woundedness. As such, I mean rethinking the functions and the ontology of power as epiphenomenal to power's own *impotency* while also attending to what power must *encounter*—namely, the *wounded life*. I have further shown how the exposure of life offers a starting point for thinking of how woundedness can become mobilized as a colonial asset, which might be able to wound but nonetheless is never more than a mobilization of wounded claims to power. While this means starting our inquiries from a life that is originally exposed (cf. Harrison 2007), it also means understanding relations and forms of power so enabled as inherently impotent, as indebted to *woundedness*. This is not, however, to reference a "pure indigeneity" originally free of the contaminating realm of power; rather, it is thinking of life as originally exposed and so wounded to influences that operate, in the very sites where they come to being, by mobilizing the woundedness of life. Being there means being wounded—a life that already is there, as exposed to (colonial) powers that can never be but a *claim* to power.

This chapter has shown that the ambiguous woundedness of/to power captures the way in which the indebtedness of power to woundedness comes into being. As the discussion of wounds and wounding in Palestine details, on the one hand, woundedness *grants* power its abilities to influence and to become powerful, while on the other hand, woundedness *ungrounds* all power and so reveals the way power always remains bound up with its own impotency. Woundedness, in other words, does not simply nullify power but makes it indebted, so it is destined to seek new forms against the wounds and impotentialities it cannot ever overcome but that it nevertheless needs to deal with constantly. In this regard, woundedness illustrates how colonial systems of control are, to return to the opening words of Foucault (1989, 258), always unfinished processes constantly seeking to develop new "power relationships" and, I would add, so fundamentally indebted to what makes colonial regimes inherently cracked, fragile, and utterly incapable endeavors that are always open to de-colonial counters and non-colonial excesses. Here, power is not approached as *a type* or *a form* that is *capable of* implementing certain, predominantly eliminatory functions and mechanisms but as wrapped up in its own *impotentiality*. Yet, settler colonial regimes in Palestine and elsewhere should not be taken only as open to failures and (often small-scale and mundane) ways of decolonization but rather as originally ungrounded and inherently impotent in the move to reduce and order Palestinian life. Geographies of Palestine should not be reduced to the eliminatory functions of one prevalent form of colonial power—settler colonialism—a priori: not only are these framings secondary to the original exposure of Palestinian life, but also they should be seen not as forces *capable* of eliminating but as *impotent claims* that are always cracked open to various ways of countering, refusal, dismissal, avoidance, and plasticity. By moving the focus to the life of the wounded, we can see this ungrounding and enabling of power at play in its colonizing claims and decolonizing functions, its failures and mobilizations, its forms and cracks, its pursuit of novelty, and its own impotence.

Notes

1. The women, between the ages of twenty and fifty years old, took part in the workshops organized with a Bethlehem-based nongovernmental organization (Psychology Spa) in the two villages and two refugee camps located in the Bethlehem region in 2020. The aim of the workshops, which held four meetings with four different groups at four different sites (each meeting with ten to nineteen participants), was to offer a venue to talk through everyday insecurities of living under military occupation.

References

Abu Hatoum, Naurouz. 2020. "For 'a No-State Yet to Come': Palestinians Urban Place-Making in Kufr Aqab, Jerusalem." *Environment and Planning E: Nature and Space.* https://doi.org/10.1177/2514848620943877.

Abu-Lughod, Ibrahim. 1971. *The Transformation of Palestine: Essays on the Origin and Development of the Arab-Israeli Conflict*. Evanston IL: Northwestern University Press.

Abu-Lughod, Ibrahim, and Baha Abu-Laban, eds. 1974. *Settler Regimes in Africa and the Arab World: The Illusion of Endurance*. Wilmette IL: Medina University Press International.

Amir, Merav. 2013. "The Making of a Void Sovereignty: Political Implications of the Military Checkpoints in the West Bank." *Environment and Planning D: Society and Space* 31 (2): 227–44.

Anderson, Ben. 2014. *Encountering Affect: Capacities, Apparatuses, Conditions*. Farnham: Ashgate.

Ash, James. 2020. "Flat Ontology and Geography." *Dialogues in Human Geography* 10 (3): 345–61.

Azoulay, Ariella, and Adi Ophir. 2009. "The Order of Violence." In *The Power of Inclusive Exclusion*, edited by Adi Ophir, Michal Givoni, and Sari Hanafi, 99–140. New York: Zone Books.

Barakat, Rana. 2018. "Writing/Righting Palestine Studies: Settler Colonialism, Indigenous Sovereignty and Resisting the Ghost(s) of History." *Settler Colonial Studies* 8 (3): 349–63.

Bayoumi, Moustafa, and Andrew Rubin. 2019. "Introduction." In *The Selected Works of Edward Said, 1966–2006*, edited by Mustafa Bayoumi and Andrew Rubin, xix–l. New York: Vintage Books.

Blaser, Mario. 2014. "Ontology and Indigeneity: On the Political Ontology of Heterogenous Assemblages." *Cultural Geographies* 21 (1): 49–58.

Braverman, Irus. 2019. "Silent Springs: The Nature of Water and Israel's Military Occupation." *Environment and Planning E: Nature and Space* 3 (2): 527–51.

Butler, Judith, Zeynep Gambetti, and Leticia Sabsay, eds. 2016. *Vulnerability in Resistance*. Durham NC: Duke University Press.

Curti, Giorgio Hadi. 2008. "From a Wall of Bodies to a Body of Walls: Politics of Affect | Politics of Memory | Politics of War." *Emotion, Space and Society* 1 (2): 106–18.

Dekeyser, Thomas, and Thomas Jellis. 2020. "Besides Affirmationism? On Geography and Negativity." *Area*. https://doi.org/10.1111/area.12684.

Derrida, Jacques. 1992. "Onto-Theology of National-Humanism (Prolegomena to a Hypothesis)." *Oxford Literary Review* 14 (1): 3–24.

Englert, Sai. 2020. "Settlers, Workers, and the Logic of Accumulation by Dispossession." *Antipode* 52 (6):1647–66.

Farsakh, Leila. 2005. *Palestinian Labour Migration to Israel*. London: Routledge.

Foucault, Michel. 1979. *History of Sexuality*. Vol. 1, *The Will to Knowledge*. London: Allen Lane.

——. 1989. *Foucault Live (Interviews, 1961–1984)*. New York: Semiotex(e).

——. 1997. *Politics of Truth*. Los Angeles: Semiotext(e).

———. 2000. "The Subject and Power." In *Power: Essential Works of Michel Foucault*, edited by James D. Faubion, 326–48. New York: New Press.

Ghanem, As'ad. 2020. "The Deal of the Century in Context—Trump's Plan Is Part of a Long-Standing Settler-Colonial Enterprise in Palestine." *Arab World Geographer* 23:45–59.

Ghanim, Honaida. 2008. "Thanatopolitics: The Case of the Colonial Occupation in Palestine." In *Thinking Palestine*, edited by Ronit Lentin, 65–81. New York: Zed Books.

Gordon, Neve. 2008. *Israel's Occupation*. Berkeley: University of California Press.

Gregory, Derek. 2004. *The Colonial Present: Afghanistan. Palestine. Iraq*. Oxford: Blackwell Publishing.

Griffiths, Mark. 2017. "Hope in Hebron: The Political Affects of Activism in a Strangled City." *Antipode* 49 (3): 617–35.

———. 2022. "Thanato-Geographies of Palestine and the Possibility of Politics." *Environment and Planning C: Politics and Space* 40 (8). https://doi.org/10.1177/23996544221099461.

Griffiths, Mark, and Jemima Repo. 2020. "Women's Lives beyond the Checkpoint in Palestine." *Antipode* 52 (4): 1104–21.

Griffiths, Mark, and Mikko Joronen. 2021. "Governmentalizing Futures: Uncertainty, Anticipation, Possibility." *Geografiska Annaler: Series B, Human Geography* 103:352–66. https://doi.org/10.1080/04353684.2020.1871299.

Hammami, Rema. 2015. "On (Not) Suffering at the Checkpoint: Palestinian Narrative Strategies of Surviving Israel's Carceral Geography." *Borderlands* 14 (1): 1–17.

———. 2016. "Precarious Politics: The Activism of the 'Bodies That Count' (Aligning with Those That Don't) in Palestine's Colonial Frontier." In *Vulnerability in Resistance*, edited by Judith Butler, Zeynep Gambetti, and Leticia Sabsay, 167–90. Durham NC: Duke University Press.

Harker, Chris. 2009. "Spacing Palestine through the home." *Transactions of the Institute of British Geographers* 34 (3): 320–32.

Harrison, Paul. 2007. "The Space between Us: Opening Remarks on the Concept of Dwelling." *Environment and Planning D: Society and Space* 25 (4): 625–47.

Heidegger, Martin. 1998. "Kant's Thesis about Being." In *Pathmarks*, edited by William McNeill, 337–63. Cambridge: Cambridge University Press.

———. 2002. *Identity and Difference*. Chicago: University of Chicago Press.

Hitchen, Esther. 2019. "The Affective Life of Austerity: Uncanny Atmospheres and Paranoid Temporalities." *Social & Cultural Geography* 22 (3): 295–318.

Jabary-Salamanca, Omar. 2016. "Assembling the Fabric of Life: When Settler Colonialism Becomes Development." *Journal of Palestine Studies* 45 (4): 64–80.

Jan, Najeeb. 2019. *The Metacolonial State: Pakistan, Critical Ontology, and the Biopolitical Horizons of Political Islam*. Oxford: Wiley.

Jiryis, Sabri. 1976. *The Arabs in Israel*. New York: Monthly Review Press.

Joronen, Mikko. 2016a. "Death Comes Knocking on the Roof: Thanatopolitics of Ethical Killing during Operation Protective Edge in Gaza." *Antipode* 48 (2): 336–54.

———. 2016b. "Politics of Being-Related: On Onto-Topologies and Coming Events." *Geografiska Annaler: Series B, Human Geography* 98 (2): 97–107.

———. 2017a. "Refusing to Be a Victim, Refusing to Be an Enemy: Form-of-Life as Resistance in the Palestinian Struggle against Settler Colonialism." *Political Geography* 56:91–100.

———. 2017b. "Spaces of Waiting: Politics of Precarious Recognition in the Occupied West Bank." *Environment and Planning D* 35:994–1011.

———. 2021. "Unspectacular Spaces of Slow Wounding in Palestine." *Transactions of the Institute of British Geographers* 46 (4): 995–1007.

Joronen, Mikko, and Jouni Häkli. 2017. "Politicizing Ontology." *Progress in Human Geography* 41 (5): 561–79.

Joronen, Mikko, and Mark Griffiths. 2019. "The Affective Politics of Precarity: Home Demolitions in Occupied Palestine." *Environment and Planning D: Society and Space* 37 (3): 561–76.

Joronen, Mikko, and Mitch Rose. 2020. "Politics of the Wound: Vulnerability and the Limits of Power." *Progress in Human Geography* 5 (6): 1402–18.

Khalidi, Rashid. 2020a. *The Hundred Years' War on Palestine: A History of Settler Colonialism and Resistance, 1917–2017*. New York: Metropolitan Books.

———. 2020b. "The Worldly Exile: Edward Said's Life and Afterlives." *The Nation*, May 5.

Kotef, Hagar, and Merav Amir. 2011. "Between Imaginary Lines: Violence and Its Justifications at the Military Checkpoints in Occupied Palestine." *Theory, Culture & Society* 28 (1): 55–80.

Kouri-Towe, Natalie. 2015. "Textured Activism: Affect Theory and Transformational Politics in Transnational Queer Palestine-Solidarity Activism." *Atlantis* 37 (1): 23–34.

Laurie, Emma W., and Ian G. R. Shaw. 2018. "Violent Conditions: The Injustices of Being." *Political Geography* 65:8–16.

Lentin, Ronit. 2016. "Israel/Palestine: State of Exception and Acts of Resistance." In *Resisting Biopolitics: Philosophical, Political and Performative Strategies*, edited by S. E. Wilmer and Audronė Žukauskaitė, 271–86.

Leshem, Noam. 2015. "'Over Our Dead Bodies': Placing Necropolitical Activism." *Political Geography* 45:34–44.

Malpas, Jeff. 2006. *Heidegger's Topology: Being, Place, World*. Cambridge: MIT Press.

Marshall, David Jones. 2014. "Save (Us from) the Children: Trauma, Palestinian Childhood, and the Production of Governable Subjects." *Children's Geographies* 12 (3): 281–96.

Massumi, Brian. 2002. *Parables for the Virtual: Movement, Affect, Sensation*. Durham NC: Duke University Press.

Mbembe, Achille. 2019. *Necropolitics*. Durham NC: Duke University Press.

Medien, Kathryn. 2019. "Palestine in Deleuze." *Theory, Culture & Society* 36 (5): 49–70.

Meneley, Anne. 2020. "Hope in the Ruins: Seeds, Plants, and Possibilities of Regeneration." *Environment and Planning E: Nature and Space.* https://doi.org/10.1177/2514848620917516.

Parsons, Nigel, and Mark B. Salter. 2008. "Israeli Biopolitics: Closure, Territorialisation and Governmentality in the Occupied Palestinian Territories." *Geopolitics* 13 (4): 701–23.

Pile, Steve 2010. "Emotions and Affect in Recent Human Geography." *Transactions of the Institute of British Geographers* 35 (1): 5–20.

Plasse-Couture, François-Xavier. 2013. "Effective Abandonment: The Neoliberal Economy of Violence in Israel and the Occupied Territories." *Security Dialogue* 44 (5–6): 449–66.

Povinelli, Elizabeth A. 2011. *Economies of Abandonment: Social Belonging and Endurance in Late Liberalism.* Durham NC: Duke University Press.

Puar, Jaspir. 2016. *The Right to Maim: Debility, Capacity, Disability.* Durham NC: Duke University Press.

Ram, Uri. 1999. "The Colonization Perspective in Israeli Sociology." In *The Israel/Palestine Question*, edited by Ilan Pappé, 55–80. London: Routledge.

Rodinson, Maxime. 1973. *Israel: A Colonial-Settler State?* New York: Monad Press.

Rose, Mitch. 2014. "Negative Governance: Vulnerability, Biopolitics and the Origins of Government." *Transactions of the Institute of British Geographers* 39 (2): 229–23.

Ruddick, Susan M. 2017. "Rethinking the Subject, Reimagining Worlds." *Dialogues in Human Geography* 7 (2): 119–39.

Said, Edward. 1970a. "The Arab Portrayed." In *The Arab-Israeli Confrontation of June 1967: An Arab Perspective*, edited by Ibrahim Abu-Lughod, 1–9. Evanston IL: Northwestern University Press.

———. (1970b) 2019. "The Palestinian Experience (1968–1969)." In *The Selected Works of Edward Said, 1966–2006*, edited by Mustafa Bayoumi and Andrew Rubin, 14–36. New York: Vintage Books.

———. 1978. *Orientalism.* New York: Pantheon Books.

———. 1979. *The Question of Palestine.* London: Routledge.

———. 2000. "Diary: My Encounter with Sartre." *London Review of Books* 22 (11).

Sayegh, Fayez A. 2012. "Zionist Colonialism in Palestine (1965)." *Settler Colonial Studies* 2 (1): 206–25.

Shafir, Gershon. 1999. "Zionism and Colonialism: A Comparative Approach." In *The Israel/Palestine Question: Rewriting Histories*, edited by Ilan Pappé, 81–96. London: Routledge.

Shalhoub-Kevorkian, Nadera. 2015. *Security Theology, Surveillance and the Politics of Fear.* Cambridge: Cambridge University Press.

Shenhav, Yehouda, and Yael Berda. 2009. "The Colonial Foundations of the State of Exception: Juxtaposing the Israeli Occupation of the Palestinian Territories with Colonial Bureaucratic History." In *The Power of Inclusive Exclusion*, edited by Adi Ophir, Michal Givoni, and Sari Hanafi, 337–74. New York: Zone Books.

Shlomo, Ore. 2017. "The Governmentalities of Infrastructure and Services amid Urban Conflict: East Jerusalem in the Post Oslo Era." *Political Geography* 61:224–36.

Stoler, Ann Laura. 2016. *Duress: Imperial Durabilities in Our Times*. Durham NC: Duke University Press.

Sundberg, Juanita. 2014. "Decolonizing Posthumanist Geographies." *Cultural Geographies* 21 (1): 33–47.

Tawil-Souri, Helga. 2009. "New Palestinian Centers: An Ethnography of the 'Checkpoint Economy.'" *International Journal of Cultural Studies* 12 (3): 217–35.

———. 2017. "Checkpoint Time." *Qui Parle* 26:383–422.

Velednitsky, Stepha, Sara N. S. Hughes, and Rhys Machold. 2020. "Political Geographical Perspectives on Settler Colonialism." *Geography Compass* 14 (6).

Veracini, Lorenzo. 2006. *Israel and Settler Society*. London: Pluto Press.

Weizman, Eyal. 2007. *Hollow Land: Israel's Architecture of Occupation*. London: Verso.

———. 2009. "Thanato-tactics." In *The Power of Inclusive Exclusion*, edited by Adi Ophir, Michal Givoni, and Sari Hanafi, 587–96. New York: Zone Books.

Winter, Yves. 2016. "The Siege of Gaza: Spatial Violence, Humanitarian Strategies, and the Biopolitics of Punishment." *Constellations* 23:308–19.

Wolfe, Patrick. 2006. "Settler Colonialism and the Elimination of the Native." *Journal of Genocide Research* 8 (4): 387–409.

Woodward, Keith, and Mario Bruzzone. 2015. "Touching like a State." *Antipode* 47:539–56.

Yiftachel, Oren. 1996. "The Internal Frontier: Territorial Control and Ethnic Relations in Israel." *Journal Regional Studies Volume* 30 (5): 493–508.

———. 2002. "Territory as the Kernel of the Nation: Space, Time and Nationalism in Israel/Palestine." *Geopolitics* 7 (2): 215–48.

Zureik, Elia. 1979. *The Palestinians in Israel: A Study of Internal Colonialism*. London: Routledge.

———. 2016. *Israel's Colonial Project in Palestine: Brutal Pursuit*. London: Routledge.

Zureik, Elia, David Lyon, and Yasmeen Abu-Laban, eds. 2011. *Surveillance and Control in Israel/Palestine: Population, Territory, and Power*. London: Routledge.

Elegy for Return

Poetry by Zena Agha
Photography by Dorothy Allen-Pickard

Elegy for Return #1

Let me be clear about what I want.
I want return, yes, but more. To turn
stones back. I read once about a
mosque being made into a bar. Now,
I can forgive iconoclasm, but that did
offend. You hate when I talk about
return but some things just have to
be spoken and anyway, my father is
older than you and while he never
spoke it, he was mighty pleased to see
the lemon. I told you it's a kibbutz
now. Off route 90, near where
Jesus fed five thousand. And so, it is
perfectly right that my savage nose
of a father was born near Jesus and
my grandmother turned chairs into
thrones.

Elegy for Return #2

Everyone says it is about land, but I believe it is about time. What are seventy-some years in the grand kaleidoscope of sunsets? And, if three thousand years is what is noted, then certainly every rotation between that moment and this is noteworthy.

Elegy for Return #3

When we are alone, we talk about
return. We all think, "good, yes!"

عودة in Arabic is more urgent.

One seismic rumble from our throat.
One blast, filling our cheeks. One
tongue, rapping the backs of teeth.
And out, at last! Into this ether. Free.

Then we all speak, "tomorrow,
tonight!"

Elegy for Return #4

I am busy tonight. My love left a
watermelon on my doorstep. It
reminds me of rebellious women.
Lining their roofs. Disobeying in
RED WHITE GREEN BLACK.
A fuck you. In America, fruit has no
feeling, the black seeds bred out.
Otherwise I would have dried, fried,
and salted them. Cracked them in
displeasure. Left a trail of shells from A
to B on the re-drawn map.

Contributors

Zena Agha is a Palestinian Iraqi writer, poet, and filmmaker. She has received fellowships from the Asian American Writers' Workshop and the Millay Arts. Zena's writing has appeared in *The Margins*, the *New York Times*, and NPR, and she is the author of *Objects from April and May* (Hajar Press, 2022). She holds a masters in Middle Eastern studies from Harvard University. Zena is a doctoral candidate at Newcastle University, looking at colonial cartography and decolonization.

Walaa Alqaisiya is a Marie Curie Global Fellow working on de-colonial feminist ecologies across Ca' Foscari University of Venice, Italy; Columbia University in New York City; and the London School of Economics and Political Science. She received her PhD in human geography from Durham University, United Kingdom, and worked as a teaching fellow in gender, sexuality, and conflict at the Department of Gender Studies, London School of Economics. Her book *Decolonial Queering in Palestine* (Routledge, 2022) examines queer politics and esthetics from a Palestinian native positionality.

Wassim Ghantous holds a PhD in peace and development studies from the University of Gothenburg, Sweden. In 2021 Ghantous was the Ibrahim Abu-Lughod Postdoctoral Fellow at the Center for Palestine Studies, Columbia University, New York, and is currently a postdoctoral fellow at the Space and Political Agency Research Group at Tampere University, Finland. His research interests and focus revolve around interdisciplinary critical approaches across the fields of political geography and international relations and the subfields of critical security studies, settler colonial studies, surveillance studies, and Palestine/Israel studies.

Mark Griffiths is an academic track research fellow in the School of Geography, Politics, and Sociology at Newcastle University, United Kingdom. His work in Palestine is focused on colonial power and political violence at various sites such as checkpoints, bureaucratic mechanisms, and house demolitions and is published in a range of journals including *Progress in Human Geography*, *Society & Space*, *Transactions of the Institute of British Geographers*, and *Security Dialogue*.

Tiina Järvi is a postdoctoral researcher at Tampere University, Finland. Her research has explored the lifeworlds of Palestinian refugee communities in Lebanon, Jordan, and the West Bank, where she has conducted ethnographic fieldwork. Järvi defended her dissertation in social anthropology, "Negotiating Futures in Palestinian Refugee Camps: Spatiotemporal Trajectories of a Refugee Nation," and her research interests include themes such as temporality, belonging, kinship, and anthropology of the future.

Mikko Joronen is an academy research fellow at Tampere University, Finland. His research focuses on questions of violence, everyday resistance, and the politics of vulnerability in the occupied Palestinian territories; space and political ontology; and geographical theory. His recent publications deal with issues such as waiting, wounding, and everyday violence in Palestine and the relationships between ontology, space, and politics.

Rhys Machold is a lecturer in international relations at the University of Glasgow. He previously held research and teaching positions at the Danish Institute for International Studies, Copenhagen, and at York University, Toronto. Currently he serves as the associate editor of *Critical Studies on Security*. His research is concerned with issues of empire, violence, and policing from a transnational perspective. Based on qualitative research across Palestine/Israel, India, and the United Kingdom, his work has contributed to debates across international relations, critical security studies, political geography, and settler colonial studies.

Kathryn Medien is a lecturer in sociology at the Open University. Prior to this she was a research associate in the Department of Sociology at the

University of Cambridge. Kathryn has held research fellowships in gender, sexuality, and feminist studies at Duke University, Durham, North Carolina, and at the Institute of Advanced Study, University of Warwick, United Kingdom. Drawing on feminist and anticolonial social theory, her research focuses on how technologies of political violence are shaped, deployed, resisted, and contested.

Moriel Ram is a lecturer in politics of the Global South at Newcastle University. His main interests lie in the meeting points between politics, space, and matter. He is currently examining the colonial politics of ruination and recovery and the emergence of new separation regimes in the Global South. His work is published in *Antipode* and *Political Geography*.

Sophie Richter-Devroe is an associate professor in the Women, Society, and Development Program at Hamad Bin Khalifa University, Qatar, and is an honorary fellow at the European Centre for Palestine Studies at the University of Exeter, United Kingdom. Sophie's broad research interests are in in the field of everyday politics and women's activism in the Middle East. She has done research and published work on Palestinian women's activism, Palestinian refugees, Palestinian cultural production, Syrian refugees, and the oral histories of the Palestinian Bedouins in the Naqab. She is the author of *Women's Political Activism in Palestine: Peacebuilding, Resistance, and Survival* (University of Illinois Press, 2018).

Arun Saldanha is a professor in the Department of Geography, Environment, and Society at the University of Minnesota–Twin Cities. He is the author of *Psychedelic White: Goa Trance and the Viscosity of Race* (University of Minnesota Press, 2007) and the coeditor of *Deleuze and Race* (Edinburgh University Press, 2012). He also has published widely on race, sexuality, mobility, and the works of Gilles Deleuze and Alain Badiou.

Haim Yacobi is a professor of development planning in the Bartlett Development Planning Unit at University College London. An architect who specialized in urban studies and politics, his academic work focuses on colonial geography, architecture, and urban health in Israel/Palestine.

Index

Page numbers in italics refer to illustrations.

Freud, Sigmund, 207–8

gender ideologies, 23
Getzoff, Joe, 122
"Ghanni A'an Taa'rif" project, 224
Ghoshroy, Subrata, 129
Godard, Jean-Luc, 201
Golan, Amos, 122–23
Gold, Daniel, 135, 140
Good Night with Assaf Harel
    (show), 152
Good Shepherd Collective, 114
Gordon, Neve, 22, 107, 245
Guattari, Félix, 76, 79, 206
Gush Etzion settlement block, 252
Gutfeld, Arnon, 133, 134

Haaretz (publication), 44, 135
Hage, Ghassan, 189
Hakak, Yohai, 34–35
Hammami, Rema, 100
Haraway, Donna, 127, 139
Harel, Assaf, 152–53
Har Hevron Regional Council, 100
Harker, Chris, 245
Hart, Gillian, 156
hatafas dam bris ceremony, 20
"Hatikvah" (anthem), 225
Heidegger, Martin, 241
Hoijtink, Marjin, 127
Holocaust, 27, 123
homophobia, 219–20. *See also* queering
    esthesis
hyperreality, 110

Ihmoud, Sarah, 28
immigrations, 35–36
imminent (in)security, 77, 86–88
indigenization, 8, 142, 216
inexhaustibility, 5–8

infrastructures of coloniality, 22. *See also*
    settler colonialism
innovation, 122–26, 134, 137, 138–41, 240
Institute for National Security Studies, 133
intermarriage. *See* mixed Palestinian-
    Israeli relationships, control of
International, Dana, 213–14, 217
"international," term of, 233n4
International Convention on the
    Suppression and Punishment of the
    Crime of Apartheid, 154
(in)visibility of apartheid system, 153–54
The Invisible Men (film), 218
In Your Absence (video), 230–31
Iron Dome system, 13, 123–43
irreducibility, 6, 7–8, 9–11
Israel Aerospace Industries, 128
Israeli Civil Administration (ica), 97,
    100, 117n2, 254
Israeli Defense Forces (idf), 32, 80, 122,
    128, 159
Israeli Knesset, 160
Israeli Ministry of Defense, 128
Israel Independence Fund, 114
Israelis: colonial violence by, 4–6, 12–13,
    75–77, 100; neo-apartheid system
    of, 14, 149–70; Regavim strategy of,
    13, 97–117; security "innovation" of,
    122–26, 134, 137, 138–41, 240; and state
    control of mixed Palestinian-Israeli
    relationships, 20–24; War Machine
    of, 12–13, 76, 77–86. *See also* settler
    colonialism; Zionism
Israel's Occupation (Gordon), 245

Jabel Mukaber, *166*
Jabotinsky, Vladimir, 123
Jerusalem: neo-apartheid in, 14, 149–70;
    Palestinian settlements and Regavim
    strategy in, 13, 97–117

Oslo Accords (1993), 22, 156, 208, 220
otherness, 185–86. *See also* difference
outposts, 100, 106, 117n5, 152

Palestine Liberation Organization (PLO), 208–9
Palestinian National Authority (PNA), 208–9, 220, 225
Palestinians: construction and Regavim's strategy on, 97–117; as "demographic threat," 27, 28; living of, 1–8; neo-apartheid system and, 14, 149–70; older Bedouin women as, 12, 44–47, 50–66, 67nn1–4, 100; refugees and refugee camps for, 14, 176–95; and state control of mixed Palestinian-Israeli relationships, 20–24
Pappé, Ilan, 138
Pedatzur, Reuven, 130, 143n4
permit regime, 75
Perugini, Nicola, 107
Pfeffer, Anshel, 124
pinkwashing, 14–15, 212, 213–18
Pisgat Zeev settlement, 165
Plasse-Coutour, François-Xavier, 80, 85
policing, 84–85
political resistance, 8, 64–66, 200. *See also* boycotting campaigns; decoloniality; queering esthesis; *rhizomatic sumud*; *sumud*
political violence. *See* colonial violence
postcolonial feminism, 47. *See also* feminism
Postol, Theodore, 130–31, 133–34, 136, 137, 140, 143n4
power and woundedness, 239–56
Pratt, Mary Louise, 9
pronatalism, 27–29
Puar, Jasbir, 27, 33, 39

queering esthesis, 14–15, 212–13, 220–33. *See also* political resistance
The Question of Palestine (Said), 138, 243
"quiet occupation" trope, 97, 99, 110, 111. *See also* Regavim

Rabie, Kareem, 107
racial capitalism. *See* apartheid
racially mixed relationships. *See* mixed Palestinian-Israeli relationships, control of
Rahat Bedouin, 52
Rancière, Jacques, 215
Raytheon, 128
Razack, Sherene, 219
The Red Balloon (film), 205
refugees and refugee camps, 14, 176–95
Regavim, 13, 97–117
rehabilitation programs, 34–38. *See also* rescue missions
Repo, Jemima, 23, 25, 26
reproductive control, 24–29, 49–50
rescue-empathy logics, 220
rescue missions, 20–21, 24, 28–39. *See also* rehabilitation programs
rhizomatic sumud, 77, 79, 89–91. See also *sumud*
right-wing radicalism, 97, 157
Rome Statute (International Criminal Court), 154
rupture, 9, 10

Safiah, Ayman, 213, 230–31
Said, Edward, 2, 138, 141, 200, 243
Second Intifada (2000–2005), 80, 208
security "innovation," 122–26, 134, 137, 138–41, 240. *See also* start-up nation trope
segregation, 14, 45, 149–70. *See also* neo-apartheid

137–38, 143nn2–3; settler indigenization in, 8, 142, 216
un/making power, 6–7, 11, 239–56
urban apartheid, 14, 149–70
urbanization project, 44–46, 52. *See also* East Jerusalem settlements; land expropriation
urbicide, 150

Vertommen, Sigrid, 27–28
victimhood, 34–35, 218, 246–47
violence. *See* colonial violence
violence, soldiers', 81–85. *See also* War Machine
vortical violence, 77, 86–88, 89, 91
vulnerability, 5, 15–16, 177, 183, 240, 251–53. *See also* woundedness

War Machine, 12–13, 76, 77–86. *See also* colonial violence; Israelis
"war of maneuver," term of, 76
The Weapons Wizards (Katz and Bohbot), 133
wedding celebrations, 225, 227
Weiss, Meira, 35
Weizman, Eyal, 21, 80, 85

Weizmann, Chaim, 216
West Bank settlements, 97–117
witch hunt logics, 12, 49–50, 68n10
Wolfe, Patrick, 48, 62, 239
women: bodies and reproductive control of, 24–29, 49–50; informal networks of, 64–66; loss of mobility of, 51–57; older Bedouin, 47, 49–52, 55–57, 60, 63–66
"wounded life," term of, 240–41
woundedness, 239–56. *See also* vulnerability
Wurst, Conchita, 217

Yad L'Achim, 20–21, 23–24, 28, 29–39
Yatta, 100–105
"Ya Zarif Al-Toul" (song), 225, 228
Yemenite immigrants, 35
Yosef, Raz, 26
"Youth Cruelly Cut Off from His Mother . . ." (L'Achim), 20

zajal, 225, 229
Zionism, 97–117, 216–17. *See also* Israelis; security "innovation"; settler colonialism
Zuriek, Elia, 243–44

In the Cultural Geographies + Rewriting the Earth series

Topoi/Graphein: Mapping the Middle in Spatial Thought
Christian Abrahamsson
Foreword by Gunnar Olsson

Negative Geographies: Exploring the Politics of Limits
Edited by David Bissell, Mitch Rose, and Paul Harrison

Animated Lands: Studies in Territoriology
Andrea Mubi Brighenti and Mattias Kärrholm

Mapping Beyond Measure: Art, Cartography, and the Space of Global Modernity
Simon Ferdinand

Encountering Palestine: Un/making Spaces of Colonial Violence
Edited by Mark Griffiths and Mikko Joronen

The Begging Question: Sweden's Social Responses to the Roma Destitute
Erik Hansson
Foreword by Don Mitchell

Psychoanalysis and the GlObal
Edited and with an introduction by Ilan Kapoor

A Place More Void
Edited by Paul Kingsbury and Anna J. Secor

Arkography: A Grand Tour through the Taken-for-Granted
Gunnar Olsson

A Different "Trek": Radical Geographies of "Deep Space Nine"
David K. Seitz

To order or obtain more information on these or other University of Nebraska Press titles, visit nebraskapress.unl.edu.

www.ingramcontent.com/pod-product-compliance
Lightning Source LLC
Chambersburg PA
CBHW032139081125
35146CB00040B/156